Wake Up, Women!

Other Books by Florence and Fred Littauer

WORD PUBLISHING
Silver Boxes
Dare to Dream
Raising Christians—Not Just Children
Your Personality Tree (also in video album)
Hope for Hurting Women
Looking for God in All the Right Places
Wake Up, Men!

THOMAS NELSON PUBLISHERS
Freeing Your Mind from Memories That Bind
The Promise of Healing
I've Found the Keys, Now Where's the Car?
Get a Life Without the Strife

FLEMING REVELL, BAKER BOOKS
Personality Plus (also available in French, German, and Spanish)
Personality Puzzle (with Marita Littauer)

HARVEST HOUSE PUBLISHERS
Blow Away the Black Clouds
After Every Wedding Comes a Marriage
It Takes So Little to Be Above Average
How to Get Along with Difficult People
Out of the Cabbage Patch

HUNTINGTON HOUSE
Personalities in Power

CLASS BOOKS
Christian Leaders, Authors, and Speakers Seminar (tape, album, and
    manual)
The Best of Florence Littauer

*For information on the Promise of Healing Workshops, CLASS Seminars,
or other conferences conducted by Fred and Florence Littauer, please call
1-619-471-0233.*

Wake Up, Women!

SUBMISSION DOESN'T MEAN STUPIDITY

FLORENCE LITTAUER

WORD PUBLISHING
Dallas • London • Vancouver • Melbourne

Library of Congress Cataloging-in-Publication Data

Littauer, Florence, 1928–
    Wake up, women : submission doesn't mean stupidity / Florence Littauer.
       p.   cm.
    Includes bibliographical references.
    ISBN 0-8499-3830-9
    1. Assertiveness in women.   2. Sex role—Religious aspects—Christianity.   3. Women—United States—Social conditions.   4. Women—United States—Life skills guides.   I. Title.
HQ1206.L56 1994
305.42'0973—dc20   93–42471
                                               CIP

Printed in the United States of America

4 5 6 7 8 9 LB 9 8 7 6 5 4 3 2 1

Contents

ACKNOWLEDGMENTS

In publishing, as in other fields, men have traditionally been the business leaders, making decisions on production and marketing services to be used by women. In my experience in working with five different publishers I have frequently found that men edit my books, men choose the titles, and men design the covers and colors while women purchase 85 percent of the books sold, including those written for men. This occurs even though it is widely accepted that women have an intuition men don't have, as well as a sensitivity to others' feelings and an understanding of what women want that men can't hope to duplicate.

In light of this male-dominating tradition, I'm grateful that Word, Inc., the publisher of this book, allows a group of female staff members to participate on editorial boards and in marketing meetings. By breaking tradition, Word shows recognition that the female mind can add insight the most brilliant of men couldn't hope to create.

In particular, my thanks go to Word project managers Nancy Norris and Laura Kendall, whose work led them to conclude that a book needed to be written to urge women to wake up. I also thank the male executives at Word who dared to let us women wake up and move on.

I'm grateful to my friend and CLASS colleague Marilyn Heavilin, who typed the manuscript and worked on collecting and verifying many of the stories included in the book. Marilyn was also willing to share her own stories, which I believe are very enlightening; most of the names in this book have been changed to protect identities but, as you will see, Marilyn's real name is used.

Pam Stephens and Francine Jackson were also of immense help in completing the research for this book. Their patience and persistence have been invaluable in bringing this book to publication.

My thanks to all these bold men and women for their willingness to support me in saying what we believe needs to be said:

Wake up, women!

INTRODUCTION

This book discusses problems that are not supposed to happen in Christian homes. Deception, divorce, financial mismanagement, abortion, physical and emotional abuse—these and other heartbreaking issues are front-page problems that we would like to believe plague other people's families, not ours.

But we know better, don't we? These traumatic miseries occur in homes throughout the land, including Christian homes. In fact, some of the pain and calamity caused by these problems may be worse in Christian families because Christian women learn from an early age that they are to be submissive to their husbands, no matter what. But being submissive doesn't mean being blind, or ignorant, or victimized. It doesn't mean a wife becomes a doormat.

This book is not meant to redefine the term *submission*, to debate the scriptural basis for women in Christian leadership, to condemn the divorced, or decide whether men are evil creatures. It is intended to help women face the facts of where they are and help them to wake up from their long Christian nap. In no way am I trying to instigate dissension but to challenge women to face reality and show them that submission does not mean stupidity.

The chapters ahead do not cover every problem area a woman faces. Instead, they focus only on those areas where I find that women don't feel they have a right to question, areas where they have been taught ignorance is bliss and stupidity is next to godliness. We can no longer assume we deserve to live happily ever after. We have to wake up, take responsibility for our lives, and move on to the best God has for us.

As a conservative Christian woman, a public speaker, an author, and a wife who has been married to the same Fred for more than forty years, I feel I can write from a view that is not radical but real, not women's lib but women's liberty in the Lord. If you find yourself and your situation described in these pages, I pray that you will be helped by the shared experiences and learned lessons you find expressed here. And, in the last chapter, I hope you will rediscover the source of strength that can help you turn your life around, no matter how troubled it is.

1

Back When Father Knew Best and We Left It to Beaver

Back in the fifties when I got married, life was more structured. We grew up with set rules that kept us in neat little boxes. We had two pairs of shoes, black for winter and white for summer, and we never wore the white ones before Memorial Day. We women wore hats to church, and we attended services each Sunday without question. Never did we think of saying, "I don't think I'll go to church today" or "I'd rather go to the beach." We wore our best dresses to church and never even thought of wearing slacks. No matter how poor any of us were, we all had our church clothes.

We ate routine meals and hadn't even heard the word *gourmet*. As I grew up in Massachusetts my family had set patterns for eating: Saturday night, without fail, was franks and beans accompanied by steamed, canned B & M brown bread. Apple pie with hefty chunks of Vermont cheddar cheese was always the dessert. No one ever seemed to be on a diet, and on Sunday morning we reheated the leftover beans and pie for breakfast. Before leaving for church we had to help stuff the little chicken so he'd be cooked by the time we got home. We had chicken every Sunday. Our heavy meal was at noon and was called dinner, and our lighter fare was our evening supper. Lunch was any snack at any time.

We were all expected to get married. There was no "singles scene." Looking for a man was somewhat confined to college and church. Peculiar old-maid aunts were hidden away and brought out only to do the dishes after Christmas dinner.

Weddings were major social events and were especially important if the bride and groom came from two well-known families of merit in the community. All brides wore white and were considered beautiful, at least for the day. Couples started married life in little apartments—except for those who had wealthy parents—and borrowed furniture from anyone who would donate to their cause. We brides gave up our brief careers to dedicate our time and efforts to household management and raising children. Childless couples were looked upon with compassion for their obvious deficiencies.

As soon as possible, we rented a little tract house to give the children a yard. Eventually the big day would come when we could buy our first home. We knew we would; it was just a matter of time. We fenced in the backyard and bought a puppy for the children. We purchased a little yellow plastic pool and a swing set and when we could we added a playhouse or a fort. Right from the beginning we made plans to add on to the house, and we often discussed the future with friends who were also building creative wings in their minds. Sometimes we actually built an addition, which always included a family room with a fireplace and a large, round game table where we could do puzzles and play Monopoly. We never thought of going out to dinner; the early days of TV kept us at home evenings with Milton Berle and Ed Sullivan. There was little sense of adventure, but we were comfortable, warm, and secure.

Marriage was a 'til-death-do-us-part commitment; if we weren't perfectly happy, we would never let anyone know it. "Never air your dirty laundry in public" was one of our firm family mottoes. Men earned the money, paid the bills, and decided who got what allowance. If a man looked at another woman, people commented on his roving eye; if he had an affair a cloud of shame engulfed the whole family. Wives were expected to be dutiful homemakers. Flashing a seductive smile at the butcher could brand one as a fallen woman. Nice people never thought of divorce, and all we knew about stepmothers was confined to the wicked one in *Snow White*.

What we laugh at today in reruns of "Leave It to Beaver" and "Father Knows Best" was the norm for the time. We left our doors unlocked and never imagined that someone would steal our car. Drugs were aspirin and cough drops; social drinking, for nice people, was sipping champagne in the fruit punch at weddings. We didn't talk about morals and values; we lived them.

We loved God, motherhood, and apple pie, and we trusted each other. Our children knew their limits, and they learned that money didn't grow on trees. We'd all come out of the Depression and lived through the war and we appreciated each new possession we acquired. We liked living where we grew up; we all knew each other and we would ultimately retire and enjoy our forever friends into eternity.

Looking back, it all sounds so simple now.

Christians in a Crazy World

What's happened since Eisenhower smiled serenely over the fifties? Young people whose parents worked hard to provide them with substantial homes and quality education rebelled at the family's emphasis on keeping up with the Joneses and wandered off to spartan settings, scattering daisy petals along the way. These flower children became the Me Generation. Forget the old standards, they said. If it feels good, do it.

By the seventies the drug culture had emerged, but it was not considered a real problem; marijuana was thought to enhance clear thinking. The seventies were labeled the Age of Anxiety as people got increasingly nervous about finding themselves. Too late they realized that free love hadn't set them free.

By the eighties the baby boomers had grown into the yuppies. They put on suits, got real jobs, drove BMWs, drank Perrier, and seemed to like the feel of money. According to *Time* magazine, in the last ten years twenty-two thousand magazine and newspaper articles have featured the word *yuppie*.[1] The eighties became the Age of Avarice and produced corporate raiders and junk-bond kings. The Greed Generation was in recession by the birth of the nineties.

Walter Shapiro, a yuppie columnist, put it this way: "The yuppie mystique was built around a sense of generational entitlement that had its roots in the prosperity of the 1950s and '60s. In these more parlous times, there is an undeniable tempering of wanton consumption, but affluent baby boomers cannot cast off the experiences of a lifetime merely by switching outfits at the Gap."[2]

As sociologists look at the nineties they see the end of financial games and high living. Already they are calling this the Get Real Generation: "Let's face the facts and begin to help each other instead of searching selfishly inside." If looking at ME didn't make it, can the WE Decade succeed?

Where does the church fit into all these changes? Have we zipped along with the world? Have we compromised our standards to keep up with the happy hedonists? Have we held our Christian standards high? As the yuppies have searched for self-identity and asked "Who am I?" have we had the right answers?

We seem to have developed different directions in these last decades. The church appears to be somewhat like an odd, oversized Dr. Seuss ostrich with three heads facing in opposing directions. One head is buried firmly in the sand of the fifties, another is stretching to reach the year 2000 unshackled by old-fashioned rules of virtue and fidelity, and the third has decided to get real, face the issues of the day, not compromise standards, and look to Scripture for answers.

All three of these heads, or views, will be illustrated in the stories of the women in this book. And as a convenience Appendix A offers a summary of how these views are carried out in many of the challenging issues today's women must face.

The media feature the buried-in-the-fifties head as often as possible. They love to find negative, sour-faced, ignorant people holding a Bible in one hand while setting fire to the local adult bookstore or shooting a doctor who does abortions with the other. These people, when interviewed, look like the pair in the American Gothic picture. Holding up a pitchfork, they spout damnation scriptures while appearing to be underpaid actors in the *Grapes of Wrath*. At best they come across as hapless victims of a cult leader who has obviously wiped out their minds and brainwashed their children.

Unfortunately, these characters often catch the media's attention, purporting to represent all Christians. One afternoon I flipped on the TV only to see a noted talk-show personality interviewing a group of nudists. They were sitting relaxed and confident while stark naked before the audience. For us home viewers they had placed little blurry spots over each person's strategic areas, but the dots didn't take the place of clothes. At the point I tuned in and stood shocked at the subject of the day, the host said, "And now for the Christian point of view on nudity in public." I held my breath as the camera panned to an overweight man in a T-shirt and plaid shorts. He was carrying a Bible and wearing a Donald Duck hat. As he began his astonishing monologue I decided he had to be an actor; no one could have been that bad spontaneously.

Was there any basis of truth in this caricature? Was the audience hissing at Christianity as well as this pathetic person? Are we still out of step with reality?

I couldn't help but feel that way recently when I talked with a pastor who explained why he was canceling the popular singles Sunday school class at his church. "It was growing so fast, and I could see it was bringing in people with problems. What we want here is sweet little families who will give to the church," he said. Don't we all!

The church's second ostrich head, which the press also loves to feature, is the one that has thrown all standards to the wind in an apparent orgy of sexual sin and financial finagling. How the media love to prove that pious believers are just like the rest of us—only more phony! As one respected leader after another falls off his or her Corinthian column, the cause of Christ is increasingly diminished. As the church labels unrepentant adulterers as good people who had a "momentary indiscretion," we give our young people elastic options they shouldn't be offered.

And what about that third head of our ostrich, the balanced attitude that is moral yet not legalistic, real without abandoning rules, positive but not preachy, compassionate without running mascara? Where do we women fit into this picture? Is it possible to be a positive, real, and intelligent woman and still stay in the church? Or should we remain the drab, dull, little damsels who become doormats for the church foyers? Should we have no greater desire than to wash and dry communion cups in the church basement? Or should we throw in the towel and head out into the world to find ourselves? Can we have a sense of submission without being stupid?

This book has the answers.

Wake up, women!

2

They Just Don't Get It

In the early nineties a new expression was used by politicians to show that their opponents were out of touch and not really with it. "They just don't get it" was noticeably applied to the fourteen white senators who sat in lofty judgment as law professor Anita Hill testified at the Senate confirmation hearings considering Clarence Thomas for a seat on the U.S. Supreme Court. Their own flawed backgrounds seemed not to bother them as they inferred that Anita Hill was lucky to have had an important man come on to her from any direction. In response the public cried out, "They just don't get it!"

Dan Quayle didn't get it, either, when his comment about TV character Murphy Brown's impending motherhood caused a national uprising from single mothers and provided a spate of comic material for Jay Leno.

Bill Clinton and his advisers didn't believe for a minute that the American public would care a whit about her illegal nanny when they proposed Zoe Baird for U.S. attorney general. They just didn't get it.

Somehow men don't seem to have the same "get-it" factor that women have. When any potential social pitfall is mentioned, we run it through our minds quickly and get intuitive feelings about how each person involved in the scenario will react. We instinctively know that Melissa will feel left out, Mother will drop into a depression, Susie will scream, and we will be left trying to pick up the pieces. Our mates are bewildered. "How did you figure that out so quickly?" they ask in amazement. Some add, "That's ridiculous!"

Yet when you get together at Susie's for Sunday dinner Melissa feels left out because she has to sit at the card table with the children, Mother is depressed because she wasn't invited until the last minute, and when the men begin to argue over politics, Susie screams. You're left to break up the fights, cheer up Mother, and make Melissa feel part of the crowd. You're also left with the dishes as Susie runs sobbing to her room and the others quickly leave. They just don't get it.

What Makes Women Different?

Are you involved with people who just don't get it? Do you wonder why, when you drop hints big enough to wrap up and sell, that your man doesn't get it? Do you have children who have been told one hundred times not to stand on a particular corner and when you catch them there, they reply, wide-eyed, "Oh, I didn't know you meant *that* corner!" Why do we get it and they don't?

Trust Your Intuition

One reason is that we have a sixth sense, intuition, that tunes into relationship problems. For the most part, women's intuitive powers are not understood by men. Often in our marriage Fred would have a business deal I didn't feel right about. He would have charts and statistics to prove his point, and I had nothing to offer but my feelings. In the long run, though, my feelings were usually better than his facts. As I have listened to thousands of women's problems over the years I have validated the worth of a woman's intuition and have suggested to men that if their wife has a creepy feeling about a potential employee don't hire him or her.

I remember the suave gentleman who came to an interview wearing a velvet jacket and silk ascot. He was extremely complimentary to me and Fred was impressed with his sophisticated manner. When I mentioned that I wouldn't trust him, Fred was stunned and asked me why I would jump to such a hasty conclusion. "The ascot for one thing," I replied. Fred thought my comment to be a potential crusade against ascots and hired him anyway to be our sales manager. Within six months he had propositioned me and embezzled thousands of dollars. Fred still doesn't know how that ascot clued me in because as a man he just doesn't get it. History, however, has proven me right often enough that now if I say "I don't feel right about this," he answers "That's good enough for me!"

We women can make feeling judgments, and yet how seldom men believe we can be right without a shred of evidence or a chart and a pointer. Maureen went to a chiropractor who was charming and attentive to her every ache and pain. When her treatment was over he patted her on the rear and told her he'd need to see her again next week. She made the appointment, but became increasingly concerned over going back. With no more facts than a little pat, Maureen called and canceled the appointment. Within a few months Maureen spotted an article in the local paper. This same doctor had been arrested for sexually abusing his female patients. Maureen was relieved that she had trusted her intuition and wasn't one of his victims.

Susan was getting her training as a masseuse and one of her required courses was hypnotherapy. She thought it would be interesting to see what went on. At the first meeting the teacher said they could all bring someone next week to work on. She brought her beautiful teenage daughter and a model friend of hers.

The instructor "helped" many of the women a little too much from Susan's perspective and he was especially attentive to the two young girls. As the group was practicing relaxation techniques Susan looked over to where the instructor was relaxing himself and noticed that he was intently perusing a *Victoria's Secret* catalog. This struck her as odd that a man would be looking at pictures of women in their undies while in charge of a class, but she didn't say anything about it.

At the end of the session the instructor announced a special drawing for two private sessions of hypnosis with him personally. Everyone got excited as he drew names from a hat and, would you believe, the two young girls won the prizes. A full hour alone with the teacher!

The more Susan thought about the situation, the more concerned she got. She shared her fears with her daughter who accepted her mother's opinion. The girls didn't go to the free appointment. Who knows what might have happened, but by not going they prevented the possibility.

Gayle moved back into her hometown and needed a baby-sitter. Her Uncle Ted was available and free, and her family insisted that she use him. Her mother explained, "Your uncle is a lonely man with nothing to do and he loves little Rebecca. It would be stupid to pay money to some unknown person when you have a blood relative available at no cost."

With such a convincing argument from her mother, Gayle gave in, even though in her heart she knew better. Each time she took Rebecca to the good uncle's house, she felt worse. Soon the little girl fussed at going and clung to Gayle's skirt. One day when Gayle stopped by to pick Rebecca up the child ran to her in terror.

"What's happened to her?" Gayle asked. As Rebecca sobbed, good old Uncle Ted confessed that he had orally abused the child along with some other nieces he had cared for. When Gayle came to me for help she was justifiably furious at her uncle, but she was equally upset with herself for being shamed into a situation she knew was wrong. "If only I'd trusted my instincts!" she cried.

Tina, my long-time friend, could certainly understand Gayle's anguish. A devout Christian who had taught marriage classes in her church for many years, Tina had seemed to have a picture-perfect Christian family. She and her husband had reared two quiet, polite sons whose intelligence and high grades earned them full college scholarships. One was studying to be a doctor; the other had hopes of becoming a missionary.

Imagine my surprise when Tina called me during a recent holiday to say the past year had been the worst of her life. Her two sons were in deep trouble, she said. The medical student had become a drug addict, and the would-be missionary had dropped out of college, announcing he no longer believed in God.

When we discussed possible causes for these calamities, she told me her husband had so tightly controlled the boys as they were growing up that they had a seething rebellion inside that burst forth when they got away at college. She admitted that she had known what her husband was doing wasn't right, but each time she tried to voice an opinion he would counter her firmly with the same three reasons: "You are only a woman and don't understand male things, you had no father so you have no sense of male bonding, and you have had so little education that you couldn't be trusted to make valid judgments. Leave the raising of the boys to me." This set of statements wiped out any alternative opinions.

Tina had gone through years of teaching on submission and thought she was the prime example of the perfectly submissive wife by meekly accepting her husband's dominance.

There's no guarantee that her sons would have turned out differently if she had been able to voice some objections, but as she looks back she says, "Why didn't I trust my instincts? I knew better and I did nothing about it in the guise of sweet submission."

God gave us women intuition. Let's not throw away the gift!

Communicating So They'll Get It

Besides intuition, the other reason women "get it" and men don't is that we sometimes can sense unspoken feelings that men can't hear. Unfortunately this can also cause trouble when we "hear" the *wrong* feelings. This ability also makes women assume men know what we're thinking when in fact they don't have a clue. We talk all around our feelings without presenting facts clearly; we belabor inconsequential details and set our mates' minds adrift. We ask for the verdict, but they don't even know they're on the jury.

This is reinforced to me every week as I listen to women who are in deep marital problems. When I ask why they didn't do something before their marriage got to a crisis point, they all reply, "Well, I told him we needed help, but he didn't seem to get it." If this kind of miscommunication is a consistent problem, what can we do about it? Are we just mumbling our way through the marriage maze? Have we never made our case clear?

In spite of my God-given ability to communicate, I realize I've been guilty of halfway hints and fuzzy phrases. Early in my marriage, because of my "Father Knows Best" indoctrination, I didn't think I had the right to point out Fred's mistakes. If he said he'd take us all on an outing next Saturday and on Saturday he left for the office, I'd moan and groan a bit as he went out the door. Then I'd tell the children, "You can't ever count on men; business comes first." They learned to never get excited over Dad's promises of trips and outings until they were actually in the car. When Fred would come home after a Saturday in the office I'd be a little distant to express my disappointment, but now that I look back on it, I know he didn't get it.

He interpreted my behavior as unappreciative for how hard he worked to support us. What I never did was sit down with him and ask him realistically how many Saturdays a month he could give to the family. If he'd settled on even one, we could have made some plans. I could have pointed out how important it was for him to be trusted to keep his word; I could have mentioned the children's anticipation several times in a positive way and probably he would have followed through. Instead I'd hold him accountable and not remind him, then wait for him to announce he was going to the office. My glares and groans made him glad he had chosen the office over a day with the children and me.

If it's true that men don't get it as easily as women, is there something we could do to help them along? Think of the last situation when you ended up frustrated over a misunderstanding. Had you made your point perfectly clear or had you approached the subject through the back door?

When Gloria got her first view of her husband's new secretary, she was upset. Entering her husband's reception area, she came upon a young woman in a skintight miniskirt leaning over a file drawer. But it was even worse when this new employee turned around. She had on a thin T-shirt and seemed to use her ample breasts to gesture as other people would use their hands. All the men in the office were focused on this creature, and Gloria was furious. She got even more upset when she found out the girl's name was Trixie. *It fits her perfectly*, thought Gloria. *This will never do!*

That night Gloria created a "don't-get-it" dilemma at home.

"I think it's important that women dress modestly in office situations, don't you?" she asked her husband, Jim, during a commercial in "Monday Night Football."

Jim, who is not into hypothetical discussions at nine in the evening, answered, "I guess so." (He didn't get it.)

"What do you mean you guess so?" Gloria retorted angrily. Jim looked up, stunned that Gloria could possibly be upset over a generic problem that had nothing to do with them personally. Now she got somewhat to the point. "How could you have hired someone named *Trixie?*"

The focus now was on the new girl's name, and because it came across as an attack on Jim's judgment, he was forced to defend himself. "I think it's an acceptable name. What do you want me to do, ask her to change it?"

"No." Gloria now tried the sulk approach. *If I look down and appear depressed, he'll have to ask me what I'm really upset about.* But he didn't. Instead he asked himself if Gloria could be losing her mind. As he pondered this possibility, Trixie came to his mind. He focused on how she looked today, then he glanced over at Gloria, who was huddled up on the couch, pouting.

As he was mentally playing with the comparison, Gloria tried a new approach. "Did you see how that Trixie looked when she bent over the file drawer?" He hadn't noticed, but the idea was not an unpleasant one. "Why are you smiling? Have you been watching her all day?"

Another attack, totally missing the original point, caused more defensiveness. "I have a lot better things to do than stare at Trixie all day. What is your problem, woman?"

"Her skirt is too short."

"If you had legs like hers you could wear short skirts."

"See, you did notice! Are you in some kind of midlife crisis or something?"

"I was just sitting here minding my own business, and all of a sudden you decide I'm in a midlife crisis!"

Jim didn't get it. But it's not really his fault. Men want the bottom line, and they don't easily pick up hints or backdoor approaches. How could Gloria bring up the problem clearly without an attack? What was she really trying to accomplish? Was Trixie's name a valid issue? Wasn't it the choice of clothing that was the problem? Let's consider another way Gloria could have presented her concerns:

"Jim, I was so glad I dropped by the office and met your new secretary Trixie," she could have said. "She seems like a pleasant person and she surely has a great figure. I did notice when she bent over that I could see her underwear and when she turned around I saw that her T-shirt was too revealing. I think for your own reputation among your clients, you had better have her dress more conservatively. It took you a long time to build this business, and you wouldn't want anyone to get the wrong idea."

In this direct approach to the problem there is no attack. The problem is made clear, and Gloria puts herself on Jim's side. The result? Jim gets it.

Here's another example. Marge has just found out that the Johnsons are going to Hawaii for the third time. She and Morris have never been, and she wants to go. She begins her approach at dinner.

"The Johnsons are going to Hawaii again."

"That's nice." (He doesn't get it.)

Silence reigns.

"Is that all you have to say?"

"About what?"

"About the Johnsons going to Hawaii!"

"I didn't know they had asked for my opinion."

"They didn't. I just told you they're going and it's their third trip. I want to go."

"Did they ask you?"

Marge is now beside herself. "No, they didn't ask me!"

"Then why are you so mad?"

"Because I want *us* to go. I want you to take me. We never do anything exciting anymore."

"Are you trying to say we should take a trip to Hawaii?"

"Yes!"

"Then why didn't you say so?"

"Well, I tried."

But not very well.

We women need to realize that the backdoor approach doesn't often work. We are dealing with men who don't get it. Some of them work hard at not getting it; others just come by it naturally. Past methods haven't brought positive results, and our increasing frustration has turned some of us into screaming shrews and others into silent statues.

Does it really matter that we are not communicating effectively on things that are not life-threatening? Isn't it easier to talk about subjects that aren't controversial? Many couples only talk about superficial topics: The children's marks in school, what restaurant to go to, who will rule Cuba once Castro is gone.

What Fred and I have learned is that when we shut down discussions on emotional topics and become pleasantly agreeable to stay happy, neither one of us really knows what the other is thinking. For example, when I just went along with things without showing interest or asking questions, Fred entered into business ventures without telling me the risks involved. We both recognize that I have a sixth sense about hiring people, but since I wasn't involved in the interviewing I had no input in the hiring decisions. Because I had let minor things slide with no meaningful discussion, Fred saw no reason to involve me in major business decisions. It took some extreme losses to make us see that we were both wrong. I could easily have put all the blame on him (it seemed so obvious, at least to me!) but then I realized I was at fault too. By setting a precedent and not making my feelings known—not making sure he got it—I had given him silent permission to hide anything that might be bad news.

Our changes did not come overnight, but as Fred could see his pattern of shielding me and I became willing to discuss matters instead of pulling back, we began to climb up the hill to meaningful communication.

Dropping hints and beating around the bush lead to frustration. Hot tantrums and cold shoulders block reception. Whether it's your husband, child, or friends who haven't heard the truth, help them.

They'll get it.

3

Filling Our
Emotional Vacuum

When Fred and I got married in 1953, there was no such thing as premarital counseling. But we wouldn't have needed it anyway. We knew the right answers to everything. We looked good, we were equally educated, and we were faithful church attenders. It would have taken a pastor of depth and insight to have spotted our problems ahead of time for they were hidden in our emotional needs.

We now know there are two major sources of emotional needs. The first is based on our inborn desires that stem from our natural personality, and the other is rooted in our individual family background.

Understanding the Personality Types

How can we spot each other's emotional needs so we can meet them? We begin by understanding the inherent needs felt by certain personality types. I have written numerous books on the four basic personalities, so I will just review them here to refresh your memory or give the basics for those of you who have not read *Personality Plus*, *Personality Puzzle*, or *Your Personality Tree*.

The Popular Sanguine is the fun-loving, outgoing, optimistic, talkative personality. By nature these people have emotional needs that make them seem like perpetual children, and if these needs are not met in their family when they're young, they may never grow up emotionally.

They may have adult bodies and minds, but emotionally they remain three years old. People say behind their backs, "Why, she's just like a child. Will she ever get her act together and grow up?"

No matter what age a Sanguine is, his or her needs are still inside, waiting to be met. The fewer needs that were met as a child, the more grabby he or she will be as an adult. Sanguines are desperate for *attention*, yet they usually marry Melancholies, who soon grow sick of listening to them. They want *approval* for every bit of trivia they manage to achieve, but their mates won't give them any compliments unless they become perfect—like they are. They want touchy-feely *affection* in front of their friends, but their Melancholy mates are repulsed by public displays of showy love. Sanguines have never felt *acceptance* from their family; they believe a true friend will accept them as they are right now, not as they might become years later if they happen to improve. When we look objectively at Sanguines' childlike emotional needs, we can see why they will do anything to please others. They are the most needy of all. "Wake up," the Sanguine says. "Love me as I am!"

The Perfect Melancholy is born desiring perfection and even as a child he or she gets depressed when things aren't right. Melancholies born into dysfunctional families are almost assured of emotional problems as they grow up. Because it's a natural tendency for them to want things done properly, they are often disappointed in people who don't seem to care. The Melancholies are highly organized, detail conscious, and analytical. They are usually the most artistic, musical, poetic, or philosophical in any group and tend to see things from an intellectual level. They can't find anyone perfect enough to marry, but they usually settle on the bubbling Popular Sanguine who they hope will cheer them up. Melancholies are desperate for *sensitivity* to their inner feelings yet they marry Sanguines, who don't see too far below the surface. For example, Fred used to say to me, "If you really loved me you would know what I am thinking." But I had no idea what he was thinking, and I'd come out with some funny comment that would show him I was hopelessly out of touch. Melancholies also want *support* when they're down, which tends to be frequently, but their Sanguine mates, who can't stand gloomy people, tend to flee instead of lifting up their sagging spirits.

Even Melancholy children like their possessions in order and don't like people to touch their things. Just imagine how depressing it is for a Melancholy to be married to a Sanguine who can't even find a pen that works or pair of scissors and who therefore rummages through the Melancholy's perfectly arranged drawers.

Melancholies also like *silence*. Surely a Melancholy must have written the Swiss slogan, Silence is golden. For Sanguines silence is dead air to be avoided at all costs. "Wake up," the Melancholy says. "Please understand me."

The Powerful Cholerics are the great achievers in the world. They love to work and need to be in control in order to feel secure. Where Sanguines love to talk and Melancholies like to analyze, Cholerics love to be in charge of whatever is available, whether or not they were asked to do so. The Choleric doesn't need to read the bylaws to become president.

Even though Cholerics don't appear to be emotional, they crave *appreciation* for all the work they have accomplished. If you don't notice what they've done, they'll point it out to you: "While the rest of you were wasting time, I finished building a wing onto the house." If you know what's good for you, you will rise up quickly and stand in awe: "I can't believe you accomplished so much in such a short time." With this comment the Choleric recognizes you as a person of discernment. Cholerics also demand loyalty among the troops, whoever the troops may be. Any sniff of mutiny will bring their wrath to the surface, so it's important that you throw in occasional sentences such as, "We're with you" or "We're on your side," even when you don't know what the side is.

The Choleric who sees life in black and white—you're either with me or against me—usually marries the Peaceful Phlegmatic who lives in a fog of gray. "It doesn't matter. I don't care. Whatever you like. You choose. Whatever's easy." The Phlegmatic is usually the only personality who can live with the Choleric and stay sane because he or she really doesn't care most of the time. "Wake up," the Choleric says. "Notice how much I've done while you've been resting."

Phlegmatics are the easygoing, laid-back, agreeable people who get along with everybody and have no enemies. They know how to agree with whatever the Choleric proposes and appear to go along with them. They will smile and nod and say, "I'll be glad to do it" while underneath they're mumbling, "That'll be the day."

Phlegmatics bounce well with joy or adversity and all they want is a little *peace and quiet*. They have learned to smile when unhappy, listen without hearing, and sleep with their eyes open. They will put their greatest effort into saving effort. They would like to be accepted as decent people whether or not they do anything spectacular and they hope in the long run to be considered of *worth and value*. "Wake up," the Phlegmatic says. "Notice me."

Can you see just from this peek at the personalities how close to hopeless it is for us to try to live together in harmony without an understanding of why we are so different from each other? As we have gone over the personalities and their inherent emotional needs, I hope you have spotted yourself and those other people who are nothing like you. Ask yourself what your emotional needs were as a child. What was missing in your home that you cried out for? What lack or dysfunction warped your personality? What were you looking for as a teenager? Did this desire get you in any trouble? Did you choose a mate who was equally needy? Did you meet each other's needs in a positive way or a sick way? Did this marriage last? If not, did you repeat your mistakes? Are you handling your friends and co-workers with understanding?

If you need additional help in analyzing your personality type, read *Personality Plus, Personality Puzzle*, or *Your Personality Tree*. As you assess your personality, keep in mind that you may have elements of more than one type. For example, because of my Sanguine nature I needed Fred to pay attention to my every word, approve of everything I did, rave about me in public, and accept me as I was without constantly correcting me. And because of my Choleric nature I also wanted him to appreciate how hard I worked and to keep his eyes loyally on me alone. Since we didn't understand any of this and I couldn't articulate these needs, Fred didn't begin to meet them. His Melancholy nature made him believe if he worked hard enough on me I would become perfect and have no peculiar needs that he would have to meet. He also had Choleric needs for credit and loyalty. He felt I was insensitive and unsupportive and I of course had no desire for the silence he craved. When we look back on those first fifteen years of each of us wondering what was wrong with the other one, we are amazed that we hung in there. We also see why so many couples with no tools of understanding give up on each other and come to believe they could be happy if they had a different mate. Because of the changes that came to us when we began to study the personalities, we have dedicated the past twenty-five years to helping other couples see the light.

Differences in Family Backgrounds

We have said that personality is one of two sources of our emotional needs. The second source comes from our individual family background. Adding all these needs together can create people who are looking desperately for emotional fulfillment without being able to articulate what they're after. The broader our differences, the less apt we are to understand each other's needs. This is especially true when it comes to needs generated by different family backgrounds.

Fred grew up in the lap of luxury from my point of view. He had all the things I didn't have: the huge English Tudor home, separate bedrooms for each child, imported German domestic help, expensive cars, and plenty of money. When I first saw where he lived, I said to myself, *Florence, this is for you!*

What I didn't see was Fred's need for someone to love him and make him feel significant. He was the middle of five children and somehow he seemed to continually fall through the cracks. What we didn't know about until recently was the sexual abuse by the maid that had occurred when he was two years old. Anytime abuse occurs, whether the child remembers it or not, he or she feels rejected, dirty inside, and unloved. Even if the offender says, "What we're doing is because I love you," the child instinctively knows it's wrong.

When we add up all of Fred's needs, we now realize I married an emotional time bomb who wanted someone to love him and support him. Under his charm and sophistication was a boiling anger. He kept it under control almost all the time but I knew it was there, and I also knew how to tiptoe around it to prevent eruptions.

I came into this marriage wide-eyed and innocent, just wanting to have a good time. I had been forced to grow up early in life as I had been responsible for meeting many of my two brothers' needs and for mothering my mother when my father died. Since we lived in a store with people around us from 6:30 in the morning until 11:00 at night, I got plenty of attention; people praised me for everything I did and I was considered the most intelligent girl around. My report cards were posted in the store and my father bragged on how well I did each term. My natural Sanguine and Choleric needs were met, but we had none of the things I wanted and read about in romance novels. We had no car, no phone, no bathtub, no hot water, and no money. I frequently wished, *If only I could have a normal house with a front door, a lot of clothes, and plenty of money* . . .

So many of us marry someone who appears to fill our emotional vacuum wherever it appears within us. Here I was, hungry for houses and money and willing to love someone who'd give it to me, and Fred had the money and was desperate for love. As we look back on it, we see our attraction to each other was partly because of our perception that the other person had what we needed.

So many of us, having no knowledge of the differences in personalities and the collection of emotional needs we carry around with us, have no healthy way to analyze ourselves. Fred and I are so grateful that after fifteen years of a deteriorating marriage we began to study the personalities. This concept gave us the tools we needed to rebuild our lives. Later we came to understand our different emotional needs, and we began to repair the hurts we'd put upon each other. I could see that when Fred gave me plenty of money and clothes and we lived in a big house I was willing to give him a portion of the love he needed, but when he had financial problems, I withdrew my love and support at a time when he needed them the most. We didn't mean to be self-centered and emotionally greedy, but we had no wisdom to call upon, no course to take, no books to read.

We are so grateful today that the Lord has blessed us in spite of ourselves and has used our mistakes, our misunderstood needs, and even Fred's childhood molestation to give us a sensitivity to others' needs and a desire to be used to help others.

Emerging from Never-Never Land

Our work in helping troubled husbands and wives would be much simpler if couples came to us *before* the wedding. Then we could help them understand the personality types and the potential impact of past memories on their lives. With that understanding they could anticipate and resolve problems those issues might have on their marriage. But far more often we get cries for help after the honeymoon (and after several months or years of marriage). That was the case with Lynn and Ben.

Lynn came out of an abusive childhood and an abusive marriage. She was glad to escape with her two children and finally be free. She had no choice but to work hard to support them because her ex-husband had left the state and she had no way to find him. She had been a victim all her life and she accepted her plight as what she deserved. Her husband had been an atheist and wouldn't let her go to church, so somewhat in a late rebellion she decided to join a local church. She was so angry over her circumstances that she refused to participate in any activities until she read in the bulletin about a support group for the "Depressed and Done In." Immediately she mused, "If anyone's been depressed and done in, it's me."

The support group was more depressive than she had anticipated, and Lynn wouldn't have returned a second week if it hadn't been for that one single man who sat quietly, appearing to analyze the rest of the participants. He had smiled at her once and somehow that one smile was enough to make her go back the next week. She spent a little extra time on her hair and makeup and tried to appear happier than she really was. Lynn managed to sit next to Ben this time and she tried to engage him in conversation. He was so quiet and shy and such a contrast to her ex-husband, who beat her up every time she didn't please him.

In the following weeks as the group members opened up and shared their individual traumas, Lynn learned that Ben's wife had left him for a younger man and yet had managed to strip him of all his possessions. Lynn's heart went out to him. Here was someone who needed her; here was a gentle, soft-spoken Christian. Lynn thought to herself, *Finally, a male who's not out to control me.* Ben was not only not controlling, he didn't want to make any decisions at all. "Whatever you want to do" or "Whenever you want to go" seemed to be his mottoes. Lynn liked this Phlegmatic attitude and was so thrilled to have found a man with a passive personality. Cheerfully she activated a relationship with this man who needed her. She was able to sublimate her hate and bitterness over her first husband as she put her energy into salvaging this downtrodden soul.

From an objective point of view we can see several potential problems in this relationship. First, Lynn was looking to a new marriage to solve her problems and make her happy, but she had not yet begun to get over the emotional toll the past marriage had taken from her. She had not dealt with her own anger or the results of the abuse she had suffered for years. She had not even asked the question, "Why did I stay in that marriage so long?" let alone found the sick need she had to be abused.

Lynn had gone back to church for the wrong reason; she wanted to show her ex she could go to church if she wanted to, even though he was not around to observe her rebellion. Lynn had not even tried to apply the Scriptures to her life problems; in fact, frequently she got angry at the pastor when he inferred all Christians could be joyful.

"If he'd lived my life he wouldn't be so happy," she would mutter.

Lynn felt she couldn't pray to a God who had allowed her to be beaten, and she knew that reading a few verses a day wasn't going to make that much difference either. The best thing about church, she thought, was finding a new mate who would make her happy. She could put the past behind her and start anew.

The second foreseeable problem Lynn faced as she began her new relationship was that she lacked knowledge about the basic personalities. She didn't understand that she was Sanguine, the fun-loving type, and also Choleric, the one who wants to be in control. Lynn was not only depressed by her circumstances but also because her life had never been fun and had been constantly out of her control. She didn't realize that she had perked up because she saw some ray of fun in the future and she had found someone who seemed willing to let her be in control.

If she had been aware that Ben was Phlegmatic, low-key and inoffensive, and also a little Melancholy, desiring perfection and getting depressed when not finding it, she could have foreseen the future potential problems. She could have thought through the possibility that while she liked his gentle spirit she might have trouble living with his weaknesses. He might be lacking in ambition and frequently feel defeated and depressed. Was she prepared to handle his collective problems on top of her own untended bitterness and anger? Would it all somehow work out in the long run?

The third problem was Lynn's lifetime of victimization. History shows us that there is a downhill spiral of repeated victimization. Scripture tells us that the sins of the fathers are visited upon the children up to the third and fourth generation. The stench of abuse that has not been dug up, looked at, prayed over, and thrown out will rise to overwhelm future relationships. Lynn had put her energies into suppressing her hurts and trying to pretend they'd never happened.

Although victimization takes a toll on everyone, the personalities handle it differently; Phlegmatics and Melancholies like Ben tend to withdraw, say little, become introspective, achieve below their ability, and manifest depressive symptoms. Sanguines and Cholerics try to deny it ever happened, charge forth to overachieve, show themselves that these past problems can't hold them down, and become the saviors of other lost souls. This latter problem has been labeled recently as *codependency*: the process of being responsible for the destructive behavior of another person.

Lynn had no understanding of victimization and did not realize that her desire to pull Ben out of his miseries was feeding her own sick needs of rescuing someone in worse shape than herself. Lynn also didn't realize the principle that Fred and I have repeatedly seen proven over the years, that people tend to marry mates of opposite personality but are on the same level of emotional pain. Lynn, by nature an optimistic Sanguine with Choleric drive, was attracted to the gentle Phlegmatic with the Melancholy reserve. Unfortunately, in marriage we wed the opposite strengths and don't realize we have to live with opposite weaknesses. When we understand this ahead of time, marriage is not such a rude shock, but when we don't we fall into unexpected disappointments.

On the emotional level, we are attracted to people who have a similar amount of personal pain. Even though one mate may appear to be more stable than the other, underneath there is usually a well of bubbling symptoms seeking out a balancing pool of pain. We have found that an emotionally stable, mature, responsible individual will not be attracted to an emotional wreck.

Looking at all of these potential problems with knowledge, any one of us could have predicted what was going to happen to Lynn and Ben. Pour all their problems into a large mixing bowl and add to it a portion of misdirected Christian platitudes on submission, money matters, and husbandly headship and you will produce a partnership of hot potatoes.

Lynn proposed marriage to Ben. She told us she had to as he wouldn't have thought it up on his own. The truth is somewhat different. She thought marriage would heal her hurts and make her happy. He didn't want to get married because he was still in pain from the rejection he'd experienced. He was in deep financial trouble and couldn't bear any additional responsibility. Lynn wouldn't hear of his objections and in a foolhardy spirit of love conquers all, she dragged him to the preacher, who gave them a booklet on the perfect Christian marriage—the husband works to support the family, handles all the money, and makes the decisions. The wife is submissive to his every whim, never questions his handling of the money, and stays home to prepare him nutritious meals. These are certainly pleasant principles that should work for a sweet spiritual couple who get married for the first time, understanding each other's strengths and weaknesses and carrying no emotional baggage from the past. But does that represent Lynn and Ben?

Lynn was so eager to get married that she didn't discuss many of the basics of life with Ben. Naturally he didn't initiate any questioning of his disastrous finances and hadn't mentioned the child-support payments he was obligated to keep current. Lynn had an hourly job that barely fed her. She hated the work she was doing even though she had been promoted to supervisor, so once she married Ben she quit her job. She took the little booklet to heart and stayed home in the apartment to cook and clean.

Ben didn't tell her he was in debt and couldn't support her, so when she quit her job he panicked. But instead of confessing to her, he withdrew and got increasingly depressed. She tried to be the happy housewife and cheer him up, but the more giddy she became the more miserable he was. As the unquestioning, submissive mate she was trying to be, Lynn didn't meddle in the finances. She just handed him the bills once a month. After all, aren't husbands supposed to support and protect their wives? Didn't the booklet talk about the priest, provider, and protector?

While still in never-never land, Lynn came to one of our seminars where she learned about the personalities for the first time. She saw her desperate need for fun and attention and realized she was getting neither. She saw that she had been out of control her whole life when her Choleric nature wanted so eagerly to be in charge.

That day we spoke on victimization as well as personality types, and I made the statement that those who were abused in childhood develop a victim personality and continue to be victimized throughout life. This thought kept playing in Lynn's mind—especially the conclusion, "Wake up, women. Don't spend the rest of your life waiting for him to change. Get hold of your life and ask the Lord to show you what He wants you to do."

A few days later Lynn's world fell apart one more time. The lights were turned off, the phones were disconnected, and the bank called to report that several checks had bounced. All of Lynn's years of bottled up anger came spewing forth when Ben walked in the door that night. She jumped on him in a rage, beat him over the head with a chair, knocked him to the floor, and jumped on him. She screamed, swore at him, and collapsed in an hysterical heap. Although Lynn uttered not a coherent word, Ben gathered that his fears had come to pass. Lynn knew about the money problems.

Ben locked himself in the bathroom and refused to come out to face his hostile, screaming wife. Here were two well-meaning people in what appeared to be a hopeless situation. It was that night that Lynn called our office. She didn't know what to do and we were the only people she could think of to call. She had the number from our book list and we happened to be in the office late. Fred explained to her and to Ben over the phone the four areas of problems that wouldn't necessarily be solved even if they had an abundance of money.

1. They got married too quickly and for the wrong reasons. They didn't take time to get to know each other and especially didn't talk about money. They avoided touchy issues before marriage and then handled each one explosively as it reared its ugly head later. They had no basis for honest communication, and neither one wanted to discuss money.

2. They had no understanding of their own personalities and even less of each other's. They didn't know that under stress she would attack and he would pull back. They didn't realize that personality weaknesses burdened by the additional load of victimization become accentuated in a negative direction. Thus, what would have made a normal Choleric person angry infuriated Lynn into a wild display of temper and attack. What would have merely upset a Phlegmatic facing a confrontation threw Ben into a panic and caused him to run for cover.

3. Neither one thought their childhood traumas had any bearing on their adult emotions. They had each buried the past. Ben had refused to even think about his, and Lynn had pushed her past under a flurry of activity and codependent behavior. Even though Lynn had married a man who didn't beat her, she was being quietly victimized by his lack of financial responsibility and his hiding of the truth rather than facing it.

4. Lynn wanted a Christian marriage so badly that she did everything the booklet said without balancing it with common sense. She quit her job without looking at their finances realistically. She put all the responsibility

onto Ben with no knowledge of whether he wanted to handle it or was able to do so. She thought avoiding reality was part of submission and that her wishful thinking of having a strong, sound reliable husband would make it all come true.

How could we help this distraught couple?

It's too late to repair problem number one. They are already married. Had we met with them before, we would have recommended they read *Freeing Your Mind from Memories That Bind* and ask each other the questions on pages 87 to 137. Couples who have done this have found that what they learned about each other was so informative that they had a new and deeper level of emotional communication. We suggested they both do this in a better-late-than-never effort.

We explained their personality strengths and weaknesses, reviewed how opposite they were from each other, and reminded them, "Just because you're different doesn't make you wrong." These were new thoughts, especially to Ben, and understanding them helped both spouses see the reason behind their behaviors.

We started them on a program of disciplined daily writing of their prayers, getting honest with themselves and God for the first time, and getting their anger out on paper. They began to work through Fred's book *The Promise of Healing Your Hurts and Your Feelings*, and later Fred prayed with them individually in a memory-retrieval time to uncover whatever the Lord wanted them to see. Lynn found that she had been sexually abused by several relatives and Ben saw that he had felt rejected from early childhood when he'd heard his mother say, "I didn't really want him." Getting to the core of their problems helped them to see why they put themselves into positions where they could be revictimized.

Perhaps the most painful part of their recovery was taking a realistic look at their finances. When they put the figures on paper there was no hope but bankruptcy unless they were both willing to get to work and budget out a way to pay off the debts. They had both lied to each other over the money situation (Lynn also had some debts she had been reluctant to discuss). Neither one was totally right or totally wrong, but they both had to grow up, become responsible, and communicate daily about their problems until they were settled.

When you put two hurting people together you don't automatically produce a happy marriage, as Lynn and Ben found out. But with God's help mismatched mates can overcome the odds that seem to be stacked against them. This begins with each spouse's taking responsibility for his or her recovery from the past. Lynn is taking control of her own life in a healthy way whether or not Ben changes. She recently told me, "I'll never forget that day at your seminar when you said, 'Wake up, women.' I didn't know then how much I had to wake up to!"

4

Who Are All Those Dysfunctional People?

We like to think that dysfunctional families live somewhere else. They drink a lot, have children on drugs, and never go to church. Books are written about them, but we don't need to read them. Some of them are labeled codependent, and many of them are involved in twelve-step programs and support groups. Like the Pharisees, we are so glad we are not one of them!

But look again. Is there any chance that we, dedicated Christians that we are, could possibly be living in a situation that is somewhat off balance? Is there a chance that we are living in a state of denial, smiling as we refuse to look the truth in the face?

So many of us quote verses on honesty to our children. We know God wants us to be truthful in our innermost parts. We know the truth will set us free. We can recite the Ten Commandments and teach Sunday school, but some of us hope no one will peek underneath our blanket of deception and catch a corner of the real truth.

It's not that we ever intended to lie, but our circumstances have caused us to cover up the truth in order to cope. Some of us have come out of contentious homes that we told ourselves were normal. Some of us are in marriages where we are demeaned and verbally abused, and we're hoping the children won't notice and the church won't find out. Some of us are single mothers trying to raise our children, earn enough money to support them, and not be bitter that our ex-husband is living happily in a comfortable lifestyle that's way above our means.

Whatever our situation, we need to wake up and face the truth so we can move on. We can't have faith in the future until we can acknowledge the present and look at ourselves with a realistic and appraising eye.

Are you in denial about your past and present?

Are you pretending that life is better than it is or that it will clear up tomorrow?

Are you deceiving yourself and others by twisting the truth?

Could you possibly be one of those dysfunctional people?

The Barrier of Denial

The definition of *denial* is "refusal to accept the truth or disclaiming responsibility for unpopular or negative actions." Denial is the major barrier that prevents women from seeking counseling to uncover the root of their problems. When it is suggested that perhaps there was some childhood abuse or dysfunction, they often dispute the possibility and won't go back to the counselor.

Until the seeker is willing to face the truth, whatever it may be, there is little a helper can do. Conversely, when someone is willing to find the truth it is amazing how quickly the Lord will bring it forth.

Tuning Out Abuse

Virginia grew up in an extremely religious home. The mother was spiritually submissive, and the daughters were trained to have "the attitude of a servant." The father and brothers were considered superior to the docile females and were never held to any accountability. Virginia never married and felt ill at ease in the presence of men.

When she came to CLASS (Christian Leaders, Authors, and Speakers Seminar) and Fred prayed with her, Virginia uncovered childhood memories of sexual abuse by her older brother. This behavior had never been talked about with anyone. She had suppressed the painful memories. After her memories returned, Virginia listened to us teach on the personalities at CLASS. Then she went home and explained them to her Phlegmatic mother as a way to open up some genuine communication and put an end to her years of denial. Here are Virginia's words:

> Last week my mom and I had the first deep talk we've ever had. Three members of my family are rather low emotionally just now, and Mama asked about them. Talking about their

situations really opened the door to explaining and discussing many things that had occurred in our family, including the many rejections, both verbal and more subtly. Mama remembers so few of these incidents that I realized anew how Phlegmatic she really is. I believe she tuned out and never really heard or absorbed the harsh statements and controlling threats Pop so frequently made to us.

She doesn't remember things I recall happening when I was five or six. She doesn't realize how abused her children have been and therefore has never raised a finger in their defense.

She listened so well as I explained about personalities. She could pick herself out as a Phlegmatic with some Melancholy in her. The outline of temperaments gave me an excellent background for two and a half hours of talking. I could sense the things I'd heard during CLASS coming out of me—flowing out of me—and it was exhilarating! There were flashbacks where I could see Florence standing up there speaking and it was thrilling to realize that I, too, was able to speak in a confident, caring way.

Virginia's words about her mother describe the denial we hear from so many. They tell us, "My mother looked the other way and tuned out on the abuse going on in the family." As mothers we must be aware of what's happening to our children and watch for signs of emotional or sexual abuse. We cannot look the other way when our children show signs of abuse; it's imperative to take action because the results of it don't go away, as we might have thought in the past. The symptoms grow worse and often seem to reach their peak around age forty, suddenly causing the childhood victim to have sexual, emotional, and even physical problems that seem to appear without explanation. Many women tell us about years of counseling and medical tests that have not yet uncovered the source of their symptoms, which include failed marriages, migraine headaches, depression, PMS, and general dysfunction.

No one likes to think that his or her child could be abused. The tendency is to hope for the best, and optimism is always good; but we must be aware of the possibility of abuse, read up on the symptoms, and not leave the child with someone he or she pulls away from or reacts against. In our book *Get a Life without the Strife* we have a chapter on how to tell if your child has been abused. Feedback from readers and workshop participants tells us this information has already been helpful to thousands.

When I ask mothers who suspected their children were being abused why they did nothing about it, they say, "It was easier to look the other way." Some add, "I didn't want to do anything that would upset the family" or "my husband" or "my mother." They say, "It was just better to pretend everything was all right and not to bring it up." Another excuse is "I didn't know how I could support the family without him," a realistic problem if the father ends up in jail. Another excuse is, "If I told him I suspected anything, he'd kill me." And those mothers who were victimized themselves as children say, "I lived through it so I guess she can, too."

There is no easy way to deal with these problems when they invade our homes, but we must put the safety of the child before money, fear, indifference, or keeping the peace. We must come out of denial and seek the truth because while we are in denial, our problems continue to grow. We need to watch for the symptoms and not put our religious heads in the sand.

Looking the Other Way

Marie came up to Fred at a lunch break during a workshop and told him about her daughter. He listened as Marie shared bizarre tales of the thirteen-year-old who was depressed and suicidal, who cut herself with razor blades and stuck pins through the ends of her fingers. She and her friends dressed totally in black and went to secret meetings. When she came home she seemed drugged and went immediately to her room, which was covered with posters of rock stars and witches. Her best friend at that point was in the hospital recovering from a suicide attempt. Would you say we had a serious problem here? No matter what your knowledge of satanic groups might be, could you not see that this child's behavior was way beyond any normal teen activity?

Fred explained the severity of the situation, telling Marie her daughter was probably involved in some occult and/or satanic activity. Her clothes, posters, behavior, and depression added up to some form of mind control. Fred asked the mother what she'd done for the child and she said her doctor had given her mood-elevating drugs.

"Did they help?" Fred asked.

"I don't really know," Marie replied. "I found out she sold the pills at school."

"What did you do when you found that out?"

"There was nothing to do; she'd already sold them."

In frustration, Fred explained what she had to do to save this child. But when he challenged her to action, she responded, "My husband would never believe any of this. We're Christians and he doesn't take any stock in this satanic stuff." When Fred emphasized the seriousness of the suicide attempts Marie shook her head. "My husband thinks it's just a phase and since I'm a submissive wife, I can't do anything about it," she said.

Marie would rather live in denial than salvage her child.

Wake up, Marie! Wake up before it's too late!

Facing the Truth

When I first met Georgia she was pouring all her energy into rearing her children and working as an artist. Emotionally she was just beginning to realize her life was coming apart at the seams. The denial system she had utilized for so many years was no longer working. Yet when asked how she was doing, Georgia would smile and say, "Just fine." As a Christian, Georgia put up with the pain of an abusive marriage because she felt she had no choice. Afterward, she wrote the following letter:

> I put off confronting my situation for way too many years. I am so blessed that the Lord is restoring those years and heal-ing the pain in my life and my children's, but many of the painful experiences could have been avoided if I had had the tools and the healing I have now.
>
> Because of the life patterns I felt comfortable with, I could not see beyond the denial. That's why getting help is of the utmost importance. To be set free, TRUTH is the only av-enue. Perhaps your book will open women's eyes to truth. Our Lord did not intend for us to be victims. Without truth we do not even know that we are VICTIMS. It has been a journey for me, and with each new truth there is new pain. But each time the pain is less, the JOY more exhilarating. Hope and trust are new roads that I now travel with excitement and new expectation.
>
> Write your book. If it sets but one person on a journey to truth and the freedom that truth promises then you will have been an instrument in the hands of our Lord. For He came that we might know the truth and be set free. And when one knows the truth then others follow. Because I've finally faced the truth, the lives of my children are being changed, and I know my grandchildren will someday experience a better way to live.

Pretending

In an article titled, "Psyched Out," author Mary Kay Blakely writes of the state of denial we seem to be in as a country. She tells of another article she wrote in which she suggested that people with problems face their true issues and not look for a quick fix. But the magazine editor wouldn't print the article because it wasn't optimistic enough, an attitude Blakely calls the Valium Theory of writing, giving people what they want to hear. This theory suggests that "prose should numb the blues without trying to name the problem."[1] She realizes the fallacy of teaching the public that happiness is within everyone's reach forever. Our first task in getting our lives together, she writes, is to get out of denial and "acknowledge reality."

The word *pretend* comes from Latin roots that literally mean "to stretch in front of like a curtain." If we picture life as a theatrical production where we all live happily ever after, we are pretending. We create a fictional fairy tale and step out from behind the curtain for our final bow. No one could have acted this out any better than I did. As a perfect candidate for Cinderella, I read all the fiction about the poor waif who married the handsome prince—and I did it. When Fred constantly corrected me and tried to make me perfect I just smiled and moved on.

When We Could No Longer Pretend

When our first son was diagnosed as fatally brain damaged, both Fred and I made the best of it. In fact we did our best to deny it! Our families could handle it much better if we didn't talk about our producing this hopeless child, and few of them ever came near. It was easier to look the other way. We went to a healer who told us if we would only believe this child was perfect, he would be healed. I worked hard at pretending, but when the baby was screaming in convulsions, my faith in the faith healer fled.

We couldn't actually deny the reality, but we worked at pretending that tomorrow would be a brighter day. Optimism is a blessing, but as I said earlier, while we are reaching for it we need to deal with the realities of today.

Our family had a double dose of reality when our second son was diagnosed with the same disease. I wanted to stretch a curtain over this second scene, but I had no choice. There was no happy ending. Both boys died. There was no curtain call, just an empty crib. We had to accept the fact that we had lost our two sons and make adjustments in our plan for our life together. Through this experience we both accepted the Lord and found *true reality*.

We talk with people every day who are not in touch with reality. Some are denying they have problems; they have stuffed their memories in a dark corner of their mind. And even though they have symptoms and sickness, they'd rather not seek the truth. Some recognize the sad situation they are in but pretend it's not there so they won't have to deal with it. But neither denial nor pretending is an answer; we must face the truth, work positively toward a solution, and learn from the experience.

Lives Built on Dreams

One morning I tuned into a talk show where the host was interviewing a young lady, I'll call her Leslie, who seemed to be attracted to charming men who would sponge off her and never go to work. Leslie wasn't a stupid woman academically. She had an MBA degree and a high-paying job. She had lived with one particular man for five years and had a child by him; she had given him money, checks, and credit cards. She looked the other way when he had affairs and broke up with him only when his lavish spending on other women caused her to go bankrupt. But Leslie didn't seem to learn from this disaster. She soon went into another relationship with a man of culture, refinement, and the arts who sat home and thought about what he might write or paint.

When asked what she had learned from all this she said, "To look at their bank accounts and employment records before I get involved." Leslie had built her life on a dream, living a life of pretense even when the truth was standing in front of her, waving a red flag.

Leslie was just a passing face on TV, but I have met many women whose stories are similar to hers, women who built their lives on dreams and refused to see the truth. Like me, many women grew up optimistic, wanting the best and expecting to get married and live happily ever after. We were instructed to compliment people who weren't attractive, to smile when we felt like crying, and to deny that we had any problems at home. So is it any wonder now that we look the other way when our dream husband disappoints us and our children are far from perfect? Don't we also hope that if we hang in there one more day our circumstances will change?

Dr. Harriet Lerner, author of *Dance of Deception*, says, "Pretending is so closely associated with femininity that it is, quite simply, what the culture teaches women to do." In her book she issues a call for women to become honest with themselves if they wish to have any kind of positive, intimate relationship with anyone. "Lying erodes trust," Dr. Lerner points out. "Closeness requires honesty."[2] How can you have a genuine relationship with someone you can't trust?

Becoming Real

Some of us grew up in homes where we didn't like the balance of power and vowed when we got married things would be different. But how many of us have repeated our family's mistakes without even realizing what we were doing?

When Margaret was in her teens she analyzed her parents. Her mother was the powerful Choleric personality, angry, bossy, and dominating. Her father was Phlegmatic, peaceful, and quiet, and would go to any lengths to avoid conflict. Margaret saw him as weak and her mother as strong; she felt her mother was the problem. "Didn't she push everyone around? Didn't Dad and I have to escape into work and school in order to keep away from her?" Although Margaret could identify the various personalities, she didn't really understand how they worked. She determined not to be like her mother when she grew up—when actually she was already like her mother. But instead of learning to understand her weaknesses, she decided to change and become the dear, sweet, submissive type she'd heard about in church.

Unfortunately when we try to shift personality types and pretend to be something we aren't, we cross up God's plan for us and we actually start working at odds with what we were created to be. Ultimately this can end up causing not only personality problems, but social and emotional troubles and even physical pain. I've never met a truly happy woman who was functioning outside of her birth personality. Rather than remake herself, Margaret should have analyzed her mother's weaknesses. Then she would have seen how much her father's reserved personality caused her mother's extremes, and she could have determined to avoid the pitfalls herself.

Instead, Margaret watched TV, pretending to be the lead in each show, and aimed to have a marriage like the one in "Father Knows Best." She wrote, "In my teens I formed ideas of what kind of marriage I wanted. It certainly wasn't going to be like my parents'. I didn't want to be bossy like Mother or have a weak husband like my father. I would seek out the opposite!"

And she did! Once Margaret started playing the demure heroine role, she attracted a strong Choleric man who was certainly in control of himself and soon of her. For many years she played her part well, covering up her frustrations and depression by doing and saying all the right things. In spite of her positive pretending, however, Margaret knew her marriage was failing.

Margaret remembers, "The day I realized I was being my dad and I had married my mother was a shocker! But once I could see the source of the problem, the healing began."

It was at this point that Margaret came to CLASS and began to study the personalities. She started to pray that the Lord would restore those lost years of confused identity and make her a genuine person. Her husband was stunned when his submissive wife began offering opinions, but he did begin to notice her in a new and positive way. To change a long-term marriage is not easy, but Margaret knew it was worth working for. She said, "It was a long ten years, which included several sessions of CLASS, Southern California women's retreats, a day of healing prayer, and almost a divorce, but our power structure and roles eventually became much more balanced. My husband even told the counselor that he likes me 'brassy!'"

Margaret's being brassy isn't what he likes, but that Margaret is finally *real*. No one likes to live with a phony, even if he or she isn't discerning enough to recognize the disguise.

Margaret has worked prayerfully and with outside help to become her true Sanguine and Choleric self, to be fun-loving and humorous and to be able to state her feelings clearly, firmly, and lovingly. I have personally been involved in the changes and have seen the spiritual and emotional growth as Margaret has determined to be real.

Uncovering Deception

While *denial* is often an unconscious act of covering up the truth, and *pretending* is a conscious act of believing things are better than they really are, *deception* is a plot to fool and trick ourselves and others or prevent the truth from being known. Initially we deceive only ourselves, but after a while we extend the cover-up to others. Remember when, as children, we told a white lie about a friend and then had to continue lying to keep the first lie secure? Remember how confusing it became and how we ultimately were caught in our own story? It's like the lines in that classic poem:

> Oh what a tangled web we weave,
> When first we practice to deceive![3]

How many of us well-meaning women are living a lie today and hoping no one will find out? So many of the women who come to me start with the sentence, "I've never told this to anyone before." After that comes an assortment of confessions:. "I was abused as a child." "My son is on drugs." "My husband's a church elder but he beats me." "He's a closet alcoholic." "He's been having a series of affairs." "He's a compulsive gambler." "He's gay!"

In all these cases the woman has been living a lie. She didn't mean to or want to, but she got caught in a tangled web of deception. Many of these women believe if they brought the truth out in the open they would be ostracized from the Christian community. Yet keeping it hidden is causing them to have headaches, stomach upsets, or nervous exhaustion, to overeat, and often to withdraw from any meaningful relationships. When we are living in a deceptive environment, it is as if we are constantly onstage in a theatrical production twenty-four hours a day with no intermission. We are worn out.

We don't need to live this way any longer. No matter what our problems are, there are others who have similar burdens who will understand. There are support groups and twelve-step programs for almost every type of emotional or addictive situation imaginable. The first step is always to recognize we have a problem and want to do something about it, humanly and prayerfully.

When we continue to deny the possibility of repressed trauma, pretend things will right themselves tomorrow, and deceive ourselves and others, we become one of those dysfunctional people we always believed lived in someone else's neighborhood.

Hiding Adoptions

Frequently I find family deception surrounding adoptions. Since Fred and I adopted a son after the loss of our two, we minister with understanding to others who have brought a child into their home by adoption. Although I don't profess to be an authority on the subject, I do feel strongly that adoptive parents owe it to the child to let him or her know from the beginning that he or she is adopted. If we don't, we begin a tangled web of deception that may disintegrate our relationship when the child inadvertently learns the truth. When that happens the child not only has the belated shock of finding that Mother and Father aren't his or her birth parents but that they aren't honest either!

We told our little Fred that God had chosen him for us over all the children in the whole world. He knew he was adopted before he had a real concept of the word's meaning. When he was eighteen, we told him he could search for his birth mother if he wished to. At that time he didn't, but at twenty-five he changed his mind and found both his father and mother. He was mature and stable enough to handle a new family without turning away from us.

In contrast to the openness we had about our son's adoption, some parents hide the adoption as a dark family secret. This was the case for Audrey, who grew up in what appeared to be a normal Christian home with a mother, father, and two older sisters. She was fifteen years younger than her sister June and never could figure out why June didn't seem to like her. She tried so hard to get June to play with her but June always shoved her off and grumbled about how difficult it was to have this little pest of a sister.

June grew up and left home and when Audrey was seventeen and about to graduate from high school, she visited a cousin who told her she had been adopted. Audrey was shocked and didn't believe the cousin. She went home and asked her mother if that were true. Unwillingly, the mother told Audrey that her sister, June, was really her mother and that she was her grandmother. Audrey was devastated. Not only was she not her mother's child, but she had been lied to for seventeen years and her real mother didn't even like her. Is it any wonder that by the time Audrey came to me with this tale she was depressed, overweight, in a miserable marriage, and angry at God?

How important it is for each one of us to live in truth, for only then will we be set free.

Dysfunction

I saw a cartoon that showed an auditorium with a banner that said "National Convention for Children of Normal Parents." There was only one child in the audience! The cartoon wouldn't be convicting if it did not represent the current thinking that nobody is normal anymore. But if we are all somewhat dysfunctional, does that include you and me?

According to the *New York Times*, "Americans participated in an estimated 100 million therapy sessions with licensed practitioners in the year ending June, 1992 and paid approximately $8.1 billion, not counting prescription drugs, to relieve this national despair."[4]

One hundred million therapy sessions. That seems like enough to take in all of us, yet the writer points out this does not include those who went to pastors, lay counselors, physicians, or friends for advice or those who stayed home and read books on codependency and mental health. The total doesn't even pretend to include Christian books and seminars.

If we as a nation are in such a bad emotional condition and we as Christians are to be examples for the rest, then we had better check ourselves out. Are we living in denial of our pain, pretending we are happy Christians, deceiving ourselves and others?

When Submission Becomes Codependency

Some of us Christian women are so steeped in the need to be submissive that we make our husbands into fathers who must take care of us. We appear to be the most devout of wives, worshiping our husbands. Gina was like that. She adored her husband and praised his every move. "Isn't he handsome?" she'd ask, and we all had to say, "He's the handsomest man we've ever met."

"Isn't he wonderful, intelligent, spiritual?" Yes, yes, yes. When together at social functions Gina would cling to Daryl's arm and coo at his every word. While the rest of the women were in the kitchen, Gina would be with Daryl and the men, who frankly wished she'd buzz off.

She never made even the tiniest decision without calling Daryl at work. She didn't seem able to plug in the coffeepot without his instruction. When he was out of town on business, Gina was a wreck; often she got physically sick awaiting his return. Gina was without a doubt the most submissive woman in the church—and proud of it.

Imagine her total shock on the day when she was kissing Daryl good-bye and clinging to him and he shoved her away. "I'm so sick of your whining all over me," he snarled at her. "When are you going to grow up and be a real woman?" With that he slammed the door and drove off to work.

"What am I doing wrong?" she cried to me over the phone. "You know what a good wife I've been. I've put him first in everything."

What was wrong here? Gina had a distorted view of submission and when I talked to Daryl he said he felt suffocated by this child-wife who couldn't move without his direction or talk without his words. It took a time of separation and counseling to help Gina grow up and become a responsible adult, one who could think through a problem and come up with a rational decision.

When submission becomes a codependent relationship, we women may be drowning our husbands.

Kay prided herself on being the submissive wife. She worried over every little thing and always looked to Sam to fix whatever was wrong. He was strong and capable and always made things better when times got tough. He felt this was his responsibility as the head of the house. Sam was a self-employed builder and the picture of physical health and strength until he turned forty-nine and began to experience chest pains. After several tests he learned the main artery to his heart was more than

95 percent blocked. The doctors did three angioplasties that didn't hold and eventually tried experimental surgery not yet approved by governmental agencies.

As Kay sat alone in the motel near the hospital, she read 1 Peter and was struck with the thought of being called to suffer with and glorify Christ. Kay feared her husband would die, and she wondered how she could ever function without him, let alone be used to glorify Christ in her suffering.

Kay tells what happened next:

> Alone in my motel room I cried out to God, "I'm afraid, God! Don't let Sam die. I love him; I need him!" I remembered the theme of 1 Peter. I didn't like having to suffer with and glorify Christ. But then I felt God telling me to rest in His arms, put my trust totally in Him, and He would do the glorifying through me. I realized I had not been the submissive little wife; I had been the codependent little wife. I needed to put God first. I could trust Him and find comfort in His arms. Submission to God comes first; submission to one another under the headship of Christ follows.
>
> My husband is doing very well physically now, but our lives have changed. You see, the more I depend on God the more freedom it gives my husband to not have to always make things better for me. When I find myself slipping back into putting Sam first, I remind myself that I can rest in my Savior's arms, that He is worthy of my total submission to Him.

Kay is now a staff minister to women in her church, teaching them how to be submissive to the Lord Jesus Christ and not be codependent to their husbands.

Gina and Kay are finally *awake*.

Could you be one of those dysfunctional people you keep hearing about? Remember:

Denial—refusing to acknowledge the past,

plus

Pretending—hoping the future will be better,

plus

Deception—hiding the truth in the present,

equals

Dysfunction—abnormal behavior.

We women are the emotional cords that hold our families together. Are your cords frayed and about to break? Answer the following questions on the Self-Analysis Quiz honestly and begin to think about yourself from an objective point of view.

Self-Analysis Quiz

	Yes	No
Are you living in a dysfunctional situation?	___	___
Does one person control the rest of your family?	___	___
Is there one person whom everyone's afraid of?	___	___
Is there one person who causes problems for the others?	___	___
Are you unhappy when you are with one certain person?	___	___
Are you more yourself when you are apart from this person?	___	___
Are you restricted in your social life by the demands at home?	___	___
Do you sometimes feel like a prisoner in your own home?	___	___
Have you been denying your emotional pain and problems?	___	___
Do you often say, "Well, others have it worse than I do"?	___	___
Are you afraid of someone's angry outbursts? of being beaten? of retaliation?	___	___
Are there alcohol or drug problems in your home?	___	___
Are you pretending things are better than they are?	___	___
Are you taking abuse by hoping it will stop tomorrow?	___	___
Is your optimism really self-deception?	___	___
Do you think submission means you have no rights?	___	___
Do you think that enduring abuse is suffering for Jesus?	___	___
Do you think Christians should pretend to be happy no matter how they feel?	___	___

	Yes	No
Do you rationalize and make excuses for the behavior of your family members?	___	___
Would you admit to yourself that your household is a mess?	___	___
Are you prevented from getting the healthcare you feel you need?	___	___
Are you kept ignorant of family finances?	___	___
Do you sometimes feel there's just no hope?	___	___
If no one held you accountable, would you pack up and take off tomorrow?	___	___
Do you feel tangled in a web of deception?	___	___

If you answered yes to more than a few of these questions, you are not living the abundant life the Lord Jesus wants for you. If you've been living a lie even though it's not your fault, it's time to wake up to the reality around you and take steps to get beyond and above your situation. You don't have to be a victim of circumstances any longer.

Untangling the Web of Denial, Pretending, Deception, and Dysfunction

This book is intended to help you get in touch with reality, to quit pretending, and to face the facts. Until we women wake up from our own fairy tales, we can't establish meaningful relationships with anyone.

I met with one couple who pretended their problems "weren't all that bad." When I got around to asking some specific questions she said, "Would it be all right if he left the room for a while?" He agreed to go, and after he'd shut the door she explained, "I had to get him out of here because everything I've told you so far is a lie." She then poured out a story of a lifetime of deception including a sexual relationship with her father, affairs during her marriage, and a Christian daughter who was living with an abusive man. This last problem bothered her the most and she was working hard to keep it from the church in hopes her fellow Christians would never know her perfect family wasn't perfect. No wonder this lady was overweight, a compulsive talker, exhausted, and a nervous wreck. She was working so hard to protect the truth that her tangled web was in knots.

How about your life? Is it time for you to unravel some of the knots in your past and present so you can get control of your life in the future? Look at the chart in Appendix A comparing three prominent views of current issues affecting Christian women. Which view represents the way you look at potential dysfunctions in your life or your family? Is yours the world view, the balanced Christian view, or the legalistic view?

You don't want to be one of those dysfunctional people. Wake up!

5

Managing the Money

One of the major areas where Christian women need to wake up is in finances. Over the years we've expected our husbands to earn and control the money, but in these difficult times, we need to understand things we never thought we'd have to handle. Father may know best, but what if he's not around? What if he's dead or divorced? What if he's injured on the job? What if he's never been good with money? We cannot hide from responsibility or turn our heads in the other direction.

Personality and Money

Before we look at examples of women who have handled money both right and wrong, let's examine the different personalities and their ability to work with figures. We are each born with certain talents. The question is not whether a male or female is best at certain tasks, but which personality can do the best job. Not all men have a feel for finances and not all women have a fear of figures.

No matter how little or how much our families have, we want to use it wisely. To do this most effectively, it is helpful to know the personalities of all family members so we can understand their differences.

Before Fred and I understood the personality differences we wondered why we had one child who analyzed her allowance and apportioned it correctly and one who spent it foolishly and had no money for lunch on

Friday. Hadn't we taught them both in the same way? Hadn't they each received the amount they needed?

Until we studied the personalities we had no explanation for their behavior. But when we learned the family members' individual personalities we understood their financial characteristics.

The Popular Sanguine loves money and the things it will buy. Sanguines tend to be lustful after possessions and greedy to have more of everything than their friends. Since their basic desire is to have fun, money guarantees a ticket to happiness. In this quest for pleasure the Popular Sanguines have little thought for tomorrow, and the idea of a budget or discipline never enters their heads. They have little natural interest in numbers; balancing checkbooks is a chore to be postponed.

If the husband in the family is Sanguine, he will need some kind of assistance in handling finances or the family may be bankrupt before anyone knows what's going on. The Sanguine male picks up the check for everyone at the table even if he knows he's overdrawn at the bank. Sanguines are so desperate for people to love and admire them that they will do whatever it takes to be the good guy in any situation. Sanguines' combination of natural generosity and poor grasp of figures causes them to go quickly into debt. When checks start to bounce they are genuinely surprised—and their mates are furious. "Didn't you know you didn't have anything in the checking account?" they rage.

"No—I guess I forgot to write in the amounts."

"I can't believe you are so stupid!"

Since the Sanguines want praise and don't want to be called stupid, this comment so depresses them that they have to go shopping to cheer themselves up. The cycle starts again.

The Sanguines love excitement and want to go on every outing or vacation that comes along regardless of cost. They will gladly go into debt for the pursuit of pleasure. They are frequently living today off of what they hope to earn tomorrow. They buy equipment for every sport or hobby before they know if they even like it or can do it. If they're going to take up golf, they'll buy the best clubs available. If they plan to take piano lessons, they'll purchase a piano.

Judy told me her Sanguine husband decided to take up woodworking during their long Canadian winter. She bought him a little kit in a hobby shop and he began to carve wooden figures. He had such fun that he decided to get better equipment; soon he had the best money could buy. "He could have competed with Michelangelo!" Judy said in disgust. Typically, when spring came his interest left with the daffodils. He hasn't carved ever since.

Opposite of the spending Sanguine is the meticulous Melancholy, who watches over every cent like a hawk. Money is doled out carefully, and an accounting must be made of every expenditure. When married to a Sanguine, the disparity is so obvious as to cause major marriage problems. The Sanguine thinks the Melancholy is stingy and is out to ruin his or her life. The Melancholy asks, "What did you do with what I gave you yesterday?"

"I don't know, but I do know I didn't give it to charity."

This comment is supposed to be funny, but it doesn't amuse the Melancholy. Until you understand the personality differences, there doesn't seem to be an explanation for these behaviors. But once you understand the forces behind these attitudes everything comes into focus.

Melancholies love figures, charts, graphs, and budgets. They can stare at ledger books by the hour. They find errors in everyone else's work, causing others to refuse to work with them. ("If that's the way you're going to be, you can do it yourself.") They have high standards, and when the rest of the family bounces along, blithely indifferent, it puts the Melancholies into a depression. "Am I the only one who cares?" they fume. "This whole family is like a kindergarten."

Melancholies rarely get into financial problems on their own; if they do buy over their heads, it's not for a trivial pleasure but a superior machine or computer that will enhance their pursuit of perfection. Sometimes they spend so much time analyzing all the different products, reading *Consumer Reports*, and asking for other people's opinions that the item is outdated by the time they've chosen the right model.

It is easy to see why the frivolous, fun-loving Sanguine loses patience with the nitpicking Melancholy. Ideally, since this pair usually gets married, the Melancholy should keep the books but not be fanatical about it. The Sanguine needs to have some "fun money" that doesn't need to be accounted for but also needs to work on curbing his or her spending habits. The Sanguine can loosen up the Melancholy and the Melancholy can rein in the Sanguine but only if they understand their differences and communicate on the subject without hostility.

For the Powerful Choleric money spells success. Cholerics don't spend foolishly nor do they sit around and meditate over it. Money is a tool, a bargaining chip. Cholerics want to be thought of as successful and they will use money to impress others with how well they have done in life. Usually they are the movers and shakers, but they are not beyond manipulating others to achieve their own goals. They believe that the end justifies the means of getting there. Others see them as cold and calculating, but they feel they are doing what any person with intelligence would choose.

Cholerics love challenges, and they seem to do the impossible. It just takes a little longer. The words "it can't be done" move them into action. "I'll show them," they mumble under their breath. Because of their need to be heroes they sometimes take risks that lead to financial ruin, but even then they find ways to borrow and start over again. They have such confidence in their ability that events that devastate their mate are only a bump in the road for them. They can usually see the big picture and move on toward it.

Their aggressive attitude toward success is frustrating to a more conservative mate who tries in vain to tone them down, only to see them throw caution to the wind and enter into a new and dangerous business opportunity. One of Cholerics' biggest weaknesses is to think they don't have any! They never seek counsel or listen to anyone with a different opinion. Their mate tries in vain to get them to talk to the banker or Uncle Harry before jumping into a new venture, but they refuse. "Why should I listen to him when I know what I'm going to do anyway?"

When Cholerics are successful, they can be great achievers and provide a lavish lifestyle, but all too often they keep their family hanging over a cliff for so long that even the ravine below looks better than living on the edge.

The conservative Phlegmatic is often married to the daring Choleric, and their life together is chaotic. The Phlegmatic, whose aim is to keep peace and avoid problems, can't stand the adventurous mate and yet can't seem to deal with impending disaster. After a few protests, the Phlegmatic retreats and pretends not to care. "Let the chips fall where they may."

Left to themselves the Phlegmatics are dependable and responsible with money and want to avoid controversy at all costs. They don't see problems coming as the Melancholy does, they aren't daring as the Cholerics, and they don't throw money around like the Sanguines. They'd really be happy if they didn't have to look at money problems at all. They do not share the Melancholy's pleasure in meditating over ledgers.

Phlegmatics' weakness with money is that they are trusting of others and can't say no to those who appear to be in need. Even though Phlegmatics tend to be stingy with themselves, they easily fall prey to the sob story of a friend and give graciously without investigating the probability of return. When the mate finds they have once again been a soft touch without discussing it, he or she gets furious and rants and raves. "How could you do this to me?" This attack causes the peace-loving Phlegmatic to retreat, build a defensive wall, and vow never to be nice to anyone again. Phlegmatics need to be needed and because their mate usually can function adequately without them, they seek people who need them outside of the family, reopening the possibility of financial victimization.

The Phlegmatic usually doesn't make decisions quickly. This caution is good in questionable investments but annoying when the mate wants quick answers. Since the Phlegmatic and Choleric are usually married to each other, it is easy to see their area of financial conflict. The Choleric wants support for his or her daring ventures and the Phlegmatic is running scared, pleading, "Can't you wait and think about it awhile?" The Phlegmatic abdicates responsibility to the aggressive Choleric and then is hurt when things don't turn out right. "I should have known," the Phlegmatic says. But when the Phlegmatic is victimized while trying to be the nice guy the Choleric tears into him or her and leaves the peace-lover in pieces.

In her book *Money Makeover* Rosemarie Patterson suggests that we pair ourselves up with a person of opposite nature to review our financial situation and to make plans for the future. As a bankruptcy attorney she deals with people when it is already too late. She says if people could only see their personalities and their financial weaknesses, they would not continue to make the same mistakes. So if you are a free-spending Sanguine, find a meticulous Melancholy who will help you analyze and plan; you Melancholies find a Sanguine who will insert some fun into your budget. If you are Choleric, find a gentle Phlegmatic and listen to his or her caution; if you are Phlegmatic, team up with a Choleric who will add a sense of adventure to your life.

These personality types and their typical attitudes and behaviors about money are shown in the chart on page 48. Find yourself and your mate on the chart, then think about how you can use your differences to complement each other's strengths and weaknesses in managing your finances.

Let's all wake up together!

Recovering from Financial Chaos

One of the main reasons I decided to write this book was to help the endless numbers of fine Christian women who seem to know very little or nothing about finances and are ignorant about their husband's business affairs. Some have been left alone by death or divorce with no understanding of finances and no way to support their families. Others have been brainwashed to think that to be submissive they need to be a little bit stupid. They have been told they have no need to know their financial

---

Money Matters According to Personalities

The Popular Sanguine
Feels money buys FUN
Goes in debt for pleasure
Loves to party and possess
Cheers up the Melancholy
Needs to curb spending
Needs to become disciplined

The Powerful Choleric
Feels money is POWER
Goes in debt for risk
Loves to wheel and deal
Activates the Phlegmatic
Needs to listen to advice
Needs to think before
  investing

The Peaceful Phlegmatic
Feels money prevents PROBLEMS
Goes in debt for others
Loves to be needed
Restrains the Choleric
Needs to say No
Needs to get involved

The Perfect Melancholy
Feels money is to MANAGE
Goes in debt for the best
Loves to analyze and correct
Tones down the Sanguine
Needs to loosen up
Needs to accept others as
  they are

---

status; that is man's work. They've been to seminars where they've been instructed to give up their checks, credit cards, and common sense and trust the Lord. This might be acceptable if these women could also trust their husbands to do their part, but what of the wives who have played dumb and lost it all?

In the rest of this chapter I'd like to share some stories of women who have overcome trying circumstances to restore their families' financial difficulties. In many cases they denied their own skills in money matters and let their family slip into financial chaos because they thought they wouldn't be good, Christian, submissive wives if they stepped in to advise their husbands. (This legalistic view of money matters is compared with the world view and the balanced Christian view in the capsulized summaries in Appendix A.)

I'll also offer some sound, practical advice on how to get a handle on your financial status and how to protect yourself in case of your husband's death, divorce, or financial ineptitude.

Millie Misses the Mark

Millie, a Melancholy young woman, approached me with this scenario. Since she was the mathematical and analytical one, she had always taken care of all the finances, giving her Sanguine husband, Mark, a certain amount to have fun with each week. They were both happy with their roles until they went to a Christian seminar on money. This particular speaker explained that God would only bless families where the man was firmly in charge and handled all the money. He had charts and graphs to prove God's plan and at no time did he even infer that some men have no feel for finances. The speaker also didn't take inborn personality patterns into consideration.

This couple went home under a cloud of guilt, thinking what they had believed was all right was actually all wrong. Reluctantly, Millie gave Mark total control of the bills and the checkbook. She was not supposed to check up on him because that would show a lack of faith. When she came to me six months down the line, the mortgage was overdue, the lights had been turned off, and the phone disconnected. Mark had bought exercise equipment on an installment plan and, typical of the Sanguine male, had run up huge bills taking people out for dinner. She was furious, and he was a bit ashamed of how poorly he'd done.

"Do you think the speaker was right?" Millie asked me.

I reviewed her own story back to her and said, "If someone came to you with this problem, what advice would you give?"

Millie answered, "I'd tell her to take back the responsibility for the bills and the checkbook." And she did.

Unfortunately Christian women have been led to believe they shouldn't be too bright or, heaven forbid, "usurp authority." I've never met a good Christian woman who woke up one morning and said, "I think I'll go usurp authority." But I've met many who must have said, "Woe is me. In me is no good thing."

"I Should Have Stepped in Sooner"

From the time Caitlin and Alex became believing Christians they sincerely desired to serve the Lord and be positive witnesses in their community. They went to church every time the door was opened, attended and then taught Bible studies, and ran eagerly to every seminar that passed through town. In spite of their intentions, they didn't understand two things that were not taught in their church: their personality differences, especially as they applied to money, and that submission doesn't mean stupidity. Caitlin recalls:

We didn't find any scriptures telling us who was to handle the checkbook, or how. I guess there were no banks set up in Bible times and no payment books or credit cards either. We argued over this subject until Alex heard two radio talks that told him the man was the head of the house and should handle the money. The personality studies had not made their way to our church yet and evidently not to the preachers giving the messages. Because I had a great desire to be a good, submissive Christian wife, I didn't feel I had the right to challenge my husband's decision to handle the finances but I hated the bill collectors' calls, and when I mentioned them to my Sanguine husband he'd reply, "No problem. It's my responsibility; don't worry. I'll handle it." Bounced checks didn't bother him, and he couldn't understand why the banks got so upset.

When the first bank closed our account I was mortified with embarrassment, but he happily moved to another bank. He learned it was even more fun to have more than one account. By writing deposit checks back and forth to each bank he could actually keep things from bouncing longer. At the time neither of us knew this game was called *kiting*. When Alex did write checks, he failed to record them and he never was certain if there was money to cover them. He just wanted to get this no-fun, nonprofitable task over with in one fell swoop. If I objected or made suggestions, he would remind me to be submissive as the radio speakers had taught. Our efforts to follow God's direction, as those speakers presented it, have been disastrous in every way and, in my opinion, a terrible witness.

Caitlin wrote ten pages of financial crises they had gone through trying to follow what they thought was God's will. Finally, when no bank would give Alex an account, he had to allow Caitlin to take over the finances. By then Caitlin had no respect for Alex's financial abilities and didn't care what any male speaker had to say about finances. As Caitlin got involved in the money problems, she found unpaid taxes, huge interest payments, and general mismanagement.

Soon Caitlin and Alex were studying books on money matters and also reading my *Personality Plus* and Tim LaHaye's *Understanding the Male Temperament*. "Why don't those speakers on male headship know anything about the personalities?" Caitlin asked. "Alex's a great guy and everyone loves him, but he should never have tried to run our finances and I should have used my brain and stepped in sooner."

In addition to taking over their household money Caitlin encouraged Alex to hire a Melancholy manager at the business who would not write checks on empty accounts. Alex is much happier now that he is freed from responsibilities he hated. He spends his time selling new accounts and has increased the business more than enough to cover the salary of the manager.

Caitlin and Alex are not totally out of the red yet and they still owe the IRS, but they are heading in the right direction. They are current on regular bills, and all their personal charge cards are at a zero balance. Caitlin concludes, "We've updated our wills, prearranged our funerals, and established trusts. Honest, open, noncondemning communication has been the key. I am at peace with my relationship with God, my husband, and our creditors. I know that the Lord will not send more than I can handle. I'm not playing the submissive ostrich anymore. I am outspoken and firm where needed. But I will stand by my man, "for better or for worse, for richer or for poorer, in sickness and in health, til death do us part."

Starting Over Again

Just as Caitlin struggled with the happy-go-lucky Alex, Marcia tried to rein in her Powerful Choleric husband, Bill, who was always ready to take on a new challenge. Marcia had been initially attracted to Bill because he was so exciting to be with. There was never a dull moment. Bill made a lot of money and didn't need any advice from Marcia—or anyone else for that matter. As a dedicated Christian, Bill shared everything he owned with Marcia. He put Marcia's name on property, credit cards, loans, and checkbooks, and he frequently had her sign documents, but he refused to explain anything to her, saying, "this is man's work." Marcia told me, "Out of my desire to be a good, submissive Christian wife and obey him in all things, I held back a lot of the time from saying what I really felt."

Bill started out by selling life insurance, and at twenty-three he was the youngest man in the company ever to sell a million dollars' worth in a year, a feat he repeated five times. Then he started opening new businesses on the side and soon had five different businesses going. But he had no time for the details of running them.

Marcia explained, "My husband is optimistic to a fault. He never sees obstacles or problems, only challenges. I describe him as a guy who leaps and then looks for a place to land. Usually he lands on his feet but not always. He's a fast mover and tries to cover all bases himself. He never hesitates to take a chance. In our twenty-three years of marriage he has made a lot of money, spent a lot of money, and wasted a lot of money.

Bill had exceptional ability, but when he spread himself too thin he couldn't keep his hands on everything. His new businesses demanded constant cash infusions to keep them afloat, and soon Bill was having to borrow money. Marcia didn't realize there were serious problems and as the dutiful wife she signed on the loans without question. Soon the whole empire was collapsing around him. As creditors came calling Marcia was unhappily surprised that her signature stood for responsibility. For the first time in their marriage she had to pay attention to their finances. Bill was forced to talk to her about money and admit that he had made mistakes in his desire to keep his life exciting.

At Marcia's suggestion Bill agreed to hire some capable, detail-oriented people to help him in his businesses. From that point on Marcia and Bill discussed his ideas and Marcia helped him put his ambitions into perspective. She signed nothing she didn't understand, and she became his partner in every sense. Marcia is a submissive Christian wife, but she isn't stupid.

Father Knew Best

Kathleen had a different reason for ignoring family finances. She had grown up in a home where her military father had been in charge of all family decisions and especially financial ones. He had been fair with her and her mother, who wrote checks whenever she wished to purchase anything and never had to worry about the balance. The father's theory was to keep plenty of money in the account and let Mother enjoy life. He was generous and she didn't abuse the privilege. Neither parent ever explained money matters to Kathleen, and she accepted her parents' pattern as the norm. Since they were all Christians, she assumed that if she married a Christian she would have a similar situation.

She met Don at a Christian college and knew he was the right man for her. She never questioned his finances, nor did she express what she expected from him as a husband. Kathleen had no idea that he had some previous debts, so when he suggested a certain ring she opted for a more expensive one with a bigger diamond. When he wanted to use some hand-me-down furniture, Kathleen chose a new couch and matching love seat. Don, not wishing to appear cheap or dampen his bride's enthusiasm, let her charge her purchases.

The happiness over her new couch faded when Kathleen found notices of bounced checks and statements with big interest charges in the mail. Don resented her asking about these problems and thought to himself, *If she hadn't wanted the ring and the couch we wouldn't be in this mess.*

He thought the money problems were her fault since she had desired too much. He did not add in the burdens and bills he brought to the marriage. Kathleen was resentful that he didn't find money somewhere out of the blue to keep her happy as her father had always done for her mother.

It's easy for us to look at these examples and see objectively how these nice, well-intentioned Christian couples got themselves into financial difficulty that led to marriage problems, but when these spouses were in the throes of quiet anger neither one could see clearly. Each one buried the resentments he or she felt. Some couples push these hurt feelings down and don't deal with them until the day one of them irritates the other beyond his or her ability to handle it. *Bam!* One explodes and hysterically reviews a litany of mistakes, sending the other into a torrent of angry language that evokes an equally emotional response from the first. Then the cycle continues until doors slam and the combatants withdraw.

Fortunately, in Kathleen and Don's case, the spouses were mature enough to pause and assess their problems. Kathleen took over writing the checks and paying the bills. By doing this she got a realistic view of how much money came in compared to what was going out. No more hoping Daddy would just keep filling the well. Kathleen began to look at life as it is. By handling the money Kathleen has more security and she is no longer angry at Don. He is much happier, too, because he is not being compared with Daddy and he doesn't have to buy things he can't afford to make his wife content. Their finances are now a team effort and Don feels the pressure is off.

Kathleen says, "Many Christians buy foolishly on the faith that God will provide. God will bless us much more when He sees we are using common sense."

"You're a Crook!"

Joe called our office early one morning, desperate for immediate help. His wife, Janice, had thrown him out the night before and she wouldn't let him back in until he got some counseling. When he arrived he seemed like a nice enough person, though slightly disheveled from sleeping in his car all night.

"What is your problem?" we asked.

"I can't understand it. I hadn't done anything wrong and she screamed at me and told me to get out."

"Does she do this often?"

"No, she's usually rational and sane."

"But you can't think of anything that triggered this?"

"Well, it could have been about the money."

The story that followed was what Sanguine/Phlegmatic Joe saw as "no big deal." Janice's father had died recently and Janice had received an insurance payment of fifty thousand dollars. She put it into a joint account in the bank and left it for a rainy day. Janice and Joe had never had any extra money, and Janice, who was a Melancholy, finally felt comfortable to know they had a cushion to fall back on.

One day Janice got a call from the bank to say they were fifteen thousand dollars behind on their house payments and the bank was going to foreclose. Janice was stunned; she couldn't believe this had happened. Joe was responsible for paying the bills, but since he was out of town at the time, Janice told the bank to take it out of the fifty thousand dollars until she could find out what the problem was. They checked and came back to say, "There is no more money in that account."

Janice was incredulous. Where had the money gone?

When Joe came home, Janice was hysterical. She asked if he knew what had happened and he told her the same thing he told us: "I took out a little when I needed it, but I had no idea it was all gone."

"You're a crook!" she shouted.

Joe always had a look of innocence about him. As a Sanguine who loves to spend money and a Phlegmatic who doesn't bother to keep accounts, Joe had somehow dissipated fifty thousand dollars and run the mortgage into serious arrears. He didn't think he'd done anything that wrong and couldn't imagine why his wife would throw him out.

When Janice came in to see us, she was beside herself. "Did you find out from him what he did with the money?" she begged. We didn't have an answer.

Joe was the bad guy here, but both spouses needed to make changes. Joe didn't like the word *crook* applied to him. He was just *borrowing* the money, he said, and he could legally sign on the account so he wasn't actually outside of the law. When asked how he planned to pay back the "borrowed" money, he had no answer. He hadn't saved fifty thousand dollars in his life, or even fifty! When we pointed out that this was stealing, he winced. "I've always been very honest," he insisted.

Here was an upstanding Christian man on their church's board of deacons who did not see that taking fifty thousand dollars of his wife's money without asking or mentioning it was dishonest! Nor did he see that while happily spending it all on things that were not additions to the household he had been totally selfish. When we ultimately found out he had gambled with much of it, expecting to pay it back with his winnings, he didn't see that gambling was really a problem. "Not as long as you don't do it a lot," he said. Not paying the mortgage when it was his responsibility didn't strike him as too terrible, either, as the house hadn't been foreclosed on yet.

All of these things added up to a selfish, irresponsible, gambling, spiritual thief who couldn't figure out why his wife was upset with him. Janice was the innocent victim, but what could she have done differently?

First, the fifty thousand dollars should have been placed in an account that was not easily accessible, and Joe and Janice should have discussed what it was to be used for and agreed that neither should touch it for anything else. Second, the account should have been in Janice's name only or in an account where two signatures are needed to withdraw money.

But when Janice talked with her pastor about a separate account, he told her that idea was not Christian. He said she needed to be submissive and show her husband she trusted him. She would ultimately receive more money through her father's estate, and the pastor suggested she put it in the same joint account and pray that her husband wouldn't do the same thing again. Janice asked us if that sounded right to us.

Wake-up, Janice!

Eliminating Financial Stress

No matter who is writing the checks and keeping the finances in order, there needs to be a simple chart that shows what has or has not been paid each month. For years I asked for this and Fred said it was too much work. "Just trust me," he said. I did trust him, but I wanted one place where I could look to see what had been paid. When I had learned that certain bills had added interest charges if paid one day late I didn't want to be paying one cent extra. Even though nothing was hidden and I could have gone through the checkbooks, I didn't have time to do that. I wanted the information to be on one piece of paper in a simple chart.

Your bills may be very different from mine, but there are certain expenses we all have. The sample chart on page 57 will give you some guidelines. We've divided the types of bills, noted when they are due, and left space where a date can be written in when they were paid. Once you begin to use this chart, you will see how easy it is to keep track.

As you can see, the left-hand column lists the bills. In the "Due" column we indicate whether the bill is due on the first or twentieth of the month, twice a year, quarterly or yearly, etc. If a bill is due less often than once a month we put a little X in the box under the month when it should be paid to serve as a reminder. The person who pays the bill jots down what date he or she paid it so the other person can double-check.

Assuming you both do your part, this method will simplify bill-paying and eliminate the question, "Did you pay the rent?"

There are many bookkeeping procedures far more complicated than this and you may be using one, but add this simple record; it will help eliminate stress over money matters.

Learning the Laws

Because each state's financial laws are different it is important to know what they are. Do you know if your state is "common law" or "community property"? In simple terms common law means the owner of property is the person whose name is on the title. That person can sell, mortgage, or borrow on it without his or her mate's knowledge. Neither partner has a right to the other's wages or belongings.

In contrast, in community property states, including Arizona, California, Idaho, Louisiana, New Mexico, Oregon, Texas, Washington, and Wisconsin, each partner owns half of what was acquired in that marriage and he or she needs the other's signature to sell. You are both responsible for debts, no matter who signed; if he has charged up a storm and then leaves you, you are responsible for half and may be sued for the rest. A friend of mine in a community property state was stunned after a divorce to find that she was responsible for an expensive painting her husband had bought without a clear title (it was actually stolen property). To stay out of court she ended up paying more than half of the value to the original owner.

Another friend, upon questioning why her paycheck was smaller than usual, discovered her wages were being garnisheed by the IRS to pay for her portion of her ex-husband's back taxes.

No matter which kind of state you live in, a devious husband can find a way to do you in if he sets his heart on it and gets to work on his plan before you know about it. I talk to so many women who say, "My husband is so kind that he'd never do any of those bad things." And I've observed some of the finest Christian men, under the passion of a new love, who lie, cheat, and steal to get all they can. Since their surprised wife is not prepared, feels helpless, and is in a state of shock, the plotting husband and his usually overbearing lawyer can have her begging for any little scrap from the table.

I know one lawyer's wife who didn't even have a table to get scraps from. During dinner one evening, when she was still in shock from the divorce surprise, Joan's husband walked in with some moving men and removed the dining room furniture. The children were left crying on the

BILL PAYMENT SCHEDULE

	Due	Jan.	Feb.	Mar.	Apr.	May	June	July	Aug.	Sept.	Oct.	Nov.	Dec.
HOUSE													
Mortgage													
Homeowners Fees													
Yardwork													
Gas													
Electric													
Trash													
Water													
Cable TV													
Phone													
TAXES													
IRS													
State													
CREDIT CARDS													
MasterCard													
Visa													
Department Store													
Other													
INSURANCE													
Life													
Health													
Homeowners													
Car 1													
Car 2													
CARS													
Car 1 Payment													
Car 2 Payment													
Car 1 Tag Renewal													
Car 2 Tag Renewal													

floor with their plates in their laps. "At least he didn't take the plates out of their hands," Joan said, trying to gain some sense of humor over it all.

Another lawyer sold off property by forging his wife's name and putting the money in his girlfriend's account. By the time the divorce papers came he was officially destitute and the wife, Peggy, was so confused she couldn't swear she'd not signed the deeds. Under oath she was asked, "Did you ever sign things he brought you without reading them?"

"Oh yes, all the time," she answered, wide-eyed and innocent.

"Then you could have signed these?"

"I guess I could have."

It was all over for Peggy.

While she was on vacation Frannie discovered her husband had been seeing another woman. The following week she came home from her Bible study and found the locks changed on her house. When she located her husband at work, he coldly told her he was divorcing her. His business was about bankrupt, the house was in foreclosure, and she had better find some place to live, he added.

When they got to court, he had nothing and the house was to be auctioned off the next week. The day before the auction, his brother came forward with the money to redeem it. Frannie got nothing but her clothes; her ex-husband now lives in the house with his new wife and her children.

All of these men are Christians who amazingly have all stayed in the church as leaders. Why do I tell these sad tales? To wake up women and let them know we must be aware of what's going on with our family finances before it's too late. Not one of these women expected to be divorced. All of them were intelligent Christians, living in lovely homes and what they thought were solid marriages; yet the surprise came to each one. As I talked with them later they had to admit they knew nothing about their husbands' money; they had signed whatever he had handed them and always hoped for the best. It's too late for Joan, Peggy, and Frannie, but how about the rest of us?

Wake Up, Women, and Care about Money

"Today no woman should be ignorant of her husband's finances or her own. If a wife doesn't share financial decisions regardless of who earns the money, her husband will act as the powerful daddy. By having to ask, you give up control and then money is used as a reward. Do what your husband would like and he will get you the car you want."[1]

So writes Shelby White in *What Every Woman Should Know about Her Husband's Money*, her best-selling book designed to wake women up about the status of their family finances.

To jar us into becoming interested, she quotes statistics from many jour-
nals, surveys, and articles that show us we may well need to know more
than we do or we are going to find ourselves in trouble. Here's a sample:

- Two-thirds of all recent first marriages will end in divorce.
- One-third of all widows in 1985 were under age fifty when their
  husbands died.
- In 1990 there were 11.5 million widows between the ages of
  thirty and seventy; the median age was fifty-six.
- Seventy-five percent of all nursing home occupants are women.[2]

Looking at the possibility that many of us someday may be alone due
to death or divorce, hadn't we better know a few of the basics? Even if
we refuse to anticipate problems, there are facts of our financial life we
should know. Excellent books are available today that are simple and
understandable. But we must take the time to read them and apply what
we learn to our own situation. Some recommended titles are included in
the Bibliography.

Those of us who have better business sense and intuition than our husbands need to get involved in financial decisions that affect our families.
Some husbands prefer that we know nothing; if we try to ask questions,
they won't give us good answers. Do we accept that, shrug our shoulders,
and give up?

When Fred and I Woke Up

For the first twenty-five years of our marriage, I knew nothing about the
money—and I didn't care to know. But as Fred made business mistakes, I
realized we had some financial problems. When he informed me we had
to sell my dream house, I couldn't believe it. What had happened? The
business had steadily lost money, the creditors were pushing, and Fred
had to raise cash; that's what happened. I came up with every alternative I could imagine, but the only true solution was to sell the house.

At that point I took a hard look at what I did and didn't know. For
example, I didn't know if we had insurance on anything, if we had savings, stocks, bonds, etc., or if we were up to date on our taxes. When I
asked questions Fred took it as an attack on his honesty and we got nowhere. Since then I have learned I'm not the only intelligent woman
who has little information of her family's finances. I've also learned that
a man who has nothing to hide is usually willing to go over the money

matters with his wife. The more he has to hide from her the more resistant he becomes.

Before we insist on participating in financial matters, however, we need to have some basic idea of what we're talking about. This step takes some preparation, and we often think it isn't worth the time and effort; but I can tell you personally that being informed is worth every minute we spend doing it.

A young lady came to CLASS who was a lawyer. As we talked I could see that she knew a lot about money, wills, loans, and all the things I had avoided. She was willing to come to our office and sort out our finances. Fred was accepting of the idea even though he was a little ashamed that I had to bring someone in to check on what he knew he should have shown me himself. There was no dishonesty, but Fred had made some poor choices that I didn't know about, and he had opposed my better judgment in decisions we had discussed.

In his book *Wake Up, Men!* he shares how important it is for men to heed their wives' discernment in decisions that affect the future of the family. Discussion and unity are needed before making such decisions. Our major money losses have been on ventures where I was strongly opposed and Fred did it anyway.

We women have a sixth sense, our intuition, but we also have a responsibility to supplement that intuition by becoming knowledgeable enough about money and business to discuss them intelligently. If we know nothing, we can't expect our husbands to value our opinion. Just because we have a high IQ doesn't mean we can be counted on for financial wisdom.

The major achievement the lawyer accomplished was to get me involved in Fred's business. She also gave me a list of business papers I needed to collect and put in a safe place. It wasn't an overnight job because Fred didn't know where many of them were, but we located the essentials and gave our daughter Lauren a list of them, specifying where each was kept. As I paid attention to what was going on, it became apparent that we needed to get rid of the business. It was constantly losing money and draining Fred's energy.

At that point I was already traveling on weekends and Fred often went with me. It became clear to both Fred and me that we were to get out of business and go into full-time Christian ministry. We had no idea if we could support ourselves and we knew we didn't want to ask other people to support us. The ministry had to pay for itself, and it has. We cannot believe the changes that have come in our attitudes toward each other as we have worked together instead of separately.

In the past few years we have reviewed our insurance needs and purchased the correct policies, including "key person" insurance on me; we have written wills, set up trusts, and arranged for long-term medical coverage. These were all things we knew we should do—but we hadn't.

Since we are both on the road together now, we can't personally handle the monthly bills, but our office manager gives each of us a statement every month showing income and expenses. Because we both review this statement individually there is little chance for a major mistake. We've both had to learn some new ways to manage our finances and make sure we have covered our needs for now and for the future.

Wake Up and Ask

Why don't women know more about money? Check off your reasons.

_____ I trust in the Lord and His provision.

_____ I wouldn't dream of questioning my husband.

_____ He would never tolerate my interference.

_____ He's such an honest man, I don't need to know.

_____ He's always handled the money.

_____ He makes it; he's got a right to spend it.

_____ I don't have time to think about it.

_____ I've never been good at figures.

_____ As long as he pays the bills I don't care.

_____ I wouldn't know what to look for.

_____ It's easier to sign things than to read them.

_____ He wouldn't tell me the truth anyway.

_____ I hate responsibility.

_____ If he decides and it's wrong, it's his fault.

_____ He says I'm too dumb to understand.

_____ I didn't think I had a right to know.

Did you check off some of these reasons? Were they about your unwillingness to learn—time, inability, fear—or were they that your husband doesn't want you to know? If it's your lack of desire, think about the possibility that you might become widowed or divorced or that your husband could become ill and unable to continue bringing in income. If it's because he won't tell you, talk with him about the family finances again, without emotion, and ask him about the important papers on the following list. Let him know that if anything happened to him you wouldn't know what to do. Have him read *Wake Up, Men!*

If you needed to, would you know where to find:

	Yes	No
Birth certificates for each member of the family?	___	___
Your marriage certificate?	___	___
Title to each car?	___	___
Insurance policies?	___	___
Mortgages?	___	___
Stocks and bonds?	___	___
If you lost your wallet, do you have a list of all credit cards and their numbers?	___	___
Do you have your driver's license number and social security number written down where you can find it outside of your wallet?	___	___
Do you know about each bank account, whose name it's in, and who can withdraw from it?	___	___
Do you have a savings and checking account in your name that no one else can touch?	___	___
Do you have a major credit card and at least one card from a department store in your name?	___	___

Establishing a Credit History

If you were to be divorced or widowed you might have difficulty establishing credit as a single woman. If your credit card is in both your name and your husband's he could cancel it without your knowledge. If your savings are in both names, he could withdraw the money unless the card in the bank calls for both signatures.

To establish credit you need to have a major credit card in your name and a record of having used it. If you make a purchase on credit, use your card and make each payment on time. Don't postpone establishing credit. Tomorrow could be too late.

Sometimes we think we have credit in our own name when in reality we don't. My colleague Marilyn Heavilin went shopping at her favorite department store to choose a present for her husband's birthday. As she started to pay for her purchase, she realized she had left her charge card for that store at home. Since she shopped there often, the clerk knew her well and said, "No problem. Just go over to the office and ask them for a temporary card."

Marilyn made her request at the customer-accounts window, but sensed there was a problem when the clerk at the window told her the manager needed to speak with her. As Marilyn sat down at the manager's desk, several thoughts went through her mind: *Did I forget to pay my bill? Can't they find my records? What could be wrong?*

The manager squirmed in her chair as she said, "Mrs. Heavilin we can't give you a temporary card."

"Why not?" Marilyn queried.

"We can't give you a card without your husband's permission because the name on this card is *Mrs. Glen Heavilin.*"

Marilyn exclaimed, "That account has only been used by me. Glen doesn't even have a card! If you look at the records, you will see that every payment has been paid from my personal checking account. I don't even sign Mrs. Glen Heavilin on charge slips; they are always signed Marilyn Heavilin. Glen has nothing to do with this account."

The manager was very embarrassed and offered to open a new account in Marilyn's name. Marilyn was quite upset by all of this confusion, but she finally agreed to fill out the forms to open a new account. At that time Marilyn was the author of three books and had a very busy speaking schedule and a good income of her own. She had two checking accounts, two savings accounts, and an American Express card in her own name. Two days later the department store called and said her request for a charge account had been denied. They said she had not had the American Express card long enough to establish a pattern of credit stability.

It took another visit to the manager of the department store and some strong discussions before Marilyn was granted a credit card in her own name. It is hard to understand, but even though she had made all of the charges and all of the payments on the old account, all she had done was establish good credit for her husband and none for herself!

Insurance, Tax, and Inheritance Issues

Ask yourself the following questions:

	Yes	No
Does your husband have life insurance and do you know where it is?	___	___
Do you know how much you would need?	___	___

	Yes	No
Do you know for sure you are the beneficiary?	___	___
Do you have enough personal life insurance to cover minimal funeral expenses ($3,000)?	___	___
Do you have health insurance for yourself?	___	___
Do you have health insurance for your family?	___	___
Do you know what it covers, how much per day, for how long?	___	___
Do you carry an insurance card with you in case of an accident?	___	___
Do you and your husband have disability insurance?	___	___
Do you know that it only provides about 60 percent of your monthly income and there may be a three-month waiting period?	___	___
Do you have enough money put aside to cover three months if necessary?	___	___
Do you have fire and homeowner's insurance?	___	___
Do you know how much coverage you have and is that enough?	___	___
Does it cover earthquakes, hurricanes, floods, or other natural disasters?	___	___
Do you have dental insurance and know what it covers?	___	___
Do you and your husband each have a signed power of attorney for each other?	___	___
Do you know what retirement provision you have and who gets what when?	___	___
Do you have Keoghs or IRAs, and do you know how to use them?	___	___
Do you have your tax returns on file for the seven years the IRS requires?	___	___
Do you know that if your husband cheats on your joint income tax return and you sign it, you could get in trouble even if you were innocent?	___	___

	Yes	No
Do you know if you have trusts, where they are kept, and who gets what?	___	___
Do you have a list of all your possessions, an estimated worth, and instructions specifying who should inherit each item?	___	___
Does your husband have an up-to-date will? If he does, do you know where it is and who inherits what?	___	___
Do you have a will?	___	___

These questions are some of the things every woman should know to protect herself from possible disaster. The more Yes checks you have, the more you know and the fewer surprises you'll have. If you have checked No on any of these questions, you need to start a learning program *today*.

Unfortunately, we have met widows who found too late that the life insurance went to the first wife and the will was nowhere to be found. We've met divorcées who were done in by their ex-husbands and who were unable to establish any credit.

We don't want to focus on the negative, but we do want to prevent ourselves from being caught off guard. The following stories will illustrate how necessary it is to take these precautions.

Trouble with the IRS

Adrian is forty-five years old and totally broke. She and her husband both worked and took care of their own finances. She assumed he was doing everything correctly on his part as she was on hers. When he died, suddenly she was notified she owed the IRS thousands of dollars. He had not paid his taxes for seven years, and even though she hadn't signed a joint return, the IRS froze her bank account, sold her house, confiscated her cars, and forced her to pay a fine for his negligence. She is now penniless. It had never occurred to her to even ask him if he'd filed his returns. Now she is paying the price.

Trouble with In-laws

Gladys came to our Promise of Healing Workshop to help her daughter overcome her problems, but as we sat and talked she poured out her

own story too. Her husband's family had a manufacturing business, and
when the father died, Gladys's husband, Ray, inherited two-thirds of the
business and his brother one-third. Ray was the salesman and his charming personality was the ingredient that doubled the business in five years'
time. Gladys was thrilled with the additional income they received and
happily spent it on new furniture, jewelry, and cars. She knew nothing
about the business or the prospects for the future. Ray felt invincible and
didn't like to focus on the negatives. But suddenly Ray dropped dead.

At the funeral his brother mentioned to Gladys that he was in charge
now and he hoped Ray had adequate insurance to keep her going. Gladys
was in a double state of shock, first with the sudden death and then with
her brother-in-law's casual comment. As soon as she was emotionally
able Gladys went to the office to straighten out the finances and find out
what her share was. Her in-laws let her know she had no share. The
business was the family's and she was no longer a part of it.

"What am I to live on?" she asked.

"That's your problem," they answered.

"But Ray inherited two-thirds of the business," Gladys cried.

"What proof do you have? Do you have any document that says so?"

She didn't. In fact Gladys had no idea what she did or didn't own. In
checking she found Ray had minimal insurance and had never increased
it when he started making more money. The IRS put a hold on his bank
account and Gladys found herself with high mortgage payments, cars
bought on credit, and no cash in hand. When she appealed to her in-laws
they scoffed at her and loaned her a thousand dollars—with interest.
None of her friends took pity on her as she had the biggest house of the
group; they soon tired of what they called her "poverty pleading."

Gladys ultimately found a lawyer who thought she had a case against
her in-laws. It took eighteen months and twenty thousand dollars to finally
get a legal subsistence allowance from the business. By that time Gladys
had been forced to sell the house and all but one car in order to stay alive.

Wealth and Control

When Marilyn Heavilin was speaking in Massachusetts, Carrie met
her at the airport. Carrie was driving a very nice, top-of-the-line sedan,
and she took Marilyn to a lovely home in a very posh neighborhood.
Carrie shared with Marilyn that her husband was an attorney, and by all
of the amenities, Marilyn gathered he was very successful in his profession.

That afternoon while they were driving to the church where Marilyn
was speaking, Marilyn pulled her cellular phone out of her purse to see

if it would work in the area where they were. Carrie asked Marilyn some questions about her phone and then said, "It was nice of your husband to buy that phone for you."

Marilyn said, "Oh, I bought it myself."

Then Carrie commented, "Well, it was nice of Glen to *let* you buy it."

Marilyn laughed, "Well, he was with me when I bought it. But it wasn't a matter of his letting me buy it. I bought it myself with my own money."

"How did you get your own money? Don't you put all of your money in Glen's account?" Carrie asked.

Marilyn chuckled and said, "My goodness, no. I have two checking accounts and two savings accounts of my own and credit cards in my own name. We share financial details with each other and I pay many of our expenses, but I am responsible for what I do with the money I make through my speaking and writing. Glen encouraged me to get the cellular phone. He said if I had an auto club card and a cellular phone, he would feel much better about my traveling alone. But I paid for it myself."

Carrie sighed and said, "I suggested to my husband that I would feel safer on the road if I had a cellular phone and he said 'You'll be fine. We don't need to spend money on such silly things.' You're really lucky Glen worries about you and is concerned for your safety. He must really love you."

As Marilyn continued to talk with Carrie she discovered that despite the wealth apparent in their home, Carrie was given a grocery allowance but had to ask for any additional money she needed, and she had no credit cards available to her. Carrie had no idea how much her husband's income was or how he spent his money. While it was true that Carrie lived in a beautiful home, drove a nice car, and her physical needs were generally well met, she felt no independence and had no idea whether she could make good financial decisions or not. If Carrie is ever left alone, she will be as lost and confused as Gladys was when her husband died and left her to deal with her selfish in-laws.

Marriage Contracts

It was when Lisa was thirty years old that reality hit. She had four children ages six, four, two and six months, and her husband was in a new business that wasn't making any money when her mother died in a car crash. When she was grieving over her mother's death her husband said, "We all have to die sometime."

She told me it was as if a light had come on in her brain. She realized her husband had not said a kind word to her in years and her mother had been her comforter. When things got too bad she could always call

Mother. Now Mother was gone and her husband didn't care. She had all these babies and she suddenly saw the truth. She packed up the children and drove to a girlfriend's house. Her friend took her in and gave her one room to live in with the four children.

When Lisa went to a lawyer to see what her options were he told her because she'd only been married five years she could expect no alimony. Ten years seems to be the magic number for any leverage and Lisa didn't have it. Lisa told the lawyer she had helped start her husband's business. Didn't that give her an edge? Evidently not. The lawyer assigned her to do some research looking up the papers and information we have discussed in this chapter. She had no idea where anything was, but she began a search. She learned that both the cars and all the credit cards were in her husband's name. She checked the joint bank account and found all the money was gone.

Lisa had no degree, no job, no expertise, and in effect no husband. The lawyer didn't give her much hope since her husband had put everything into his business. Lisa said, "I realized I had suddenly become one of the great American homeless living below the poverty line."

At that point Lisa's husband called and wanted her to come back. Some women would have run right back on the first call even if there was no improvement, but Lisa knew better. She insisted they go to a lawyer and have a contract set up. She said she realized she had been "all messed up by my religious upbringing about what *submission* means. I had let him do whatever he wanted and this had led to both financial and sexual problems. I allowed him to treat me like a piece of property."

Lisa doesn't do that anymore. Their contract specifies that her husband would buy her a car in her name, and he did. She now has a separate bank account, and at the end of each year she and her husband review their finances and divide the assets in half. "I am now with him by choice, not by control."

Their business has prospered since they got their finances straightened out. "I could leave tomorrow," Lisa writes, "with over $150,000 in assets all my own, but I don't want to leave a man who has given me freedom to be an intelligent wife and an equal partner."

One other agreement they have in the contract was a new thought to me. The bedroom is Lisa's and she chooses to share it with her husband. Before, he demanded sex no matter how Lisa felt; now he courts her and treats her like a lady. Not a bad idea!

We women have no idea how our lives could change for the better. Until we wake up!

6

Where, Oh Where, Have All the Good Husbands Gone?

I often conduct informal surveys of CLASS participants and other groups of women so I can stay current on women's experiences and attitudes on modern issues. During one recent survey, a group of exemplary Christian women from many different denominations wrote about how blessed they were and how happy they felt. They seemed to be content with their lives. But when they were questioned more closely, one on one, they told different stories. Some admitted they had poor marriages, some were being emotionally abused, some had financial problems, some felt put down by their husbands or by men at work or in the church, and some thought other Christians were judging them. When asked why they had not written this on the survey, they said that since they were Christians they couldn't let themselves put any negatives in writing. Someone might figure out who they were and think they weren't spiritual enough, they said.

Such surveys have taught me that honest Christian women tell the truth less often than people of the world. It's not that they lie, exactly; it's that they feel they are hurting the cause of Christ if they give the facts of their lives as they really are. Women often keep apologizing for their husband's behavior as they tell me the awful acts he's performed. "He beat me black and blue, but he's really a nice man and I know he doesn't mean to. I wouldn't want you to think negatively about him," they might say. Sometimes I have to stop them and say, "I'm sure he means well, but if he's doing this he is not a nice man. Stop apologizing and give me the truth." Until women get honest and face their problems with no denial, they are helpless to act upon them.

The following true stories have been shared with me by women who have had to deal with major problems that none of them anticipated. These are women who, like those in the survey mentioned earlier, would have said they were joyful Christians, not because they *are*, but because that is what we are supposed to be. Their stories are fascinating when they are not our stories; yet as we think about them there may be a little of these women in each one of us. Let's examine our lives honestly as we look at theirs.

The Bigamist

Cynthia had a master's degree in English literature but hadn't used her common sense in years. Her husband handled everything and gave her an allowance that was more than adequate. She had no checking account or credit cards but always had enough cash. Cynthia had no idea where the money came from or how much there was in reserve. She was even a little hazy on what Al actually did for a living. He said he had an importing business and had to go out of town frequently. As the children grew up, he occasionally missed important holidays, but as long as the money was there Cynthia didn't mind, and she made excuses for his absence.

Whenever her church had a fund-raiser, Al gave a large contribution even though he rarely had time to go. Sundays were particularly busy days for Al; he always seemed to have emergency calls from the office that day that required him to go in to work. Cynthia's friends envied her comfortable lifestyle even though it was a little lonely.

When Al was about forty he came home from having a physical and said he had been proclaimed impotent. This surprised Cynthia because he had not seemed to have any sexual problems before the exam. From that time on, though, he seemed embarrassed to sleep with her and "sacrificed" by moving into another bedroom.

One day Cynthia's thirteen-year-old daughter Jody came home from school and told Cynthia about this new girl in class who looked just like her. The child seemed disturbed about it, but Cynthia passed it off as a coincidence until Jody brought the girl home with her. The resemblance was uncanny and unchristian thoughts went through Cynthia's mind. She chastised herself for even thinking that Al could have somehow fathered this child, but she surely did look like him and Jody. She wanted to ask him about it, but he hated to be questioned about anything. She did ask the child where she lived and found it was only a few streets away. Cynthia started driving by the house frequently—until one Sunday when Al was supposedly at the office handling another emergency call, but she saw his car in the driveway.

Cynthia felt sick to her stomach; she didn't know what to do. She drove home and went straight to his desk. The first thing she found was two sets of checkbooks. One set was labeled A, the other, B, and neither was imprinted with an address. A had carbons of checks to pay her mortgage and bills, and B had similar checks made out to a different mortgage company. She could hardly wait until Monday to call the mortgage company and check the address of the second mortgage. Sure enough, it was for the other woman's house!

When Al came home Monday night he found Cynthia and their pastor waiting for him. When they confronted him he confessed to leading a dual life and having another wife and family for fifteen years. The other family had been in another state but it had been too inconvenient for Al so he had brought them closer. Somehow he never thought they'd find each other.

When Cynthia told me this fascinating story she was divorcing Al, who had chosen to stay with Lady B and her young family. Cynthia kept as quiet about it as possible to save her children from shame; she plans to move away at the end of the school year.

"Was I ever naive!" Cynthia said. "I didn't want to question where he was on holidays and Sundays. I didn't know anything about our money. It turned out the life insurance was in her name, and although I didn't know it, I'd had no health insurance for two years."

Why didn't Cynthia wake up?

One reason was her basic trust in mankind, which is a positive trait in all of us. Another was that she was living well and had no obvious clues about Al's hidden life. It's a lot easier to look the other way when you're not hungry. Cynthia would have known earlier about Al's deceitfulness if she'd spot-checked his Sundays in the office or his nights in distant hotels.

When Al proclaimed himself impotent at forty, Cynthia just accepted it as a medical fact. She didn't ask the doctor's name or suggest they go see him together for further diagnosis and treatment. In truth, there was no doctor's visit at all; but Cynthia didn't even ask, making Al's lack of sexual interest in her a lot easier to excuse.

Because Cynthia never questioned his finances or asked to be shown the insurance policy, Al was able to leave the "paper trail" right under her nose in his desk at home.

Their children are not only humiliated and angry at Al, but they're also furious at Cynthia for her years of blind indifference. "How could you be so stupid?" they asked. But Cynthia wasn't stupid. She just didn't wake up.

Probably none of you have a husband who's a bigamist, but would you really know if you did? Do you have access to all of the insurance policies, checkbooks, investments, and the will? Do you accept his absences without checking? Are there gaps in his life that don't add up? If this is your situation it's time to wake up!

The Workaholic

Jennifer described how hard her husband worked. "Poor man. He doesn't get home until two in the morning and he's off again at seven." Since she had brought up the subject, I asked if she had ever checked at midnight to make sure he was at the office.

"Oh no! I wouldn't do that," she gasped. "He told me that a real Christian wife is trusting and has faith in her husband. He's really big on trust."

I didn't want to burst her little bubble, but I don't know any men who can work that hard for long. One day Jennifer called to say, "He's divorcing me. He wasn't working after all." What a surprise!

The Stripper

Several times Martha wondered why her doctor husband didn't answer his page when she tried to reach him. He always had excuses of emergencies that had come up, but somehow his words didn't ring true. One day he turned on her and snapped, "Don't ever try to check on me again. What I do is none of your business."

His reaction frightened her, but it also made her more determined to find out where he was in these missing hours. She hired a detective and fully expected to find her husband was having an affair. She was dumbfounded when the detective came back with pictures of her fine Christian husband coming out of a huge cake and doing striptease shows at women's parties. He had a post office box and ran ads in the personal columns. Clients looking for such entertainment would write to the box number, then he would call and set up an appointment. He was paid in cash and no one ever knew his name.

What a shock it would be to discover your professional Christian husband is also a stripper!

The Rapist

Ronda wrote to me about the shock in her life when her husband's deceptions were brought to light:

> Eleven years ago my marriage was dealt a deadly blow. My husband of seven years was arrested for the kidnapping and rape of a sixteen-year-old girl in the small South Texas town where we were living. It turned out he was also deeply enmeshed in burglary, drugs, and alcohol. I was to discover that he was in fact a serial rapist. He had forsaken the God he once knew and loved. His double life, expertly hidden behind a wall of silence and depression, came as a great shock to me and my children. The morning after his arrest, the police searched our home. It was as if I were standing naked before a roomful of strangers. Our lives were laid bare before them. What little self-esteem I had was destroyed that day.

Ronda's husband was sentenced to thirty years in a state penitentiary, and she found herself a broken, devastated mother of two. There was no time to sit around and feel sorry for herself, no money for counseling, and few friends left to give her support:

> I found myself at the breaking point, desperate before God for a complete healing. I discovered that I had stuffed the closet of my heart with package after package of pain. The closet was full, and I could no longer shut the door and ignore it. I began rummaging through, sorting and tossing and making order out of my life once more. Through it all, as difficult as it has been, God has begun to do a work in my life. My inner strength has grown along with my character, compassion, and faith. God, who was the beloved Guardian of my childhood, has once again become Lord of my life.
>
> I watched a log burn in a fireplace one night, and I wept. "That's how my life is, Lord," I whispered. "It's been destroyed, and I'm useless." That greatest of all counselors listened, let me cry, and then soothed my spirit. Then He reminded me of Isaiah 61:3, "To appoint unto them that mourn . . . to give unto them beauty for ashes, the oil of joy for mourning, the garment of praise for the spirit of heaviness, that they might be called trees of righteousness, the planting of the LORD, that he might be glorified."

So I brought to God a rusty old bucket, filled with the ashes of my life, and He has begun to turn them into a "planting, that He might be glorified." And I stand in awe at the wonder of such a God and am humbled that He would love and care for me.

In the process of healing Ronda has come to CLASS to learn how she can help other women wake up before it's too late. She feels the Lord leading her to speak out even more; she has been on "Sally Jessy Raphael," "Inside Edition," and "Hard Copy" and is the subject of Kevin Flynn's book, *The Unmasking: Married to a Rapist*. She is thrilled when she can hold one hurting lady and give her a spark of hope.

The Sexual Deviate

We would like to believe that stories like the one you are about to read are rare. However, as I speak to groups all over the world, I hear of too many situations that are very similar to Candy's story.

Candy was married at an early age to a young man who won her over by his charm and good looks. He swept her off her feet, just as Prince Charming was supposed to do. However, her dream was severely shattered on her wedding night when Candy was forcibly raped by her husband and thrown out of their honeymoon cottage naked, an act he considered funny. Candy was humiliated and devastated. She should have been on her way to the nearest police station or at the least a bus station for a ticket home, but Candy wanted to live "happily ever after," and she convinced herself she could make it work.

And she did work at it—for twenty-two long years. During her deteriorating marriage she was expected to participate in skinny-dipping parties, nudist camps, hot-tub clubs, and X-rated movies—all aimed at improving her sexual performance. Candy set out to be the sexiest girl at these events in order to keep her philandering husband interested. But her efforts were unsuccessful. Not only did he have numerous affairs and encounters with other women, but he sexually abused his own daughters.

When Candy finally started saying no to her husband's demands, he became violent. Candy finally took the girls and left, twenty-two years too late.

Because of Candy's denial of her husband's perverse behavior for so many years, she has had to face far greater consequences than if she had faced it from the beginning. Sadly, her daughters, innocent victims, have had to endure abuse that is hard to undo, even with Christian counseling.

Often our fear of the unknown causes us to put up with behavior that should never be tolerated. Sometimes it is the dread of facing a failed relationship and the judgment of others that causes us to stay in marriages filled with violence or perversions. Too many times it's not being able to make it financially that figures into our reasons for hanging on when we should run the other way.

Candy didn't want to face the death of her dream for a happily-ever-after life. But, thank God, she finally put her trust in the right Prince—Jesus—and had the courage to get help for herself and her girls.

Candy now ministers to others who have been through similar situations. She has been a guest on many radio programs and shares her story and insights into finding victory in Jesus over sexual, emotional, and physical abuse. There can only be victory if we women wake up!

The Slave Driver

When Sally Field starred in the movie *Not Without My Daughter* we were made painfully aware of what can happen to unsuspecting women who marry into Arab families. In the movie, Sally's Arabian husband takes their child and goes back to Saudi Arabia, leaving Sally behind. Sally eventually hires sympathetic mercenaries to kidnap her child back and return her to America.

We'd like to believe this was only a fictional story, but it wasn't; it was based on a true event with real people. Unfortunately, there are many more real-life events very similar to this one.

Sarah was a student nurse when she started dating Reza. After Sarah's fiancé was killed in Vietnam her friends had introduced her to Reza. When Reza wined and dined Sarah the overt attention was extremely flattering, and Sarah was very vulnerable.

Their dates turned to talk about marriage, and they started looking at homes and rings. They decided to get married in Las Vegas and then visit his homeland for a traditional Arabian ceremony.

As the time drew closer to their marriage date, Reza said he would buy her a "huge diamond ring" in Iraq because he could get it there much cheaper. He postponed buying the home they had chosen because, he said, he couldn't see letting it sit idle while they honeymooned in Iraq.

The day they arrived in Las Vegas, Reza decided to visit the casinos before finding a chapel to have the wedding ceremony. He gave Sarah a few dollars and told her to enjoy the slot machines while he went to the gambling tables. When she asked when they were going to get married, he kept saying "later, later." Since later became still later, Reza dropped Sarah off at a motel so she could rest; he continued to gamble. When Reza returned the next morning, Sarah was having doubts whether she should go ahead with the wedding. When she voiced her doubts to him, he threatened to abandon her on the streets of Las Vegas if she didn't comply. She decided that marrying Reza seemed better than being left alone. If she'd only known!

Fortunately for Sarah, Reza decided the Mideast was too full of conflict to return there. Instead, they settled in an apartment. Still, life became increasingly difficult for her. Sarah was never again allowed to go with him to look for a new home, and after a while Reza lost interest in looking and invested the money in his business. Sarah was never allowed to see the checkbook or inquire about where the money was going.

Reza kept Sarah away from people, even making her stay in the back room of his business doing menial tasks while he dealt with customers. Sarah was not allowed to go to the grocery store until she refused to cook because her cupboards were bare. When he did allow her to make a trip anywhere, he accompanied her and told her to keep her eyes down and not to look at any men. She had to use a checkout line that was operated by a woman.

Reza insisted that Sarah prove her value and worthiness as his wife by conceiving, and he demanded that she find a woman doctor to treat her during the pregnancy because no other man should be allowed to see her body.

Sarah became more and more unhappy and depressed, but she stayed with him and had two more children. As Reza became both physically and mentally abusive Sarah feared for her life. He slept with a gun under his pillow and told her that if she ever left him, he would hunt her down and kill her. He continually accused her of having affairs if she ever went anywhere without him. She had to obey his every whim; Reza became the slave driver and Sarah the menial slave.

On trips in the car, he would leave Sarah and their three children in the parking lot in the heat and go into the restaurant to eat alone. On occasions when they were invited to come along, Sarah had to share a meal with the three children and was not allowed to order anything to drink. He would humiliate her by aggressively flirting with the waitresses and insulting her in front of them.

After eleven years of an abusive marriage, Sarah decided she had to leave. The threat of death didn't sound as bad as the thought of having to live like a slave forever.

Sarah may not have had to hire sympathetic mercenaries to steal her children away from her husband, but like Sally Field, Sarah and her children were held captive by a deceptive man who had no intention of being a good husband or father. His only concern and thoughts were for himself and for his own needs.

Is anyone holding your life captive to fill his own needs? If so, perhaps it's time for you to decide, as Sarah did, that things need to change. I hope your situation is not this desperate, but you may need to instigate some changes to make your relationships healthy.

All of the women whose stories I've shared here—Cynthia, Jennifer, Martha, Ronda, Candy, and Sarah—are Christians. Each got married with the best of intentions, and each trusted her husband too much.

We don't need to turn ourselves into suspicious, vicious women who keep our husbands under surveillance, but we do need to alert our minds to possible problems. We need to know it's not bad to want financial information or to want our husbands to account for large gaps of missing time. In each of the previous cases the situation was so far gone before it was recognized that there was little chance of redemption. Nancy's story is different.

The Philanderer

Nancy Norton's husband always kept in touch with her when he was on the road, but one day as he left he said he wasn't sure where he'd be staying that week. This sounded odd to her and made her wonder. She called his office and asked the secretary to give her the name of the hotel since he had forgotten to tell her. She called the hotel that night and asked for Mr. and Mrs. Norton. A woman answered the phone in the room. Nancy, in a burst of quick, creative thinking said, "This is the front desk. When will you and Mr. Norton be checking out?" The female voice answered, "On Thursday."

"Thank you so much, Mrs. Norton," the real Mrs. Norton said.

The next afternoon Nancy got in her car and drove the many hours to the hotel. She sat in a corner of the lobby, somewhat hidden. At dinner time the elevator opened and out stepped her husband and a sweet young thing. She waited until they were seated in the dining room and then slipped into the booth beside them.

"What a surprise to find you here," she chirped cheerfully.

She told me later that the look on their faces was worth the trip. From that point on, Nancy traveled with him as much as possible and they kept in very close touch. While their marriage was far from ideal, they were able to put their life back together because Nancy nipped the affair in the bud and was willing to forgive.

In my experience I rarely find women who are overly suspicious, although there are some; but I frequently talk with those who did not wake up to obvious red flags waving before them.

Red Flags

What are some reasonable questions to ask? What should you be alert to in your marriage relationship? When should you go looking for your lost sheep? Answer: When any of the following symptoms are evident:

1. Expenditures of money that are unexplainable. Obviously, if you have nothing to do with the family finances, you have no way to see discrepancies before it's too late, but you should have at least a basic knowledge of what comes in and what goes out.

2. Excessive amounts of time spent at work or other unaccounted-for spans of time. Many of us work more than the forty-hour week, but if your mate is working every night for more than emergencies, volunteer to go in and help. If he refuses to let you join him or check up on him, you know you are in trouble.

3. Disinterest in family functions. If a man who has enjoyed his children no longer wants to be with them or refuses to go to their programs, and if he has urgent business on holidays and weekends, you had better check up on him.

4. Gaps in accountability and discrepancies in stories. If you call and he's always out to lunch or not where he said he'd be, you have a right to ask. Don't become his mother, but ask when you feel in your spirit that his excuses don't make sense. And if his stories don't add up, do some checking.

5. Secretive behavior. If he seems to be nervous when you ask where he's going or gets defensive when you question him or gives you lectures on trust, watch out!

6. Sudden changes in looks and activities. If he has a new desire to exercise, joins a co-ed health club, buys silk underwear, and starts test-driving red Corvettes, you may be in trouble.

7. Lack of communication. If he withdraws and refuses to talk about anything but the most trivial matters ("What's for dinner?" or "Have you seen my brown argyle socks?") you have to start wondering if his mind is focused on something or someone else.

8. No interest in sex. Some women take this as a relief and not a warning sign.

9. Mysterious phone calls. If there are suspicious messages or if he talks for long periods of time off in another room with the door shut and gets upset if you pick up the phone, watch out!

Many women I counsel have lived through all of these symptoms and yet have not confronted the problem; instead they live in hopes that it will go away. They don't realize that the sooner the facts are faced the better chance there is of recovery and restoration. The longer unusual behavior is allowed to progress, the sooner it becomes a habit that is extremely difficult to break.

Wake up, women!

7

When Submission
Allows Abuse

In June 1992 the American Medical Association declared domestic violence against women as a national epidemic. This abuse in the home is the leading source of injury for women between the ages of fifteen and forty-four. One-third of the women who are brought to emergency rooms are victims of domestic violence, and over four million women each year are severely assaulted by their present or former mate. Because of these increasing statistics the AMA has issued directives for its members to guide them in looking for and reporting domestic-violence cases.[1]

Are any of these abuses taking place in Christian homes? Are we any better than the rest? Unfortunately, Christians tell me stories of domestic violence each week. I wonder when we Christian women are going to wake up. The most frequent response from a Christian leader to a victimized wife seeking help seems to be, "Just be more submissive and you will win him by your 'sweet and gentle spirit.'" How long is a woman—any woman—to be sweet, gentle, submissive—and beaten up? One pastor told a lady, "You will get your reward in heaven." She was on her way.

The stories in this chapter are based on real women in real situations. They describe the abuse of Christian wives by their Christian husbands. In most cases these wives accepted the abuse, thinking they had no choice if they were to be good, submissive Christian wives. But as I pointed out earlier, being submissive doesn't mean being victimized. (These views are summarized in Appendix A.)

Submissive Codependency

Lou Ann came from a family with a father so strict she became "a submissive codependent." That is, her passive submission enabled her father to continue his abusive behavior. When she would cry out "Why?" he would answer, "Because I said so!" She married at seventeen to get away from him and soon found her husband to be as controlling as her father. He stayed out until four in the morning and Lou Ann knew he was womanizing although he denied it. Lou Ann and her husband separated and reunited many times, but the cycle never improved. While he was drinking, carousing, and spending excessive amounts of money Lou Ann believed as a Christian she was not to question his behavior. Her approach was to have a quiet spirit so she could lead him to the Lord. But when she was passive he abused her even more.

Being sweet and submissive didn't win any points for Lou Ann because her husband left her anyway; he is now living with another woman. After thirty years Lou Ann now sees that she should have taken a stand much earlier. "Because of my being so submissive and not confronting him about his behavior, I feel our relationship has been so badly damaged it could never be salvaged."

Is thirty years of abuse enough?

Mutual Victimization

Polly grew up with a Melancholy martyr mother and a father who was Sanguine with his friends but Phlegmatic at home. The mother waited on them all, sighed often, and made frequent note that she never did anything for herself. "Your father always knows that if I'm not doing for him, I'm doing for you children." Polly was taught that women are inferior and must accept their lot in life. Being subservient, she believed, is being godly.

Polly is a Sanguine and she knew from the beginning she didn't fit with the rest of the family. Because she didn't like the quiet morbidity she felt at home with her family, she went outside to have fun and tried to be the dutiful child when she was at home. Her mother kept pointing out that Polly was different and if she'd only think of others and give more of herself she would be accepted. "If I could just be better," Polly recalls thinking, "maybe I'd be accepted. If I could just be that gentle, kind, giving, giving, giving person I *should* be, then I'd be OK in everyone's sight and wouldn't have so many problems."

Polly tried so hard, but all she got for her efforts was the warning: "You are just an ordinary person. Don't try to inflict yourself on those above you."

Polly was desperate for love, attention, and affirmation and when she found a boyfriend who seemed to like her, she was willing to do whatever he wanted. Polly got pregnant at sixteen and "brought disgrace upon the family." She was forced to get married quickly and leave town so no one would know the truth. When her sister got married in a lavish ceremony a few years later Polly was told, "You could have had a wedding like this if only you'd been good."

Polly tried to be good, and she knew from her saintly mother that a good wife was submissive and did what pleased her husband. Looking back on it now, Polly asks, "Oh, how many times as a child had I gotten hit with the belt or been grounded because I had a will of my own? When would I learn that if I was what others wanted me to be I would be accepted? When would I learn that I was nothing if I was not what others wanted me to be?"

With this distorted view of what a good Christian wife was, Polly really tried. At first her young husband criticized whatever she tried to do. "I thought if I could just stir the sauce clockwise instead of counterclockwise maybe he wouldn't hit me," she said. "If I could just cook all three vegetables he brought home maybe he wouldn't yell at me in front of my friends. If I could just learn to clean like my mother. If only . . . if only . . ."

The verbal abuse turned into hitting and shoving gradually, and Polly felt she deserved whatever she got. After all, she wasn't perfect. "With no self-esteem, no self-worth, and no self-love left, I finally gave in and did as I was told," she said.

But her obedience didn't stop the abuse. This was a husband who hadn't wanted to get married in the first place, and he took his anger out on Polly. When he threw her to the floor, sexually victimized her, and tried to choke her, she finally woke up. She knew if she didn't do something to change things she'd be dead within the year either by his hand or her own.

She called her mother, who told her she needed to be more submissive, and her pastor, who said he'd pray for her. Close to hysterics, Polly phoned her friend, who said, "Get out of there immediately and come to my house."

For a year Polly and her two sons lived in one room of her friend's house until she could save enough for a deposit on an apartment.

When Polly came to our Promise of Healing Workshop she was depressed and discouraged. She responded to our Survey of Emotions and Experiences (see Appendix B) with many symptoms of childhood sexual abuse. Later we prayed with her for her repressed memories and she saw herself being sexually abused by her grandfather. She had told her mother, "Grandpa's touching me." She remembers her mother saying, "Whatever your grandfather does is all right. We're living in his house and if you don't please him he'll throw us out on the street and it will be your fault." Not only was Polly living under the rule of conditional love but she was also being sexually abused and had no recourse. Is it any wonder Polly's adult life was a disaster sprinkled with guilt? Polly says, "As I look back on my childhood, it is not surprising that I became a battered wife, that I have suffered from depression for years, or that I fight every day, with Christ at my side, for life and happiness."

As Polly has written her prayers daily and increasingly felt the lifting of her guilt, she has begun to share her story with other women. Now she realizes her husband was probably victimized as a child because he has so many of the symptoms. What was done to him he took out on her. She wishes someone had recognized the real problem of mutual victimization that ruined her marriage; instead, the pastor's answer was to pray about it, and the mother didn't want the family to be humiliated anymore. Wherever Polly turned for help she was put down and, in effect, told again, "If only you'd be perfect, we'd accept you." It was the refrain of her lifetime theme song.

How many of you women have been made to feel you are to blame for everything that's ever happened to you or your family? Wake up! You are not the sole cause of your problems. Begin to prayerfully look at your childhood to find the root cause of your adult pain. Read and do the written work in *Freeing Your Mind from Memories That Bind*. Don't let your mother, pastor, or friend drape unnecessary guilt around your shoulders. Hebrews 12:1–2 tells us to "Lay aside the weight and the sin which doth so easily beset us" so that we can "run the race with patience and endurance, looking unto Jesus the author and finisher of our faith." Some of us women have been so burdened and so blamed that we are not even in the race. We don't feel worthy to enter a contest we know we will lose.

Not until Polly examined her childhood pain and found the core problem of both verbal and sexual abuse was she able to lay aside her weights and enter the race. As an added bonus Polly has lost some of the extra weight she put on as a wall of protection around her, and her Sanguine personality is bursting forth as she shares her healing process for the glory of God the Father.

"You Are an Abused Woman"

Caroline's story is similar to Polly's but it has a better ending. She and Peter were both expressive Christians when they met. They had similar interests and hobbies and prayed together on each date. Caroline noticed Peter's occasional burst of anger, but she could always rationalize that some circumstance had caused it. Soon after their wedding, Peter began to put Caroline down, discourage any activities she wanted to attend, and show jealousy toward her family. She tried to tell herself this was his way of expressing love but his angry tirades became more frequent and there no longer seemed to be any cause for them. As a Christian Caroline believed she had to deal with the hurts she felt as her cross to bear. She also believed she had to accept Peter the way he was.

For seven years they lived a "roller-coaster marriage, either high on the mountaintop or way down in the valley. Peter's emotions were either ecstatic or combinations of despair mixed with frustration, anger, and depression." Throughout these years Caroline was receiving mixed messages. Peter would fly into fits of rage and violently abuse Caroline; then, after he'd calmed down, he would profess love to her and buy her gifts and flowers with love notes tucked inside. "He spent an enormous amount of money we didn't have in trying to make up for the hurts he caused," she said.

Finally Caroline listened to her sister, who had observed Peter's fits of rage, and told her, "You are an abused woman. You must do something before you are killed!" Caroline hadn't thought of herself as abused, but as her sister reviewed the symptoms she listened and agreed. Caroline and her sister managed to convince Peter to go to a psychiatrist, who tried to teach him how to control his anger but never sought the source of his volatile emotions.

Caroline said, "I knew I couldn't take the abuse any longer. I had exhausted all of my personal resources trying to get along and be gentle and kind, but nothing I ever did calmed him down." At the insistence of her family Caroline moved her belongings to another town. When Peter came home to an empty house he was horrified. *She must mean business*, he thought.

Isn't it amazing how much pleading and begging a woman can do and still the husband just doesn't get it?

As Peter saw that Caroline was upset enough to leave he began to get serious about his anger problem. He knew it was God's will for them to stay married, and he began to pray, study God's Word, and seek counseling. Both Caroline and Peter went to a psychiatrist, who put band-aids over their surface problems but didn't want to dig too deeply.

By the time Caroline and Peter came to our Promise of Healing Workshop they were close to desperate. Peter was ready for God's answers, and when he prayed for his repressed memories, he clearly saw sexual abuse in his childhood. This took the cover off his anger and let him vent to the Lord the horror of the torture he had lived through, the source of his anger. Peter's abusive treatment of Caroline had nothing to do with who she was or how she behaved. It was Peter's unconscious response to what had been done to him as a child. As the pressure receded in Peter's life, Caroline felt free to search for truth in her own past, and she also uncovered childhood abuse. So often victims marry victims and neither one knows the source of his or her problems or what to do about them.

In contrast to Polly, who fled for her life and instead of getting help in restoring her marriage received only condemnation for leaving, Caroline and Peter worked together to find the heart of their abusive marriage and then put it back together again. Healing is a process, not an event, and Caroline and Peter now are on the road to recovery. Caroline wrote, "We learned that any abuse we received as children has an emotional impact on us as adults. We didn't realize that seeing the psychiatrist provided only temporary relief and didn't provide for the internal cleansing and healing we needed."

Grieving for What Might Have Been

Vera is a very attractive, middle-aged woman in full-time Christian service who looks poised and confident. However, when Vera was nine years old she was molested on a Saturday afternoon at the movies by the man sitting next to her. He told her she was a good girl and gave her two dollars. She remembers how fast she ran to spend the money to get it out of her hands. Even at nine she knew this was "dirty money." She told her father what had happened and he laughed at her. "You should be glad a man looked at you," he chided. "You're so homely. You'll never find another man who'll think you're worth two dollars."

From then on Vera believed she'd never find a man who'd think she was worth anything. Her father continued to verbally abuse her and when at eighteen she found a boyfriend who said he loved her, she married him.

Her mother begged her not to marry the boyfriend. She pointed out how rough he was with her and how they fought and argued all the time. This young man was a replica of Vera's father, and the mother could no doubt see the handwriting on the wall. But the couple went ahead with their wedding plans.

A year later Vera had a son; suddenly there was something beautiful in her life. But her husband was jealous of her attention to the son and verbally abused her just as her father had done. Then the abuse became physical; one night he held Vera down on the bed with a butcher knife at her throat for over two hours, teaching her submission. Vera was afraid she'd be killed at any moment. When she finally got loose, she began to plan her escape. Her husband told her she'd never get away from him because if he couldn't have her, he'd make sure no one else would either. One night when he sensed she might escape from the prison he had made for her, he came up behind her and strangled her. When she passed out and fell to the floor he left, thinking he had killed her. She awoke, grabbed the baby, and ran to a neighbor's house to call the police. They picked up her husband and put him in jail for thirty days.

When he got out he didn't come near her or their son. Nor did he send money. Vera had nowhere to turn. She couldn't admit to her mother that she had been right about her husband, so when he finally called and said he'd changed, Vera let the man back in. She needed money and she wanted to save face.

For a while he was better, but soon he started abusing her again. He told the little boy what a rotten mother he had and he gave the child anything he wanted. Vera didn't know where to go for help; in desperation she ran away and left her son behind. In the divorce proceedings that followed, Vera gave custody of her son to her husband, believing she'd be able to visit him and maintain contact, but once the divorce papers were signed it was all over. Each time she'd try to see her son the new wife would scream at her and the ex-husband would curse at her. Miserably, she'd stand near the boy's school and watch him go in with the others. The few times he saw her, he would look the other way. She wrote his school and asked for a copy of his report card and a school picture, which they sent. Later she received a letter from the school saying since she was not the legal guardian she would not be allowed to have his records again or come onto the school grounds.

Vera's son is now in his thirties, and Vera has not talked to him since the day she left. She occasionally tries to contact him, but she receives no reply. Nor has she received any answers to the letters she sent to him. Vera assumes he has been so brainwashed against her, the mother who "rejected" him, that she may never see him again. Vera never had another child and she grieves for what might have been. "When you are in the middle of these problems," Vera says, "you can't see the whole picture and you think you have no choice."

Vera's second husband has treated her well and they are on the staff of an international Christian organization. She has come to CLASS to prepare herself to speak to young women in the hope that she will be used to spare others.

"I haven't told my story before," Vera told me. "I didn't think anyone would believe me. But when you mentioned the idea for a book titled

Wake Up, Women!, the Lord urged me to tell it. I talked it over with my husband and we agreed if one woman could be spared the lifelong heartache I have suffered, it would be worth risking the embarrassment."

Here's some of the advice Vera now offers others:

1. Don't marry as an escape. There's got to be another way. If your living situation is abusive, go to a relative you trust or to the authorities, who are much more aware of these problems today than they were twenty years ago. Do whatever you have to do to be safe, but don't marry someone to escape problems at home and then start a family that may well be as dysfunctional as the one you left. Ask your parents and friends how they perceive the potential of this marriage and listen to what they say.

2. Look at your father's weaknesses. Ask yourself if there are any similarities between your father's and your fiancé's weaknesses. Are the things you're trying to flee already apparent in even a small way in this new person? It's tragically ironic but true: We tend to marry the same kind of behavior we're trying to escape. In case after case I see the same kind of abuse going from generation to generation.

3. Don't marry a non-believer. So often young girls in the flush of what appears to be love think it doesn't matter that much if he's a Christian. Many think, *He'll become a believer living with me!* Not so. Seldom will a young man who won't commit his life to Christ before marriage suddenly convert on his honeymoon. God wouldn't have told us not to be unequally yoked for no good reason. The Devil can use an atheistic husband to ruin the wife and spread strife in the family.

4. Seek counseling when needed. At the first sign of marital trouble, start checking with your friends or church on some available counseling. Vera kept her problems so much to herself that there was no one to help her. She had no one to call in time of emergency. Her husband wouldn't let her go to church, and she didn't know where else to go for help.

5. Know some safe places you can go. These days the Salvation Army, Union Gospel Missions, and other groups have homes for battered wives, and the local authorities have information about these and other safe havens. Don't wait until you've been strangled to find a safe place. Know where they are ahead of time just in case.

6. Don't go back into the same situation. Promises of good behavior without any evidence of a changed life don't often mean anything. Once you are out, don't return until your mate has been willing to seek counseling and apply it. Victimizers often mean well but the overwhelming urge inside them from their own abused past is stronger than their desire to do good. Take your time; don't rush back into the lion's den. Just because the abuser has prayed in repentance doesn't mean he's cured.

7. Don't leave your children behind. Vera made many mistakes out of fear of abuse and lack of knowledge, but she said her worst mistake was leaving her son. She realizes now she was using him as a pawn to get her husband to seek help, but it didn't work.

Breaking the Chain

How much abuse should a woman take? Jeraldine wrote about her family situation, "My mother worked and supported the six of us children while my father drank, ran around with other women, and traveled the country freely as he wished. My abused mother did nothing until he tried to murder her. Then she took action, and he ended up in the psychiatric ward of the veterans hospital. Why didn't she wake up sooner?"

Unfortunately, the fact that the mother took years of abuse set a pattern for her sons. It is amazing how the sins of the fathers so often pass down to the sons. Jeraldine's four brothers were in and out of the house as adults, returning each time they had a broken relationship or got into trouble. "Mother did their laundry, cooked for them, and paid their fines for being drunk in public and sometimes for having robbed taverns and grocery stores. One by one they returned home to live, and mother cared for them until they drank themselves to death."

What kind of a woman would take a lifetime of abuse? Probably one who had been abused in childhood and made to feel that she was worthless and didn't deserve to be treated any better. In our experience, every woman we've counseled who accepted years of wife abuse had been previously abused as a child.

How do you break the cycle?

You have to decide you won't take it anymore and be willing to confront the abuser. You have to refuse to be part of the system. Jeraldine's sister didn't learn; instead she followed the family pattern, repeating her mother's role as abused wife. She married an abuser and took physical, emotional, and sexual abuse from him for twenty years before she left him and ran off to the city, became a prostitute, and continued to live in abusive relationships.

Jeraldine was determined to be the exception to this sick family scene. She never married, and she prayerfully worked through the effects of her abuse. She took her sister's son to raise, and when he began to drink, skip school, and steal as a teenager, Jeraldine gave him a clear ultimatum and announced she would not fight "a war of independence" with him. She cut off his financial support and let him go out on his own. Later he went back and got his high school diploma. He is now in the construction business and recently he wrote his aunt Jeraldine a letter that said, "Thank you for granting me independence instead of enabling me to become a codependent like the rest of the family."

The chain is broken!

Superman to the Rescue

Faith was the most striking beauty in our Promise of Healing Workshop, but the pain in her eyes was in contrast to the serenity in her appearance. She told me, "If this workshop doesn't help, it's all over!" She was prepared to kill herself because life wasn't worth living. When we set aside some time to meet, Faith poured out her story.

She grew up in "a fine Christian home" and was in church every time the door opened. Her father was a saint of the faith when in public and her mother was the definition of submission. In the home, however, the father was brutally abusive to his daughters. He would speak about how much he loved his children when at church but at home he insulted them, beat them, and threw them against the wall. He taught them verses about God's love and being obedient children, but he was tyrannical and hateful. Thus Faith got mixed messages about God, about love, and about men. When she was five, her father's youngest brother abused her sexually, but because of her terrifying home life she never said a word. This began her pattern of secrecy and denial that became her way of life.

One night when Faith and her sister were taking a bath together they were making too much noise and their father made them come out naked into the living room while he mocked their bodies and shot at them with a BB gun. When they tried to run, he made them come back and stand still in front of him while he continued shooting. "Every day was 100 percent fear at our house," Faith said.

It was understandable that her mother had two nervous breakdowns. When Faith recently asked her mother why she had never protected her daughters, she replied, "If I'd lifted a finger to help you he would have killed me."

Growing up in this frightening atmosphere was enough to warp any child, but being told this behavior was Christian love was doubly harmful. It's understandable that Faith wanted to get out of her abusive home. The obvious way, Faith thought, was to get married. She met Ted when she was still in high school, and when she told him what her life was like he wanted to rescue her. Ted seemed so gentle and compassionate, and Faith knew this was her superman who had come to rescue her. Ted's mother obviously didn't approve of the young marriage and said so clearly. Faith was afraid of Ted's mother, but Ted promised they could move far away and never see the mother again.

In her desire to escape, Faith didn't think clearly about the negative possibilities. Once they were married there was no money to move anywhere except in with Ted's mother. His mother controlled their every move and was verbally abusive to Faith. It was the same tragedy played out on a different stage. She had swapped her father for Ted's mother. When Ted began to travel with a Christian rock band Faith went too—and found herself in another abusive situation.

At this point another knight in shining armor came riding forth to rescue Faith. Lance was already well known in Christian music, and he said he would make her a star. In her excitement Faith didn't stop to realize that if this fine Christian man was having sex with her while she was still married to Ted, perhaps he wasn't all that spiritual.

Lance promised to rescue her from her mother-in-law and from her wimpy husband. Lance had glamour and charisma, and Faith knew she would finally be happy. Lance helped her get a divorce, then they immediately got married. Right from the start they traveled with a well-known Christian singing group and Lance would bring Faith out on the stage and introduce her as his wife. "Isn't she beautiful? Aren't I the luckiest man on earth?" It soon became apparent that Lance wanted a showpiece and Faith fit the image.

He demanded perfection from Faith in every way so he could be proud of her. Her nails had to be freshly done each day, her clothes could have no wrinkles, and her posture had to be perfect. Faith did her best to live up to Lance's standards, but it was never enough. Even though she had a slim, shapely figure, he told her she was fat; he mocked her body as her father had done before. One day she had her hair cut in a new style, and Lance blew up at her. "The only thing you had going for you was your long hair, and now you've ruined it."

At the concerts Lance still brought her out and praised her, as her father had done at church, but back in the motel room he demeaned her. When she cried to him, "How can you call me your dear wife on stage and then insult me here?" he responded "I'm trying to do you a favor. You sure need it."

As Faith took this abuse from Lance she began to wonder why she was such a perpetual victim. Faith begged Lance to go for counseling with her and he finally agreed in hopes it would straighten her out. Because he was so well known in the Christian music field, he had to find a counselor who "wouldn't talk." He had to protect his image. He found a woman counselor in a distant city and went alone to her first to set the stage and charm her to his side. By the time Faith walked in for their joint meeting, Lance and the counselor appeared to be good friends. When the counselor asked why she wasn't interested in sex, Faith offered the possibility that it might be related to her childhood sexual abuse. Both Lance and the counselor laughed out loud and ridiculed the thought. That was the end of counseling for Faith. After that Lance had proof that he had been willing to get help and Faith had refused it.

During this turmoil Lance's friend Rob spent time with them and observed what was going on. Once again Faith's combination of physical beauty and emotional helplessness caused yet another man to befriend Faith and want to rescue her. Lance was jealous when anyone else looked at Faith even though he frequently told her how ugly she was. He threatened that if she ever tried to leave him, he'd ruin her. But when life became unbearable and the threats increased, Faith planned her escape.

She and Rob waited until Lance was out of town and then moved her personal belongings out of the house. She took no furniture, no dishes, no money—just her clothes and books. Her new rescuer pledged to take care of her forever, and the cycle began again. Since Rob was a music minister and Christian songwriter, he promoted Faith's singing talents. Soon she was doing backup vocals for recording artists along with Rob. Just at the point when Faith's life seemed to be evening out she started getting flashbacks of her childhood. But Rob didn't want to hear about it, so she tried to stuff it all back down and pretend nothing had ever happened. She started going to a counselor who ultimately put her into a hospital. Rob was humiliated to be a pastor with a wife who was "a mental case," and he let her know she had to shape up or ship out. She was shocked that her new rescuer was abandoning her. Rob felt he had valid reasons to divorce her and continue to be a pastor because, he said, Faith was obviously unbalanced and unfit to be a pastor's wife.

It was at this point that Faith came to our Promise of Healing Workshop, desperate for help. Those of us on the outside looking in can pass quick judgments and wonder how one woman could possibly make so many mistakes, but from Faith's perspective she had been trying to do what was expected of her. At the workshop, we understood the origin of her problems. In spite of her beauty Faith felt she was a homely woman with an ugly body. She had no idea what love really was; she confused rescuing with love. She had no Christian male model to look up to because every Christian man she had known had done her in. She had learned women were only good for one thing and she had tried her best to provide it—and failed. Faith was a victim of her early childhood. Her deep desire to flee problems had led her into repeated poor choices. As soon as a man said he'd take care of her, she was hooked. Then because she had such low self-worth, she allowed herself to be revictimized and didn't know what to do to escape her downward spiral. Now, in spite of her beauty and talent, Faith saw herself as a hopeless failure and was contemplating suicide. We knew she needed help, and fast.

First we allowed her to give her whole story without judgment or interruption. We prayed with her to retrieve her lost memories, knowing that until she got to the bottom of her abuse she wouldn't be healed. We encouraged her to write her prayers daily, telling the Lord honestly how she felt. As we reviewed her faulty behavior patterns they became obvious to her for the first time. As Faith says, "When you use up all your energy keeping your problems hidden and denying you have them, you have no spiritual strength left to help you make intelligent choices."

Faith realizes now that victims continue to be victimized over and over again until they see what's happening and take human and spiritual steps to halt the onslaught. She also sees that we tend to marry those who are on a similar level of emotional pain. No man who is a ten on the scale of emotional maturity is going to be attracted to a woman who's a one! Healthy people attract others who are stable; hurting people gravitate to those with similar dysfunctions.

Faith now understands that childhood victimization significantly distorts our ability to make healthy choices in life. Victimization lowers a child's sense of value, causing him or her to accept abuse throughout life that another person wouldn't take. We have not yet found an abused or battered wife who stayed in the situation who had not been initially abused as a child.

You may not be in the depths of chaos that Faith was in, but you still may have a low self-image or a distorted view of love on a godly and human level; or you may feel that you are repeatedly put down or victimized. You may be looking for a superman to swoop down and whisk you away from your pain. You may have been to a counselor who made you feel worse or who discounted your own views of your problems. You may have an uneasy feeling that there's more to your childhood than you can remember. You may wonder, as Faith did, if there is any hope. The answer is yes, but *you* have to take responsibility for finding the way out of the depths of your despair.

When I asked Faith a few months later what had made the difference in her attitude and even in her appearance, she outlined her progress for me through the following steps:

1. Look at your problems objectively. Faith had always been the victim and felt there was nothing she could do about it. She had to back up and say, "This is enough. I will not be a victim any longer." Once she allowed herself the possibility for change she began to look for help.

2. Find some godly counsel. In Faith's case a friend brought her to our Promise of Healing Workshop where she took the Survey of Emotions and Experiences (see Appendix B). The results showed that she had some hidden victimization beyond what she remembered. Seeing her symptoms on paper validated her opinion that her pain originated in childhood abuse in spite of what others had told her. Once she accepted the source of her lifetime of victimization, Faith was ready and willing to get to the bottom of her pain.

3. Pray for clear memories. Faith had spent so much of her life and her energies denying her circumstances and waiting for a superman that she felt powerless to do anything herself. Once she began to pray on paper and ask the Lord to separate her mental wheat from the chaff, she began to see her life clearly for the first time. She was able to throw off the misconceptions of her worthlessness and see herself as an innocent child, pure in God's sight. Once she asked specifically, the Lord began to give her pictures of her victimization and she was able to cry out, "It wasn't my fault. I didn't deserve it. I wasn't a bad girl." This clear view of her childhood relieved her of the blame, shame, and guilt she had carried for a lifetime. Once she placed the blame where it belonged, at the feet of the victimizers, Faith was free to move on.

4. Take responsibility for your life and decisions. Eliminating guilt does not wipe out responsibility, but it does give the victim new energy to get on with life. In just a few months of daily written prayer, Faith can look back and see the pattern of her victimized life. She recognizes herself as a helpless child unable to make mature decisions. She refuses to be a victim any longer. This step is close to impossible for a non-believer because no human has the power to make such drastic changes in direction. Only with God's help can this come about. Faith's daily reach to the Lord in her time of written prayer and her repeated reading of the Psalms, inserting her name in place of the seeker, is bringing healing in a most exciting way.

Faith gave me these words of encouragement: "If God ever brings another man into my life, he will not find a pitiful victim waiting to be rescued. I've already been saved by the real Superman!"

An Abused Missionary Wife

When we first met George and Louise at our Promise of Healing Workshop, they appeared to be the ideal Christian couple. They had recently returned from a missionary assignment, and they carried well-used Bibles. Louise was a cheerful Sanguine, but she had a somewhat frightened look about her, and George seemed to change from friendly and conversant to withdrawn and shy at the coffee breaks. When Louise asked if she could talk with me privately her tragic, hidden story began to unfold.

She grew up in a legalistic home where things looked good on the outside and where the family reputation was far more important than what went on behind closed doors. Louise's father was extremely controlling; he was never wrong, and he managed to place the blame for everything on Louise. She grew up apologizing to everyone for whatever went wrong. Her mother was so desperate to get some control of her own life that she managed to ruin every major family event and cause continual chaos. Life at home was so stressful that Louise was mentally and emotionally exhausted. When she met George, she could tell he was nothing like her father. He seemed so quiet, pleasant, and easygoing, and he even wanted to be a missionary. Louise had seen those glorified missionary movies where the natives stood in adoration as the saintly ones dole out food and blessings. What a glamorous change from "Life with Father."

Although Louise's mother accepted George as a godly man, she was not interested in helping with the wedding. In her usual way she set about to undermine the joy that should have surrounded the event. She refused to "waste a cent" of her own money on it, and she disagreed with even the modest plans Louise made. She berated Louise at her bridal shower, letting Louise know in front of others that she had better make this marriage last because divorce was unacceptable in this family. When George arrived the week before the wedding, he seemed different. He was aloof from Louise and her family, and he complained about how she was preparing the wedding even though he refused to help or contribute to the expenses. Detecting a mean streak in him that she had not seen before, she began to have second thoughts about the wedding.

When Louise mentioned to her mother that George seemed different her mother warned, "Don't you dare think of canceling the wedding and humiliating me in front of all my friends!" Louise knew in her heart that this wedding wasn't right, but to save her mother from embarrassment she went through with it and hoped for the best. George's moods fluctuated daily; Louise never knew if he'd be sociable or withdrawn. As they prepared for the mission field, Louise excused his depressions as part of the uncertainty about the future. By the time they arrived at their post George had begun hitting Louise. When anything went wrong, he took it out on her. The hitting turned to beatings, and sometimes he would pin her down and try to choke her. He swore at her, put her down in front of others, and threatened to kill her and "bash her head in."

Being far from home, Louise didn't know where to turn for help. Finally, in desperation, she called her mother. Mother told her it was all her fault; if Louise was a decent wife, Mother said, this wouldn't happen. Louise felt devastated and rejected and finally realized her parents cared nothing for her life and safety, only for their reputation. The frequency of the beatings increased, and one day George even tried to choke Louise while she was driving the car. She went to their mission director's wife, who had actually observed some of the abuse. Her advice was to pray more and persevere and God would ultimately reward her. "After all," she stated, "everyone has some problem to deal with."

Louise had done all she could and no one seemed to care. After another severe beating Louise finally went to a primitive shelter for battered women. George went to a psychiatric hospital for three weeks, and when he got out they got back together. But George was not better; in fact, he was even worse. However, he managed to convince his superiors he was healed and all their problems had been Louise's fault. No one believed either of them, and they were sent back to the States, where Louise checked into a government-run shelter. She also located some friends who believed her and became supportive in both prayer and helpful deeds. George went for some counseling, but in Louise's words, "it was a joke." One day he trapped her behind a fast-food restaurant and kicked her repeatedly.

It was at this point that Louise and George came to our workshop. Louise was an obvious victim, and through prayer she learned that she had been abused as a child even more than she had remembered. Only someone who had been victimized as a child and made to feel worthless would accept years of abuse as she had done. We also suspected that George was a multiple personality with an abusive childhood, and we helped him get counseling with someone who is an expert in MPD (multiple personality disorder). Even though George recognizes that he has this problem, the fits of rage and violence are still occurring. Louise says the difference is that now she can tell when George is changing personalities an instant before he does and she runs from his presence. Things are improving, but there is not yet a happy ending to this story. Louise wrote, "Even though I have received abuse from parents, siblings, and employers, there is no comparison between them and this man. He feels not a shred of remorse or compassion; from him there is *only* cruelty, coldness, and control."

What could Louise have done differently? How could she have prevented ten years of torture? These are Louise's thoughts about these questions, which she shares here in hope of helping others.

1. Trust your intuition. If you have the distinct feeling that you should not marry a certain person, don't. We have talked with many women who knew better but got married anyway because calling it off would humiliate their family. If you are the parent and your child wishes to withdraw from an engagement or wedding, don't be the one to say, "What would my friends think?" If you are considering marrying someone you've only known for a short while, try to find a friend or family members who can give you some insight into his background and past behavior. Obviously, this person's opinion should not be definitive, but information on abusive behavior or flagrantly immoral conduct should give you cause for concern. Each week I talk with middle-aged women who have suffered through abusive or deceitful marriages while someone who knew the husband beforehand huffs, "I *knew* this would happen. He's always been this way." We can't know everything ahead but we should try to collect all the information we can, and if we have any doubts, we should postpone the marriage.

2. Separate from your husband as soon as a pattern of abuse occurs. By staying in a situation as Louise did and being beaten down for years you allow yourself to be killed bit by bit. Separation doesn't mean divorce, but it does mean you need to take charge of your own life and not remain forever a victim.

Louise says in retrospect, "I should have had the strength to call off the wedding. But since I didn't, I should have had the marriage annulled or at least have separated as soon as I saw the pattern of abuse. Instead I hung on, thinking certainly he would come to his senses and certainly God would answer my prayers and things would improve. It has only gotten worse, though, and the beatings, swearing, lethargy, and general disinterest in a normal life continue."

Louise was at an extreme disadvantage, living in the mission field where little help was available. Those people she went to added to her guilt instead of helping her.

3. Examine your guilt. Where does your guilt come from? Did you actually do something wrong, or is it unjustified guilt put upon you by others? Louise realizes now that both her parents loaded her with guilt, saying all of life's problems were her fault. They put up a pious front with their friends, abused her at home, and then blamed her for "deserving" it. She fled from her abusive home life only to marry a man who abused her and made her feel guilty. Louise was so loaded with unjustified guilt she was unable to function. Fortunately, she brought this problem to the Lord for healing, and He took away her guilt.

Ask yourself if the guilt you feel is due to your own clear disobedience to God's will or if it is blame and shame put upon you by other people. God gives us natural guilt when we have strayed, but He doesn't want us to be manipulated by others who put their guilt on us. Examine your guilt, bring it to the Lord in prayer, and ask Him to show you your errors and lift the unjustified guilt from your shoulders.

Louise said, "I came to realize that because of my background I internalized problems and thought they were all my fault. I continued to take the blame for everything, and I played the scapegoat role, the one I was cast in as a child. I allowed a manipulator to prey on me. I've now learned to listen to and trust my own feelings. I've learned to stop accepting blame and instead expect other people to take responsibility for their attitude and behavior."

4. Seek competent counseling. Louise had little choice of counselors in the mission field, but much of what she received later in the States was poor counseling that added to her guilt. Once she found a competent counselor who could expose her pattern of victimization and uncover the childhood abuse she had repressed, and when she began to work on her healing by reading and writing her prayers, relief crept over her. Abuse that has taken years to victimize doesn't go away overnight, but as Louise's story shows, there is hope.

"I learned I should stop listening to advice from sick and dysfunctional people," said Louise. "I also realized that just because a person can quote Scripture it doesn't mean his or her counsel is godly. I have to use my head."

The average counselor would not spot the source of George's problems unless he or she was trained to deal with multiple personalities. George could always pull up one of his charming personalities to fool the counselor—and then become vicious toward Louise at home. This deception caused several would-be helpers to see Louise as the problem, adding to her guilt.

5. Find supportive friends or groups. Today there are support groups for just about everything. In one cartoon I saw, a character said, "We're starting a support group for those who don't need support groups." Test out a support group to see if it really makes you feel better. Does it deal with your issues, or is it a group where everyone focuses on the negative? Does one person monopolize the time? Do you come home feeling worse? Sometimes it's better to start your own group of people you know and trust who have been through similar problems. Have at least one friend you can call and talk with, but don't abuse his or her time or infringe upon the family. Too frequently, victims are not sensitive to other people's time, and they become pests. As a result, the friend ultimately retreats for his or her own sanity, signaling more rejection to the victim, which causes more guilt.

"I now surround myself with godly people who will support me and be my allies," said Louise. "I'm in a support group for spouses of mates with multiple personalities, and I have learned how to take care of myself and meet my own needs. I keep a list of shelters where I can go for help, and I have a few friends who know about my husband's behavior and who can hold him accountable.

6. Read and study about your problem. One of the best things we can do to hasten our healing from abusive behavior is to read books and articles on our subject area so we can become experts on ourselves. There are so many books out now on dramatic problems that many bookstores have whole sections focusing on recovery. Although we suggest Christian books, the first two that Louise read were not Christian; still, they opened her mind to her problems and gave her initial insight. They were both by Susan Forward: *Men Who Hate Women and the Women Who Love Them* and *Toxic Parents*. Later she worked her way through our books, *Freeing Your Mind from Memories That Bind* and *The Promise of Healing*. Both Louise and George read Dr. James Friesen's book, *Uncovering the Mystery of MPD*, along with others on the subject.

7. Study God's Word for His answers. Many of us don't realize how much of the Bible deals with people who are hurting until we are hurting, ourselves, and willing to look. The Psalms especially speak to those of us who are seeking help. The *Narrated Bible* (published by Harvest House) has pulled together the Psalms that deal with victimization in a section called "Psalms for the Troubled Soul." Reading and praying through these specific selections can be a special help. Many churches today have Bible studies relating to personal problems. Faithfully attending one of these groups and doing the homework will be a blessing.

Louise says, "I've finally stopped hearing the mental tapes from my sick and dysfunctional family telling me it's my fault. I've replaced those words with verses that tell me of God's love. Our marriage is not healed yet, but it's getting better. Now I feel if telling my story will wake up one woman before it's too late, it's worth the telling."

Calling the Cops on a Cop

Patsy's husband was a policeman trained to look at circumstances, people, and their actions and quickly come up with an accurate assessment and a course of action.

Patsy had always been the sweet, dutiful wife. It was not until she had been married to Pete more than twenty years that she went back to work part-time in an office. At first there was no problem with her working, but as time went on and she began to express to Pete how good it felt to be appreciated for her hard work and how much she enjoyed what she was doing, she sensed that this made Pete feel threatened.

One night Pete announced to Patsy she was going to quit her job the following month and there would be no discussion about what she wanted. When he couldn't get his point across, Pete finally accused Patsy of being attracted to her boss.

He knew in his heart that she had always been a faithful wife, but to get control of her he accused her of planning to run off with her boss. Throughout the next year, whenever Patsy didn't jump to his every desire, Pete would bring up the supposed affair, threaten her again, and leave with a dramatic slam of the door. Sometimes he stayed away a few hours, sometimes several days. Patsy, the perpetually submissive wife, was dumbfounded that after all these years of apparent harmony, Pete was playing havoc with her emotions.

She suggested counseling, but Pete refused to even consider it. "There's nothing wrong with me. If you'd quit your job and stay home, we'd have no problems," he fumed.

Pete became paranoid when none of his offers or threats seemed to work. One night he came storming in holding a cassette tape in his hand. "I have the proof!" he shouted. "I have a tape of you and your boss. I have proof you're having an affair."

If Patsy had been involved, she might have been done in by this supposed proof, but since she was innocent she was able to be strong and say, "That's a lie. There is no affair and no proof."

Pete was furious that his trick hadn't worked and he backed Patsy up against the kitchen sink and berated her in a barrage of verbal abuse. Towering over her nose to nose, he threatened to hit her. Patsy had little hope of pushing away a man who could subdue violent criminals, but she tried. As she shoved him, he hit her. They were both stunned. How could their good marriage have turned to this? What should the sweet submissive wife do at this point? Just what Patsy did.

She ran to the phone and called 911.

The whole time she was on the phone with the dispatcher, Pete was telling her how stupid she was for calling. This was the worst thing she could've done, he said. When the officers arrived, they asked Pete to leave and go to the station to be interviewed. They interviewed Patsy at home, and she asked that Pete not be allowed to come home.

Pete was a man out of control. He didn't know how to deal with a situation when control was taken away from him. The only way he knew how to handle the problem was with anger, threats, and finally violence. Patsy did the right thing; she stopped the violence at the start. Then she set down some conditions for their relationship in order for them to be reconciled: Pete would go to counseling with her until the *counselor* said he could quit coming, and there were to be no threats, no physical abuse, no accusations of affairs with her boss. Finally, decisions about her job wouldn't be made by Pete, but by Patsy; he would support her career as she had supported his.

Patsy was courageous to call 911. She realized it might signal the end of a twenty-five year marriage, but she also realized she didn't want to continue in a lifestyle she had seen so many other women put up with year after year. Sometimes love must be tough and set parameters in order to stay on solid ground. Love means allowing our mates to be who they are, accepting them, and wanting them to be fulfilled and happy. We cannot be their happiness or their all-in-all.

Patsy's friend shared with her the image that spouses are two people choosing to ride bicycles in the same direction—not on a tandem bike where one leads and the other follows unquestioningly, but on two different bicycles, choosing to go in the same direction. Sometimes one is ahead, sometimes another, and sometimes they ride along at the same pace, but they're always choosing to travel in the same direction.

Do you have some difficult choices to make? Is someone beating you up verbally or physically? Perhaps you need to do as Patsy did—set some parameters and take some steps that will get you both back on your bikes, moving in concert, and heading by choice in the same direction!

Patsy's story differs dramatically from the stories of Faith and Louise described earlier in this chapter. In contrast to Patsy, who took immediate action when her marriage took a violent turn, Faith and Louise spent many years in abusive situations. Each of Faith's multiple marriages and relationships had similar aspects of abuse. Louise's missionary husband berated her and exploded into violent behavior with little or no reason. And both Faith and Louise accepted this behavior for years. Why did this happen? Why did they seem to attract men who demeaned them and physically abused them? Was it something they were doing? Did they have offensive personalities? Were they not perfect enough?

No! This had nothing to do with it. Both of these women had been abused as children by their parents, so even as adults they felt they deserved nothing better. Why didn't either of them call 911 as Patsy did? Because they didn't know they had a right to stand up for themselves. They believed the lies told to them by parents, by friends, by colleagues: "You must have done something to deserve it" or "All of us have our crosses to bear" or "Why do *you* make me do this?" or "If you'd only behave, it wouldn't happen" or "You made your bed; now lie in it."

But Patsy knew she didn't deserve to be slapped. She knew she had the right to stand up for herself. She didn't wait to see if Pete would hit her again or if the rage would pass. Pete learned right then that this behavior would not be accepted. He would certainly think twice about ever laying a hand on Patsy again!

Are you believing lies fed to you by others? Do you *know* that you have a right to stand up for yourself? If *push* came to *shove*, literally, what would *you* do?

How to Stop Being a Victim

There are no magic tricks to restore order in an abusive marriage, but here are some positive suggestions that have worked for others.

• **Get out quickly.** Do not pass go. Do not collect two hundred dollars! Take your keys, purse, and your kids and go! If he has abused you before and you think it might happen again, take some things over to a friend's house—a few changes of clothes, extra toiletries (include some cash in this bag for safety's sake), and the children's needs for a few days (clothing, a toy, etc.). If violence does occur either go to the friend's home or to a motel, your parents, or a shelter.

• **Don't go to another man.** Think about the long-term consequences. If your marriage ends in separation or divorce, you certainly don't want your husband to be able to produce pictures, tapes, or other accusations of your abandoning the marriage because of another man. You also don't want him to convince the court that your affairs during the marriage make you an unfit mother so he gets custody of the children.

• **Don't leave the children there.** You don't want them to be subjected to any of his anger or abuse when he finds you have left. If you do your husband's attorney will bring up the fact in court that you must have abandoned them and that you must also feel your husband's fathering skills were not lacking or you would not have left them with him.

- **Get medical attention.** If you've been injured by your husband don't be embarrassed at how you look and don't be ashamed of what's happened—just get help. Be sure you get a copy of the bill for treatment or a copy of the report from the emergency room or doctor's office. You *must* document the abuse in case you need to prove it in court.

- **Don't lie.** When you report the abuse tell the story just as it happened. Professional people (doctors, police, nurses) see this abuse day after day. Your situation is not unique. Don't cover up for him, and be sure to let them know there have been other instances of violence if that is the case.

- **Make a police report.** If you call 911 this happens anyway, whether or not you want to press charges of spousal abuse. If you call the local police or sheriff directly, make sure they make a report.

- **Get a restraining order.** Go to the courthouse in your county or city (any police department can tell you where to get this) and file a restraining order against your abusive husband. Be sure to file this with the appropriate jurisdiction. If you file in a city and you live in the county, the county sheriff will have no jurisdiction on the restraining order. When you file you must explain why you need it, and you must be able to articulate a fear of violence, harassment, or threats. This restraining order is not a guarantee of your safety, but it will document the fact that you were afraid. The fee for filing varies from place to place, but several I've checked were between fifty and seventy-five dollars. Call the appropriate law enforcement agency if your husband violates the order. The only way the police can help is if they are called. If the man shows up in violation of this order, *call the police.* If your husband is violent or is threatening you, be sure to tell the 911 operator and have him or her stay on the line with you until help arrives.

- **Get a safety deposit box.** Unfortunately, if there's been abuse in the past there is a great likelihood it will occur again, so you must plan ahead. Go to the bank and rent a safety deposit box. Here is an idea of some of the things you should have in it:

  1. Extra keys to the house, car, etc.
  2. Extra blank checks from your *own* account
  3. Duplicate credit cards (your *own*, not in *his* name)
  4. Two hundred dollars in cash (more if you can afford it)
  5. Copies of the wills, bank statements, credit card bills, marriage certificates, birth certificates, and the restraining order, if applicable

6. Photos of past injuries due to violence

7. Copies of police reports, etc., detailing past violence

• **Take color pictures.** Take pictures of the house in disarray, of broken furniture or windows, and of the children, frightened and hurt. Have someone else take pictures of you including close-up shots of bruises and lacerations. A video tape with the date in the corner of the frame would also be excellent evidence. This may sound ridiculous now, but I've had so many women say later, "I wish I'd had the proof."

• **Remove known weapons.** If there is a gun in the house, temporarily remove it. You could put a small handgun in the safety deposit box, but a larger one may need to be placed in someone else's custody so your husband will not be able to use it to hurt you, your children, or himself in a moment of rage. Certainly it is hoped that, with counseling, this terrible time in your marriage will pass and you will no longer have to hide guns and worry for your safety. But wouldn't it be horrendous if you decided not to take precautions like these and the worst scenario unfolded? The newspaper is full of such sad stories every day!

• **Press charges and stick with them.** If you value your life and your children's lives proceed with the charges. Don't just assume your violent husband will reform tomorrow.

In her book *Love and the Law* Gail J. Koff says, "It is our experience that there is a continuing pattern to abuse and unless the couple seeks professional help, the problem is almost sure to recur. The frustrating fact is that most women, if they do seek the help of legal authorities, eventually drop the charges against the men who batter them."[2]

Isn't it time we women realize that we do not deserve to be abused and mistreated? We have the God-ordained right to demand we be treated in a healthy way, and if we are not, we must wake up!

Scripture tells us "Woman is the glory of the man" (1 Cor. 11:7). She is not a doormat, a victim, or a possession.

8

Sticks and Stones Can Break My Bones, and Words Can Also Hurt Me

Many women I meet are not being beaten or burned, yet their beaten-down attitudes, looks, and burned-out existence scream ABUSE. Not all abuse is physical. The dictionary defines the verb *abuse* as "to attack in words, to put to an improper use, to use so as to injure or damage."

The first part of the definition refers to a verbal attack. Men frequently feel that strong language and swearing are indications of being a real man, but this attitude on an angry man can easily lead to verbal abuse. As with physical violence, abusive words express the victimizer's need to dominate and control. In an article entitled "The Wounds of Words" in the October 12, 1992 issue of *Newsweek* the author explains that verbal abuse can take the form of anger, ridicule, undermining, constant judging, or challenging:

> The verbal abuser has a different style and a different motivation. He uses words and emotions (like anger and coldness) to punish, belittle, and control his partner and he does it compulsively and constantly. He rarely apologizes and shows little empathy.
>
> As a power play, the war on words can be devastatingly effective; many targets of abuse start to believe the put downs they hear.

Since verbal abuse doesn't leave physical scars, it is difficult for the hurting victim to find help. If you are the victim of verbal abuse and feel helpless, confront the victimizer. You may need a friend, pastor, or counselor with you for protection and reinforcement when you do this. State clearly what the abuse is, give examples of the abuse, and describe what you expect from here on. You must set limits no matter what the abuse is and let the abuser know that the next time is the last time.

A decent man will not want to be abusive once he sees what he's been doing, but a sick, angry man may not improve. In fact, he may go from verbal to physical abuse.

Just because we're Christians doesn't mean we should also be stupid. There is no special crown in heaven for the martyred women who took it the longest.

Is This Abuse?

How do you know if you are being victimized? It seems abuse would be obvious, especially to the victim, but if you grew up in an alcoholic home, saw physical violence all around you, or were sexually abused, you will tolerate behavior and language that a woman coming from a more wholesome background would not accept.

To know whether something is improper or damaging we need a norm to compare the behavior to. What is normal? In an age when sado-masochistic bars and nightclubs exist for those who would pay to be tied to a pole and whipped with chains for supposed sexual pleasure, it would be hard to come up with a norm. In a year when a popular style is labeled "Bondage Chic" and is composed of dresses wrapped in heavy chains simulating the garb of slavery, we would be hard-pressed to explain some women's acceptance of the extremes as normal.

We all know black from white and we know if we are being beaten black and blue. We also know if we have a model husband who treats us like a queen, never insults or demeans us, and has never lifted a finger to harm us. We can all grasp the extremes, but what about that gray, murky area in the middle?

Each day women give me tales of woe and then ask, "Is that abuse?" We can all see someone else's victimization better than our own. We must also realize that the victimizer often accompanies his abuse with expressions such as "It's because I love you," "It's for your own good," or "It's God's will." The difference between a worldly abuser and a Christian one is only that the Christian has a verse to back up his actions!

Here's some more information to help you assess your situation:

• The abusive person was probably abused himself as a child.

- The abuser tends to abuse in the same way he was violated. If he was beaten, he beats. If he was sexually molested, he molests. If he was verbally abused, he degrades and insults.

- The abuse is usually compulsive behavior so good intentions, vows, prayers of repentance, and even threats of jail won't necessarily keep him from repeating the offense.

- The abuse probably won't just stop because he is getting older or going to church more. When I ask many women why they allowed the abuse to go on they tell me they thought their husband would see the error of his ways and change. Not so.

- The abuser may not see what he's doing as abusive. If he lived with abuse growing up it seems natural to him. He has no doubt rationalized his behavior as necessary to keep the family under control.

- Power and control are the major motivations for abuse. The abuser, a victim himself, is scared to death he will lose control.

Types of Nonphysical, Nonsexual Abuse

With these thoughts in mind, let's look at the types of abuse that do not involve physical or sexual violence (even though these same activities are also used by the more violent abusers). You are being abused if you are living under intimidation, humiliation, deprivation, or isolation.

Intimidation

If you are afraid your husband will "let you have it" if you do something wrong, you are being abused. The something wrong could be as simple as not picking up the shirts from the laundry, not getting home when you said you would, or buying a new book. Your action is not the problem; it just gives an abusive husband justification for the abuse he was going to heap on you anyway. He may threaten, "If you don't do what I say . . ." or "I won't tolerate . . ." or "You are pushing me . . ." When you live in genuine fear of making a mistake, you are suffering emotional abuse.

Several women I know personally were threatened for years by their husband's guns. One woman was forced to sleep with a revolver under her pillow. Another slept with a shotgun between her and her husband. One dear lady in Canada who was on the verge of a nervous breakdown told me, "If I tried to head for the border, he'd have his men there to shoot me." All of these men were Christians. The first two situations, where guns were brought into the bed, ended in divorce and the men are still regarded as church leaders while the women had to leave town. The Canadian woman is still living in daily fear for her life. Legally there was nothing any of these wives could do because they weren't actually shot.

Living in life-threatening situations is abuse by intimidation.

Humiliation

Constant put-downs, insults, and derogatory statements can wear women down to the point where they lose all feelings of worth or sense of identity. The one who takes sadistic joy in humiliating others is an insecure person who feels that by belittling others he will feel better about himself. It's bad enough when a husband does this to a wife. But it's even worse when he berates their children. He is not only wiping out their self-confidence but also setting them up to be abusive parents when they grow up.

Humiliation of others is verbal abuse.

Deprivation

One of the most effective tools religious cults use to pull people into their clutches is deprivation. As the leaders are comfortably ensconced, they keep the converts in Spartan quarters, deprived of sleep, food, and social contact until they are willing to be obedient. We Christians are appalled at this, but we don't realize how many of our Christian families are being controlled in a similar manner. I talk with women who turn over their paychecks to husbands who control every cent and give them nothing or only a small allowance. Some women must account on paper for every cent they spend, and others must call their husbands from the store to get permission to buy a needed household item. I also know women who aren't allowed a credit card or checking account, women whose husbands do the marketing and control the food purchases and women who have no car and are at the mercy of others for transportation.

A young girl told me she had left her abusive father at sixteen to marry a dashing, romantic man with a red Corvette. Once they were married he wouldn't allow her to touch the car. He told her if she were ever good enough, he might let her drive, but she never got that good. The car she had expected to own, owned her.

Another example of deprivation was two young sisters who came to me for help with their eating disorders. As we talked, I learned that their father put a high priority on being slim. He controlled their eating and when he found they sneaked food, he punished them by taking away all their clothes except two school dresses.

He told them what weight they should be and would not give them any more clothes until they got to that weight. As a result one became anorexic and the other bulimic. The mother was so emotionally abused herself that she had long since given up any hint of influence. The father, a Bible-toting elder in the church, was so impressed with the girls' weight loss that he stood up at prayer meeting and suggested this method to other families with chubby daughters.

Another example of deprivation was Dawn, who was steeped in saintly submission as a young bride and right from the beginning did whatever Mason told her to do. He handled all the money and gave her nothing, saying, "As long as you go everywhere with me you don't need any money to squander." They opened a small ice cream shop together and at first they worked side by side. Once the business stabilized, though, Mason assigned Dawn to work six full days a week while he supervised occasionally. Mason bought new sport coats and bright ties and seemed always ready to take off at any time with anybody who dropped by. He decided that Dawn and the other clerks should wear uniforms, so six days a week Dawn was in khaki slacks and an orange polo shirt. When Dawn looked in Mason's closet one day she began to cry. When Mason came in to see what was wrong she told him, "You have all these nice clothes, and all I have is khaki slacks and orange shirts and two church dresses." Mason looked surprised. "But you don't need any clothes," he said. "You don't do anything but work."

How true!

A sad-looking lady in a drab dress waited until everyone had left the church before she came up to ask me her question. "I've been sick for almost a year and my husband won't let me go to the doctor. He says he loves me so much he doesn't want any other man to touch me. Do you think that's the truth?"

"What do you think?" I asked.

"I think he's hoping I'll die."

This poor lady sobbed as she sank into the front pew. During the next half-hour she told me a litany of emotionally abusive tricks her husband had conceived over their years of marriage. At the time she had not seen them as abusive but as her duty as a submissive wife; however, when we looked at the pattern objectively, she could see his manipulation as abuse.

Willful deprivation is abuse.

Isolation

One of the most serious but subtle forms of nonviolent abuse is isolating the wife and family from normal social relationships. Sometimes this is physical, moving the family to a remote area where there are few or no other people. Often the move is described as temporary, but it may last for years. The home (trailers are the frequent choices for men isolating their families) usually lacks even the basic amenities of life and makes the wife too ashamed to have a friend in for coffee. The children are too far away from school to participate in extracurricular activities, or they are home-schooled, effectively eliminating social contact. Often there is no phone and no car, and the wife becomes a recluse in the name of submission.

Sometimes the isolation doesn't appear to be this dismal. I've met women who lived in large houses, drove fine cars, and wore designer dresses but were not allowed to go anywhere or do anything without permission. People who didn't know envied them, but these women lived isolated, lonely lives. Often pious husbands convince wives they are too pure to be contaminated by friends whose doctrine may be flawed or whose behavior is not exemplary. One pastor's wife told me that every time she found a friend she enjoyed in the church, her husband would in some way undermine the relationship. When it was broken, he would say, "See, she wasn't what she appeared to be. You're well rid of her."

Some abusive husbands manage to disrupt old friendships as well as new ones. Bev and Mary had been friends for years. Mary's husband abused her and the children, and after a long period of suffering Mary left and got a divorce. Bev's husband, who had already moved her to a remote area in an attempt to isolate her, forbade her to see Mary anymore. "All divorced women run around, and I won't let you be tainted," he said. On his unfounded opinion a long-lasting friendship was broken for good, further isolating Bev and keeping her submissively dependent on her husband.

One young woman told me her husband moved her into a senior-citizen trailer park so there wouldn't be any eligible men around she might get interested in. He said he was protecting her from temptation. Another's husband wouldn't let her wear attractive clothes; he kept her in high-necked white blouses lest men should lust after her.

Isolation, whether it's physical or emotional, can be abuse.

Why Do Women Stay in Abusive Situations?

Why do women put up with this kind of manipulation and control? In many cases women don't realize that they are living in abusive situations.

That is why we are dealing with the issue here: to wake up those women who are in some kind of bondage and feel they have no choice. One of the major symptoms of a woman who was abused as a child is her feeling of helplessness to do anything about her situation. Because of this background of trauma, she is less apt to see her situation as abusive and more apt to stay in it than an emotionally healthy woman would.

If you have any question as to whether you are in a potentially dangerous relationship or whether someone you know is in trouble, read the following list and check any statements that apply. These excuses are paraphrased from actual comments women have made to me.

_____ 1. **No choice.** I have no options, no place to go, no one who cares, no money. I might as well grin and bear it.

_____ 2. **Religious reasons.** As a Christian I must stay in this marriage and hope for rewards in heaven. I'm committed to obedience.

_____ 3. **Children.** I'll take the abuse for the sake of the children. They need a stable home life and I can't disrupt them.

_____ 4. **Finances.** I can't support myself and the children; I need his income to live. I'll just keep quiet and keep going.

_____ 5. **Wifely duty.** I was taught that sex was what I had to do even though he's abusive. It's my cross to bear.

_____ 6. **Social status.** Without his name I'd be nobody. I'd be out of the country club and ostracized by his friends.

_____ 7. **The comfort zone.** It's easier to stay here where we're all settled than to uproot everyone. I guess I can stand it a little longer.

_____ 8. **Shared responsibilities.** I could never run this house on my own. At least he helps get the kids to bed. Maybe it's my price to pay.

_____ 9. **Loneliness.** I hate going places alone, and even though he puts me down in public, it's better than staying home.

_____ 10. **Fear.** If I leave he'll come after me and kill me—or the children. He scares me to death.

_____ 11. **Depression.** It's been this way forever. I'm doomed. I'm just too tired to do anything about it.

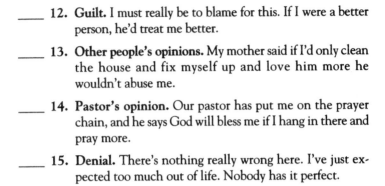

_____ **12. Guilt.** I must really be to blame for this. If I were a better person, he'd treat me better.

_____ **13. Other people's opinions.** My mother said if I'd only clean the house and fix myself up and love him more he wouldn't abuse me.

_____ **14. Pastor's opinion.** Our pastor has put me on the prayer chain, and he says God will bless me if I hang in there and pray more.

_____ **15. Denial.** There's nothing really wrong here. I've just expected too much out of life. Nobody has it perfect.

So many Christian women are convinced that being submissive includes forever accepting any kind of abuse. When they are suffering, many are afraid to go to their pastors for fear they won't be believed, or they expect that the pastor will look down on them when he hears of their abuse. Many women don't trust any men because of their victimization and they are especially afraid of an authority figure. Often their childhood abuser was viewed as a religious person, giving them doubt about pastors and even God Himself.

Some Christian women don't take action because they feel if they pray hard enough the situation will change. Isaac Black, pastor, professor, and author of *Assault on God's Image*, states that abuse is a serious problem within the church and most of it is not reported until it becomes violent. "In addition, too many people in abusive situations have been told that it is their Christian duty to hang in there and suffer as a Christian, that it is their role to be faithful and willing to endure some hardship as a good soldier of Jesus Christ."[1]

Some women feel abuse is the "poorer" part of their vow "for richer or poorer." Some have even been told that the more they suffer on earth the bigger their reward will be in heaven. Some feel that if they hold on long enough their children and Christian friends will rise up and call them blessed.

Wake up, women.
Wake up!

9

Is Someone Taking Advantage of You?

It was in 1920 that the women suffragettes, under the leadership of Carrie Chapman Catt, persuaded an all-male Congress to give women the right to vote. This victory, fought through nineteen successive congressional campaigns, was only a beginning in the struggle for women to achieve any type of equality in a worldly sense. Karen Nussbaum, director of the U.S. Department of Labor Women's Bureau, was recently quoted in *USA Today* as saying that the government over the years has been negligent and indifferent to the needs of women and "seems to have lived in a world of make-believe, oblivious to women's real circumstances."

Between 1980 and 1990 the number of women living below the poverty line increased more than 25 percent. Figures for women's unemployment, wage inequities, stress-related illness, discrimination complaints, and level of despair also have risen sharply.

According to Nussbaum, "real wages, benefits, good jobs and basic fairness have plummeted." Enforcement of laws protecting women have been "a mirage," she said. She suggests it is time for us "to confront the fantasies that obstruct our day-to-day realities."[1]

Can Women Make It in a Man's World?

One way we can overcome these obstructions is to be aware of problems in the workplace that we unintentionally create for ourselves. To make it in the male-dominated world of business we must keep some typi-cally feminine characteristics in check. While these traits, which in some instances could apply to men also, can be appealing and advantageous in other settings, in the office or workplace they can cause problems and invite others to take advantage of our ineptitude. Two of the most com-mon problem areas are intimidation and inappropriate clothing and grooming. Let's take a closer look at these potential obstacles.

Don't Intimidate

Because of our eagerness as women to make it in the big wide world, we sometimes overcompensate for the negative response we anticipate. We jump in quickly and establish our credentials in hopes of warding off any attack by the enemy. In some cases this may win points, but I have learned to speak softly, shake hands firmly, and look a man straight in the eye. Upon doing what Teddy Roosevelt advised, "Speak softly and carry a big stick," I can tell immediately whether a man is intimidated by me: If he turns his eyes away, drops my hand quickly, or shifts his feet around, I can assume he is uncomfortable. I try immediately to give him a compliment on how well I hear he's doing or how attractively he's dressed, something that will let him know my focus is on him and not on myself. The majority of men today are accepting of an intelligent, moderate woman, but I help them accept me by being gracious and not pushy. I've learned that a man who is intimidated may sneak up and attack at a later time.

One pastor who was obviously uncomfortable having a woman in the pulpit introduced me by saying, "Our speaker today isn't like a real speaker, and what our speaker will say won't be a real sermon. In fact our speaker is wearing a dress, but listen anyway and don't be deceived by her packaging."

Check Your Clothing and Grooming

Even though some of us women have read *Dress for Success* and sub-scribed to *Working Woman*, we still don't dress for the occasion. We want so much to be independent and not let men dictate our clothing choices that we often overcompensate. But somehow doing our own thing turns out to be self-destructive. If you are applying for a position and you don't know the expected dress, you're always safe keeping your clothing simple, basic, and conservative.

Check yourself out as others will see you. Try sitting down in any dress or skirt before you buy it. If it comes up so high that it exposes your thigh, it's too short. Sit in it for a few minutes in the dressing room and see if there are wrinkles across your skirt when you stand. Do you look like an opened accordion? Linen may be a lovely natural fiber, but by the end of a day you may look like an unmade bed.

Another test is to back up toward a full-length mirror wearing an outfit you would use for your job. Now bend over and look back between your legs. What do you see? This replicates the view others will have of you when you bend to pick something up. Now lean over frontward and look in the mirror. Does your blouse fall open? Can you see your bra, or worse yet clear down to your stomach?

When our daughter Marita was in junior high school she wore a blouse that was open too low. A boy told her, "You shouldn't wear such a revealing blouse."

"There's nothing to reveal," she replied.

"That's what it's revealing."

What are you revealing when you lean over? We're all very quick to cry out against sexual harassment in the workplace, but we must be sure our clothing and deportment don't send out the wrong signals.

Check your slips and slits. So often I see a woman wearing a black skirt with a white slip peeking out the slit. One way to remedy this is a "tulip slip," which has a wide-shaped slit so that the curved edges will not show. It also helps if the slip is a similar color to the skirt.

Don't overdose on perfume. It's great to smell good, but don't pour on so much that people know when they enter a room you vacated an hour ago that you were there. One man told me about a perfume-drenched typist, "She's got on so much Giorgio I can tell when she arrives in the parking lot."

As these reminders show, there are special issues women must be aware of if they want to compete successfully in the workplace. But there are also some advantages to being a woman in today's business world.

In a *Newsweek* article titled, "Women's Feminine Skills Are a Plus in Today's Corporate America," the writer notes that women have a natural tendency to be more concerned than men about people and feelings. This gives women an innate advantage over men in an economy that is shifting from an industrial base to a service orientation.

> Whereas not too long ago it might have been generally accepted that women were unstable, indecisive, temperamental, manipulative and not good team players, now qualities that men have traditionally denigrated as feminine weaknesses

(sympathy, sensitivity, and lack of killer instinct) may be to an advantage when trying to get the best out of others.

Antonia Shusta, a Citibank executive, believes that women are better able to cope with the "sometimes messy emotions of the workplace" and they foster a "greater sense of belonging in their employees," which in turn encourages loyalty and performance.[2]

How Have Women Fared in the Church?

Such trends inspire us to hope that women are finally entering an era when our intelligence, training, and inherent skills will finally come into full recognition in the workplace. If it happens, there will surely be a collective sigh of relief and a rousing chorus of voices shouting, "it's about time!" Because the truth is that all these past years of women's lib seemed to have moved women's position in the business world in the wrong direction. And if they've lost ground in the workplace, how have women fared in the Christian community?

In asking this question I don't infer that women should be marching through church conventions carrying placards and chanting for their rights but only to ask if we are being treated fairly. Or is the word *submission* used incorrectly to push us into an inferior position in the Christian world? That's not what God intended.

Paul wrote to the "foolish Galatians" (Gal. 3:1) who had become legalistic and explained to them that "Christ hath redeemed us from the curse of the law" (3:13). We become the children of God through faith in Jesus Christ, not by what church we go to or in what level of society we function. "There is neither bond nor free, there is neither male nor female: for ye are all one in Christ Jesus" (3:28).

In Genesis 1:27 we read, "male and female created he them." God was well pleased with His creations and did not change His mind later and say, "Master and female slave created he them." We are all to have humble spirits and submit ourselves unto God's direction (James 4:7). We are to submit ourselves "one to another in the fear of God" (Eph. 5:21).

When Paul described spiritual gifts he didn't say they are only for men and that women have no special talents. He praised Priscilla and commended the men to help Phoebe in whatever business she needed assistance (Rom. 16:2). Paul spent many days in the home of Philip the evangelist and observed his four daughters as they prophesied. Women do have spiritual gifts, and their function in the church should not be mindless. The male leaders should allow talented women to do more than wash communion cups and handle childcare.

I am personally grateful for the pastors who have allowed me, as a woman with the gift of teaching, to speak in their churches. The Lord has used me to impart His wisdom to men without my usurping any authority from their leadership. I praise these men for accepting me as a Christian and not just putting up with me as a female. The exceptions have been amusing.

In one church Fred and I co-taught a class on marriage that eventually drew a larger attendance than the church service. But our popularity somehow became a threat to the pastor, who pulled out a rule—hitherto ignored—that said women could not teach men. The class was promptly abolished.

At one Christian college I was brought in for a women's alumni day. The chairwoman asked if I'd be willing to speak at the students' chapel on Friday for no extra charge. I agreed. When she enthusiastically approached the dean about her idea he immediately responded, "We couldn't use her; she's a woman. No woman has ever spoken in chapel."

"What's wrong with a woman speaking in chapel?" the chairwoman asked.

The dean didn't have a logical reason. He said simply, "Women aren't allowed to pray or teach the Bible in public."

"Then why," the woman queried, "do we allow our female students to do this in chapel?"

"They're just practicing," he added after a pause. "They're not yet of age."

"Do you mean we are training our female students to do something at college that they will not be allowed to do once they graduate?"

The dean did not like the way this inquisition was going, but he couldn't back down and lose face so he curtly nodded yes. The lady, undaunted even in the face of defeat, then suggested, "If that's the case, I think we should write a letter to our girl students (80 percent of the student population) and suggest they transfer to a school where they can learn skills they can use once they graduate."

This whole conversation had become ridiculous, but the dean wouldn't change his mind.

The chairwoman gave up, discouraged over the dean's legalism. As she walked away she told him to call her if he changed his mind.

Two days later the dean called to say he had thought the matter over and hated to waste a "free speaker." However, he could not betray the tradition of the school and have a woman speak in chapel. So, to solve the dilemma, he proposed abolishing chapel for that week and instead having a "special assembly." Evidently his Bible differentiates chapel from special assembly and allows women to speak at the latter. He put a notice in the college paper canceling chapel and announcing the special assembly would be held in the same auditorium as chapel was usually held and at the same time with the same people. Proud of his obvious deception, he told the chairwoman later that he could still state, with head held high, that no woman had ever spoken at chapel.

Is this not hilarious? If God were concerned about my sharing His word at this school would He be happier if the name of the event were changed?

Does God Speak Only to Men?

Linda came to CLASS to polish up her speaking skills. She was already a motivational speaker about Christian education-development, and she taught Sunday school in her church. Let's let Linda tell what happened when the pastor called her into his office one day.

> He flooded me with compliments about my outstanding abilities as a group leader, speaker, and Sunday school teacher. This was based upon his own observation since I lead children's, youth, and women's groups in the church. He then asked me to pass these insights on to others. He asked if I would be willing to write a training seminar, to be taught in several sessions, to teach others how to teach more effectively. Naturally I was pleased and gratified. I said I would be happy to begin preparation. I simply needed to know what sort of timetable I was facing among the other obligations of my life. When would I need to be ready to begin teaching these seminars? The pastor looked up from the papers on his desk, surprised I had asked this. He quickly told me in a matter-of-fact tone that invited no questions, "Oh, you won't teach it! You may write it, but we must have a man present it publicly!" Once I recovered from the shock, I let him know, in no uncertain terms, that I could not conceive a rationale that allows my thoughts and words to be spoken as valuable and useful, but I—a woman—could not be the one to speak them. I left his office and did not write or teach his training seminar!

What a shame that because of her gender Linda was considered capable of writing but not of teaching. Similar things happen in churches across the country. One woman told me she was allowed to teach Sunday school up through the fifth grade but not from the sixth on. Another woman's church duties were taken away from her after an unwanted divorce, but her ex-husband and his new wife were allowed to teach the couples' class! Even more shocking is the case of the wife who went to the board of deacons about her church-elder husband's affair and was told they'd have to take his side "because he's the one with the money."

How can anyone believe God only speaks to men and that women have no ears to hear the voice of the Lord?

God Doesn't Need a Translator

Does it make sense that if a woman's husband dies, she must listen to her pastor and accept his leadership even if it doesn't ring true in her spirit? No, it doesn't. But it happens anyway.

It happened to Denise, such an attractive and intelligent young lady that it seems impossible to imagine what she has been through. Denise was married at eighteen to a handsome young man, and they had four children. When the youngest was one month old, her husband was tragically killed in a head-on collision that was the fault of the other driver. Denise's world was shattered. In shock, she tried to pull a funeral together but was devastated again when word came that her husband's two sisters were killed in a plane crash on the way to the funeral.

For months Denise walked around in a fog handling the daily duties of four children but not fully comprehending the measure of her grief. At this point her pastor told her it was time to "pick up the pieces and move on." He said since her husband was gone and God speaks to women through men, he was to be her spiritual leader. "God's Word tells us that women should marry so they will not have problems with lust and so people will not say bad things about them," he told her. Denise was having no lust problems, but the pastor convinced her that she needed a new husband to help raise her children. He had the right man all picked out, he said. The groom was a godly man in the church who was going to become a pastor himself. It was not mentioned that this godly man was well aware of the large insurance settlement Denise was to receive.

Still in shock and in no way ready for a new husband Denise reluctantly agreed to take the pastor's word from God and marry this man she hardly knew. She had no inner peace about the situation, but she didn't want to disobey the Lord.

On the honeymoon this new husband quoted Scripture on submission and headship—as he perceived the message. Denise was to obey his every wish, he said, and he was to handle all the finances. She could no longer wear makeup and her dress had to be modest, meaning high-necked and long-sleeved. He became a dictator to both her and the four children, who were soon in fear of him. On Christmas her five-year-old opened a present without permission, and the husband "followed Scripture" by beating the child seventy times. Denise was again in a state of shock. When she told the pastor, he said a sense of discipline was necessary in the home and this was God's way of teaching her. During this time the husband was going to seminary, becoming more spiritual, and spending her insurance money. When she became pregnant he began to abuse her physically and to spend time in "Bible study" with female seminarians.

Finally Denise woke up and realized none of what was happening could be called spiritual and surely God was not in favor of abuse or infidelity. By the time Denise took control of her own life and listened to the Lord, firsthand, the insurance money was gone and so was the husband. He went off to be a pastor, and Denise was left with no money and five children.

"Why didn't I wake up sooner?" Denise asked me. "Please tell women to use their common sense and realize that God doesn't need a human translator. He can speak to each one of us in our own language."

Denise is now married to a youth pastor and still looks remarkably youthful herself. Her new husband brought one child into the marriage and they had one together, bringing Denise's total to seven. She is dedicated to being the best mother possible to her large family and to the church teenagers who flood her home each weekend, sometimes seeming desperate for loving attention. In her spare time Denise speaks to women's groups, hoping to help them wake up and not be pushed into questionable situations, no matter how many verses are quoted as proof.

God will speak firsthand to women who are AWAKE!

Ministering Too Well for Too Long

As Christian women, we want to care for others, always be kind, and have the attitude of a servant. Our aim is to become like Christ, so we give freely, feeding the sick and offering water to the thirsty. But is it possible to minister too well for too long? Because of our good nature, are people taking advantage of us? As exemplary wives, are we being submissive into stupidity? As loving mothers, are we letting our children expect too much from us? As adult children, are we allowing our parents to usurp our authority and drain our energy?

So many women I talk with have at least one of these problems; some are mired down with people dragging on them from every angle. When does a giving spirit turn into martyrdom? Have we somehow crossed the line of rational reason and don't know how to get back? By looking at the following true stories of other people's lives, I hope you will be able to assess where you stand.

Boomerang Children

Jane took pride in the fact that she had always been a good mother. She had raised three children to be productive adults, all married and out of the house. Finally Jane and Will had some time to themselves. It was fun to travel a little in their motor home and come back to a house that was as neat as it had been when they left. Jane redecorated the living and dining areas and even dared put in off-white carpeting, which brightened up the whole house and made it seem more expansive. Jane's friends who still had children at home were envious of her freedom and opportunities. "I can hardly wait!" they often said.

But Jane's carefree days didn't last long. They ended the day her oldest daughter, Roxie, called to say she was divorcing her husband and was going to marry Greg as soon as her divorce was final.

"How could she do this to the family?" Jane questioned. "And who is Greg anyway?"

Roxie never asked her mother's opinion, however, and before Jane knew it the old husband was gone and a new one was in. Jane resented the switch but kept her feelings to herself. Greg was the tall, lanky, cool type. Roxie thought he looked like Clint Eastwood although Jane couldn't see any resemblance at all. From her perspective he was dull and a little on the lazy side. Roxie had always been the domineering type and she seemed to enjoy pushing Greg around.

Will thought his first daughter could do no harm, and he rationalized the divorce quickly. Roxie and Greg sold the house she had lived in with her former husband, hoping to get enough money to put a down payment on a new one. However, when the figures were totaled they found they had just enough money to pay off the accumulated debts they'd each brought into the marriage. There was nothing left, not even enough for a deposit on a decent apartment. Unhappy that their financial situation didn't work out right, Roxie and Greg held each other accountable.

Clint Eastwood didn't look so seductive when he couldn't make her day—or even some pay.

As stark reality overcame romance in this new marriage, the couple found themselves with no place to stay. Roxie called Jane and Will who were on a trip to Alaska, and asked if she and Greg could stay at their house while they were away. Will immediately approved the plan although Jane was skeptical of this invasion. Will made her feel selfish and materialistic about her hesitancy, so she gave in. After all, wasn't she the sweet, submissive wife? And wasn't this her daughter in need?

Jane assumed Roxie and Greg would live in Roxie's former bedroom, but when she came home three weeks later, she found the couple firmly entrenched in the master bedroom. Jane was shocked that this new man was in her bed, but Will calmed her down and suggested that she and he live in the motor home in the driveway and let the young people have the room. Once again Jane was made to feel selfish when she balked, so she gave in.

When she told me this story later, she got red in the face. "Roxie and Clint Eastwood were in my house, in my room, in my bed, and I was sleeping in the driveway!"

Will, who had just retired, suggested they take a lot of trips and "leave the kids the house while we're gone." In the next year while the kids took over Jane's house, Will and Jane crossed the country and back, looking for places to go and canyons to see. In that one year they were home only twenty-one days. But even in that short time it was quite apparent that Greg rarely worked. By the time Jane attempted to reclaim her territory, Roxie was pregnant—and angry.

"We can't throw her out now," Will explained. "We don't want to be the bad guys." And they weren't. Roxie and Greg were the bad guys. Roxie, with her hot Choleric temper, was in control of the house and no one dared cross her for fear of bearing the brunt of her anger.

Greg reacted in typical Phlegmatic fashion. He withdrew, took to Will's recliner, built a wall around himself, and watched TV.

Roxie reprimanded Jane if she laid her jacket on a chair or left a glass on the kitchen counter. Roxie liked all surfaces to be neat, but she had no interest in cleaning below the surface. That was up to Jane to do.

Will and Jane consoled themselves, believing that after the baby was born Roxie and Greg would move out. Surely they'd want their own place then. While they waited Will and Jane took more trips and were shocked when they found the baby was to be born in their bed rather than in a hospital. Jane would never have thought of Roxie's having a baby at home—especially in *her* bed.

While Will and Jane were staring blankly at the red rocks of Sedona, they received news of little Jason's birth. They tried to get excited as they drove home to see the new addition to the family, but they couldn't help thinking about the consequences of Roxie's decision to quit her job to be a "real mother." Greg was still working only sporadically in part-time jobs.

Will explained to Jane, "We can hardly throw our little girl out on the street at a time like this." Or at any other time it seemed. So Will and Jane went on another trip to Calgary to see the annual Stampede. Jane told me, "I hoped to get killed by the rampaging bulls."

When they returned home, they were greeted with the news that their daughter was pregnant again. She was also sick, so Jane became the nurse, baby-sitter, and cleaning lady. Relationships deteriorated during that time, and Will played a lot of golf. Roxie didn't like Jane and Will to turn up their TV too loud or to have company in the house; it interfered with her rest or infringed on her privacy.

By the time the second baby was born, Jane was ready to scream. While Roxie was giving birth in the hospital—not in Jane's bed this time—Jane moved Roxie's things into the guest room where she and Will had been sleeping.

She bought a new mattress and sheets and put a lock on her bedroom door. Then Jane took a real look at her house. There were spots on the off-white carpeting, crayon marks on the newly papered walls, and pink magic-marker scribbles on her toilet seat. There were teeth marks on her lipsticks, rips in her towels, and crumbs between the cushions of the couch.

When Jane told Greg she didn't like the way they let little Jason run wild, he replied, "Well, Roxie really doesn't like living here."

That did it. Jane was ready to explode. She wanted to shout, "Doesn't like living here? How does she think I like it?" But once more she bit her tongue and said nothing.

That weekend Will and Jane took off for the desert, and when they had settled into a trailer park for the evening Jane tried to explain that she could not live this way any longer. When Will once again retorted, "We can't throw them out with a new baby!" Jane yelled, "You just don't get it, do you?"

Will was shocked at her response, but not as shocked as he was fifteen minutes later when Jane emerged from the back of the motor home and brushed by him carrying a suitcase. She stopped at the door and gave a little farewell speech. "I am leaving you. If you ever decide I'm of more value to you than our children are, you may come after me."

By the time Will pulled himself together and got in the car to follow her, Jane was walking out the gate of the trailer park, trudging along with her suitcase in her hand.

"I love you more than I love them," Will called out to her. "I guess I didn't know it bothered you that much."

He just didn't get it. But he wanted to. They went back and talked for three hours, reviewing every step of what had happened and how it had gotten so out of hand that Jane felt like an intruder in her own house.

Once they agreed on what to do, they returned and met with Roxie and Greg. They simply stated they felt it was time for the couple to get their own place and they would expect them out in two weeks. Much to Jane's amazement, the couple accepted the news positively, and within two weeks Greg had found a better job, Roxie was rehired at the old job she had left, Greg's mother took on the full-time baby-sitting, and they were thrilled to be in a place of their own.

Jane could hardly wait to clean out the house and start life all over again. When I asked her what she would do if she were ever in that position again, she laughed and said, "They'd have to lock me up."

So I rephrased my question: "What advice could you give to someone whose adult children might return?" She thought about it awhile, then came up with the following guidelines:

1. Be in agreement. Before you take anyone into your home agree with your mate that you will stand together on decisions. Jane realizes that their daughter manipulated her father and caused a division between her and Will. If agreement doesn't come instantly, there at least must be unity and a willingness to talk over the issues privately. If one partner is strongly opposed to the return of this adult child, with or without a family, it will never work, and it could cause marital chaos. It would be better to put them up in a motel for a short time than allow them to move in.

2. Establish control. If it is agreed that they may come into your home, it must be made clear to them whose home it is, and if they show the first sign of bucking for control both parents must take quick action. Once they found the couple in their bedroom Will should have backed Jane up and immediately moved Roxie and Greg to another room. He should not have allowed the daughter to dictate the volume on the TV or decide when they could have company. If you are dealing with this type of situation alone, without a mate, you must still take a stand and be firm in your decisions. Perhaps you could bring in a sibling to support you. And even though the disciplining of your grandchildren is basically their parents' problem, when they live with you, you must establish what's acceptable behavior. Remember, if it's your china they're breaking, you have a right to speak up.

3. Set a time limit right from the start. Don't let anyone move in for an indefinite time. Roxie and Greg lived in Jane's house for four years. Each time Jane was ready to make them leave, there would either be a financial crisis or a new baby on the way, making her look like a heartless grandmother. If Roxie and Greg had known this invasion had to terminate in one month, they might have hustled a little harder to get their finances in order and find a Plan B!

4. Assign jobs. Make it clear from the beginning that you are not slave labor. Sit down with the boarder and establish who does what.

Don't start doing their laundry and making their bed. Put the responsibility on the right set of shoulders. You have already raised your family once; you don't need to do it again a second time. Jane got no credit for all she did; in fact, she was criticized for how and when she did it!

5. Keep your regular mealtimes. If the guests want to eat at separate times or don't like what you cook, make it clear they can buy their own food, cook it and clean up from it. I know one mother who bought a secondhand refrigerator and put it in the garage. Her son was responsible to stock it and eat from it. He was not to deplete her supplies. If he wished to eat with the family, he was to tell her ahead of time and be there on time.

6. Let them know this is not a hotel. Not only should meal times be established and clean-up assigned, but guests must not expect hotel services. You should not be in charge of their business calls, their dry cleaning, or their change of linens. The minute any requests like this are made, tell them firmly, "We have no staff for that. This is not a hotel."

7. Make them contribute financially. Granting family members a week or two of hospitality can be considered a kind maternal gift, but if there are signs that this visit will be longer, establish a time frame and ask them to share the expenses. They can either pay rent or cover some of the utilities, but this contribution, even if it is small, helps them to keep in touch with the expenses of running a home. Do not let them take you for granted or they'll never leave!

8. Don't let them criticize. Right from the start let these needy people know that if they don't like your home, your lifestyle, or your friends, they can leave. Sometimes when adult children move home, they feel like a failure and they may take out their anger on you. But you are not their problem. If they had handled their own lives better they probably wouldn't be back. Don't let them make you the butt of their misplaced anger.

9. Don't use the children as a dumping ground. Often when grandchildren move in with Grandma and Grandpa the grandparents drop on them the feelings they don't dare say to the parents. "When is your mother going to grow up, stop smoking, dress better, fix her hair, and get a decent job?" These comments may seem harmless to adults but they place adult responsibility on children. Then the little ones feel they have to do something about the complaints, yet they have no clout with which to do it. They think they are failing you if they can't get Mother to change. Similarly, if there's been a divorce, don't review how rotten the in-law parent is. Don't tell the children if their father were a decent provider they wouldn't all be crowded into your house. The children are confused enough. Don't dump your anger on them.

10. Don't assume guilt. Jane felt she had really matured when she was able to face her daughter and not feel guilty. Roxie complained when Jane didn't always want to baby-sit so she and Greg could go out more. Jane stated calmly but clearly, "I did not have these babies; you did. I love them, but I am not responsible for their care. When I do baby-sit it is a gift of love to you." Jane was so proud of herself when she told me, "I'm not going to carry her guilt any longer."

11. Relax and try to enjoy this time. This is the graduate school of motherhood. Once you make the rules, see that they are followed; then have fun with the family so they remember their time at Grandma's as a positive experience.

Roxie told one of Jane's friends, "Mother's gotten a lot nicer since we moved out."

Mothering Too Well

Charlene asked to see me after I spoke at a women's retreat. She was very upset about her son, who never seemed to hold a job very long. She wanted to know what she could do to help him become more stable.

As Charlene shared her story with me, she explained that her husband had left when her son was quite young. She had worked hard as a professional to support herself and her son, and she had managed quite well. She had even saved up a healthy retirement fund. She paid for her son's college education, but in spite of his training he never seemed able to hold a job for very long. He was always trying new business ventures that used up any money he acquired. When he was deeply in debt because of overspending on credit cards, Charlene bailed him out.

Then he got the "financial chance of a lifetime" to invest in a business with a friend, but Charlene's son had no money. When she refused to loan it to him, he badgered her, made her feel guilty, and actually threatened her physically. So, being the good mother that she was, she finally gave in and borrowed against her retirement fund so he could invest in this business venture. The business failed and the bill collectors started coming to Charlene's door. She paid off what she could until her retirement fund was completely gone.

When her son's car was repossessed, he convinced Charlene to let him drive her car. One morning he took her to her office, promising to pick her up that evening. Charlene waited and waited, but her son never came. She actually spent the night at the office without anything to eat. The next morning, she was ashamed to admit to her co-workers that she had slept on the floor all night, but it was even more humiliating to admit to them that her son had actually stripped her of her car, her money, and her retirement fund.

I helped Charlene see that her son's having to grow up without a father and the early struggles they'd had financially did not justify her son's taking advantage of her now. I encouraged her to insist that he take responsibility for himself and not give in to the guilt he tried to impose on her. Charlene followed my instructions and stopped protecting her son from the difficulties of the real world. Then she could start taking care of herself again.

It took some hard lessons, but Charlene woke up.

Fairness and Honesty

The Johnsons told me how they handled their son when he came back from college and had his first job. He wanted to be independent and yet live at home for a while. First, his mother went with him to look at a few inexpensive apartments. They were all in poor neighborhoods and he didn't like any of them. She took the amount of money of the lowest rent, cut it in half, and charged him that much for one room and bath with kitchen privileges. He didn't have to join his parents for dinner, but if he did want to eat with them he was to call and let her know. She also told him that when he got his first raise his rent would go up proportionately.

Sometimes as he paid his rent he would grumble about having to give money to his mother, but she referred back to their arrangement and suggested he could look at one of those apartments again. By the end of two years the young man was doing well enough to rent a decent apartment. He left with positive feelings that his parents had been fair and honest with him. What he didn't know was that they had deposited all of his rent money in an account for him and when he left they gave him the sum with interest.

He was dumbfounded and apologized for the times he had complained. These parents handled the situation well, made the standards clear from the beginning, and helped him see that it costs money to live. They could have let him have everything for free and hoped for eternal gratitude in return; instead they charged him fairly, taught him some lessons, and saved him money he would probably not have amassed himself. The Johnsons did it right!

Instead of a farewell with hard feelings, the son left excited about the challenges ahead. He is often heard starting a conversation with "Wait 'til I tell you what my parents did for me!"

Parenting Our Parents

Many of us who, at an early age, were put in the position of mothering our mothers grew up needing to be in control. With this tendency we very easily become the stability for codependents searching for a solid rock.

I look back on my adult life and see how I have repeatedly been the positive person picking up the people with pitiful pasts. Before I understood victimization, I didn't know why so many sad souls attached themselves to me. Now I realize that someone who was abused as a child seeks out adults who offer a measure of protection, who will take care of them. They are still looking for a mother and I seem to fit the image. There is nothing wrong with uplifting others, but we need to see what it is we are doing and why we are doing it. I realize now that I gathered pain-filled people as if I were stringing them into a strand of beads.

Now I am able to listen to the presenting problem, pull out the probable truth, suggest books, tapes, or counseling, and not have the string of beads strangle me.

Programmed to Feel Responsible

I'm not alone in my sometimes overwhelming feelings of responsibility. Thousands of women (and some men) were programmed this way during their childhoods.

Gloria Steinem, the world's most famous feminist, is now coming to terms with her childhood and realizing why she has fought so hard for causes and what she has missed out on in her life. An article in *Time* magazine reported she is searching for her real self through twelve-step programs, imagery, hypnosis, meditation, and relearning. How we might wish that in her search she would find the Lord and His power for change. At least she has uncovered the source of her pain and her reason for compulsive control.

> She traces her loss of self to the day her three-hundred-pound father, an itinerant salesman, abandoned her when she was 10 in a rat-infested, dilapidated farmhouse fronting on a major highway in Toledo. Left to care for a loving but mentally ill mother who heard voices, she was forced to grow up

too soon, to be mother to her mother. She escaped to Smith College but never escaped the trap of being the caretaker. Once she became involved in the movement, there was no campus, community group or benefit so small that she wouldn't hop on a plane and raise money for it. At times it seemed as if she had taken personal responsibility for every oppressed woman in America.[3]

If your background, like Gloria Steinem's, programmed you to bear responsibility for every oppressed woman in America (or every unhappy person in your family), wake up! While we are saving the world we are often sacrificing close personal relationships. As a result it could be lonely for us in the old ladies home when the world forgets to visit.

Those of us who lost much of our childhood in mothering Mother need to take an especially sharp look at our caretaking nature and make sure we're not gathering up too many beads that will sooner or later make us choke. And even if we did not have to mother our mothers when we were children, we may well find ourselves in that role as our mothers' increasing age and health problems reduce their independence.

The time comes when instead of them caring for us, we may have to care for our parents. While this section is not a treatise on caring for elderly parents, it includes some emotional precautions we should wake up to.

One of the things I learned through experience is to make sure there is no guilt on your part that will hang on and drain you emotionally long after the parent is gone. I remember one uncalled-for comment when I snapped at my mother. I knew I should have been more patient and I knew she had done nothing wrong, but I didn't say I was sorry. She died shortly thereafter and even though I've confessed it to the Lord, I still think of that day each time I drive by the convalescent home where she died. Why didn't I say I was sorry? How important it is for each one of us to clear up any unfinished apologies before it's too late.

Sometimes we have no choice about what we have to do when our parents are no longer able to live independently. At other times, when there are several siblings, for instance, there are also various possibilities. One decision is whether you will move the dependent parent into your home.

The right reason for bringing a parent into your home or under your care is to provide the most positive environment you can for his or her waning years.

The wrong reasons for supporting a parent are: thinking you'll get points from the family for how noble you are, still trying to win the affirmation from this parent that you've never received, or thinking you'll get more in the will than those siblings who have done nothing. Unfortunately, these hopes, subconscious though they may be, don't often come true. Instead, exhausted and frustrated, you end up with no credit, no affirmation, and no money.

When You're Mature Enough to Say No

Claire came to me in a state of disbelief. "My mother is suing me!" she exclaimed. "I'm in a state of shock!" I could hardly imagine it myself.

Claire grew up with an alcoholic mother who produced thirteen children, only four of whom were still alive. The son had divorced himself from the remaining family, and the three daughters had stayed somewhat close to the mother. Of these three, Claire and Faye had led relatively stable lives while Sara has been labeled schizophrenic. The burden of caring for their mother had fallen on Claire, who was still subconsciously hoping to get her mother's approval.

"I've done everything I could for her," she explained to me. "I've bought her groceries, prescriptions, and clothes. And she never even says thank you. One day I asked her if she could reimburse me for some of the month's food and she said, 'I only have six dollars, but if you want to take the last cent a poor old lady has, go ahead.'"

Claire started to cry at the sick control her mother had over her. "I've given my all. I've done my best, and that's all I get from her."

But there was worse to come.

Mother never seemed to have any money, even though she had Social Security and a hundred dollars a month from renting out the little family house she still owned. Claire had made arrangements for her mother to live in senior-citizen housing, but to qualify for the low-income program she could not own property. It was suggested that the mother quickly quit-deed the house to the four living children, and Claire took care of all the details and did the legwork. Once the transaction was in process, Sara sensed she might have inherited the house herself if Claire hadn't split it four ways. She decided she wanted it.

Without any understanding of how long it had taken Claire to get their mother into the housing program and what legal circumstances were involved, Sara marched in without warning, removed Mother from the senior-citizens complex, and brought her to her house. When Claire went to visit her at the complex she was gone and there was a bill for five hundred dollars that Claire had to pay. Sara got Mother to stop the process of the quit-deed, take the house back, will it to Sara, and then sue Claire for fraud and mental stress.

The day Claire received the summons she was flabbergasted. Why would Mother sue her after all she'd done for her? When Claire poured this out to me, she explained that the house was worth at most $30,000 and it was "such a pit" full of bad memories that she didn't want any part of it. She had done all she could to help her mother and for her efforts she was accused of stealing one-fourth of an old house.

As time went on Claire spent six thousand dollars on legal fees to defend herself against her mother's charges and ultimately the judge threw out the case. Mother got the house but ended up with lawyers' bills, a lien on the house, and a fine from the housing program for lying about the ownership.

A few weeks later Sara called Claire and said, "Thanks to you, Mother is having a terrible Mother's Day."

"That's when I realized I had to wake up. My mother had never appreciated anything I had done. I ended up being the bad guy and the one sister who caused the problems is getting the house."

Later, when Sara was sick of living with her mother, she had her call Claire and ask to move in with her. "I hope there's no hard feelings" Mother said.

Claire felt she had finally grown up when she was able to say, "No, Sara took you out of the place I had you in and she is now responsible for your welfare. You and she can work it out. I refuse to take the blame anymore."

Most of us will not be sued by our mothers, but we should guard ourselves from being put in any position where our emotional expectations will be dashed. Anytime we expect credit for family favors, we open ourselves up for disappointments. Anytime we expect our mothers or fathers to change their habit patterns and begin to praise us because they're getting old, we become the hurt little child again. We must do what we know is right, expecting nothing and being grateful for any thanks we may receive.

Personalities of the Elderly

If you are currently dealing with a parent situation, reread chapter 3, Filling Our Emotional Vacuum, and apply to your parents what you learn there. Perhaps you are giving them what *you* need in hopes they will catch on instead of filling *their* emotional needs. Remember that our personality types continue to influence us throughout our lives. The elderly Sanguines still want to be the star, get lots of attention, and have people listen and laugh at their stories. Cholerics hate getting old because it means life is slipping out of their control. If possible, put your elderly Choleric parent in charge of something and praise him or her for any minor accomplishment. Melancholy parents may be increasingly depressed and withdrawn. Don't try to jolly them up; just agree with them in their miseries: "Yes, this is a bad day" or "I don't know how you stand the pain!" The older Phlegmatic is usually the easiest to handle if he or she has a TV and is fed. Try to include your Phlegmatic parents in family activities and let them know you value them as persons.

The Manipulator

Chelsea was an only child who was reared by a very domineering, Choleric mother and a Phlegmatic father. Often when we think of only children, we assume they will be very self-centered and used to getting their own way, but this was not true in Chelsea's case. In her family everything centered on Chelsea's mother.

When Chelsea married and moved to another state, friends predicted she would be homesick; they doubted she would survive without her mother. Much to their surprise, Chelsea survived very well. She began to think for herself and learned to acknowledge her own personal feelings. She reared her children to be quite independent, yet they have a good relationship with her.

All was going well until Chelsea's parents retired and moved to Chelsea's town. At first it was nice that Chelsea's mom wanted to cook each evening for Chelsea, her husband, Joe, and their children. After all, they had very busy schedules and reasoned it would "help Mom feel useful while she adjusted to her new surroundings." Then the phone calls started every morning, just like a wake-up call, and they continued frequently through the day. Chelsea began to long for the freedom she had enjoyed before her parents moved to town. But how do you break a pattern when the other person doesn't want to break it?

At first when Chelsea would suggest they shouldn't eat together quite so much, her mother would become sad and teary-eyed and say, "I guess we should have stayed in New York. At least people had time for us there." If Chelsea let the answering machine take the early-morning calls, mother would leave messages that hinted of tears or imply that there was an emergency. Then Chelsea would feel guilty and worry, *Perhaps one of them is sick. What if they really need me?*

As Chelsea spent many hours in prayer over this situation, God began to show her how enmeshed she had become with her mother as a child and how controlling her mother really was. She remembered the times her mother had manipulated her until she was willing to think and behave the way her mother wanted her to.

One day as she was praying, she saw that her mother held her in emotional bondage. In her mind Chelsea saw her mother's manipulation wrapped around her just like chains. Then she saw her mother standing between her and Jesus, and Chelsea realized her mother had actually become a barrier to her spiritual growth. She said, "Lord, how do I get rid of this emotional bondage?"

In Chelsea's mind the Lord said, "Just flex your muscles. You are strong, and you can do it."

Chelsea pictured herself taking a deep breath and flexing her muscles. As she did, the chains fell at her feet. However, in her mental picture, her mother was still standing between Chelsea and Jesus. Chelsea said, "Jesus, how do I get past my mother to You?"

Jesus let her see that all she had to do was reach for Him. In her mental picture, as she reached for Jesus, her hand went right through her mother to Jesus as though her mother were a vapor. Chelsea told me, "Florence, it was then I realized my mother had taught me her happiness was more important than anything else and that I was a bad girl if I didn't keep her happy. When Jesus gave me that picture, I realized I had been manipulated by my mother most of my life, and it was up to me to stop the manipulation. I just had to flex my muscles."

"Flexing her muscles" has been a difficult process, but Chelsea has begun to set some guidelines on how often she has meals with her parents. Mother was not pleased at first, and sometimes she still threatens to move back to New York, but Chelsea is not swayed by those threats now. She keeps focused on making decisions that will be best for her and her family. The phone calls still come early each morning, but Chelsea doesn't feel obligated to answer them. She lets the answering machine take them if the timing isn't good, and she calls her mother back later.

As she has begun to heal, Chelsea has come to realize her mother never looked at her as a separate entity. She didn't affirm her as a person. This became obvious recently when Chelsea made a statement to her mother that was completely provable: "It's raining outside." Her mother's response was, "That's *probably* true." Chelsea realized her mother would not do that to other people. For example, if Chelsea's husband had said, "It's raining outside," Chelsea's mother would have responded, "Then we'll need umbrellas."

As Chelsea pondered and prayed over this new revelation, God gave her courage to challenge her mother's thinking. The next time her mother answered with "That's probably true," Chelsea very kindly said, "Take the *probably* out of that statement and you've got it right!" Her mother took a quick little breath and said, "That's true."

It's unlikely that Chelsea's mother will change much at this stage in her life, but as Chelsea has allowed God to alter her own perspective, she has become healthier and is beginning to find the real Chelsea.

Are We Entertaining Angels Unaware?

It's not always family members who take advantage of us. Sometimes it's sweet little Christian couples who are in need of a place to lay their heads. We remember those verses about hospitality and about giving a cup of cool water to someone in Jesus' name and we get close to euphoric about our spirit of generosity.

Years ago Fred and I knew a delightful young couple who looked like Barbie and Ken dolls—in fact, we'll call them Barbie and Ken. They had just left their positions on staff with a Christian organization and needed a place to stay while they decided what to do next. We had an extra room in our new home, and we let them move in.

Ken loved to decorate houses, and we agreed he would paint and paper in return for room and board. I assumed Barbie would pitch in and help, but I did not make any assignments clear from the start. I also didn't know that the Ken doll had diabetic problems and needed special meals cooked at exact times. Since I was in charge of producing the food (for eight people at that time), I had to learn about his restrictions and change my way of cooking. I just knew this was what the Lord would want of me.

Barbie couldn't get up when we all had breakfast. "I'm just not a morning person," she said, "plus it takes me so long to wash and dry my hair I can't get ready that early." She did look better than the rest of us when she finally emerged from the bathroom. Barbie had lovely nails that she filed and polished each afternoon while I prepared dinner. She couldn't do "real work" for fear of breaking one, and to this day when I hear someone file a nail, I cringe and remember Barbie sitting so sweetly on my sofa, perfecting her nails while I cooked.

Ken wasn't a lot better. His idea of helping with the decorating was going to paint stores and leafing through wallpaper books. He seemed endlessly fascinated by mixing prints and coordinating borders, and often after his afternoon nap he'd show me his ideas of the moment. Then there were those days when he was too tired to go out at all and he would sit quietly in the living room staring at the wall, getting a feeling for how it would look if it ever got wallpaper on it.

As weeks rolled into months, we all tired of the perfect, precious pair. Since we had made no rules, required no calculable work, and charged no rent, we had nothing to complain about. They were doing what they thought we expected of them: nothing. They were pleasant and inoffensive and happy to live with us. This could have gone on forever since Ken seemed in no rush to get a job.

In the fourth month of their stay, during which time he painted one wall, we had some company from out of state who wanted to go to Disneyland. I informed Barbie that I was taking these friends to Disneyland and that we would be back by six o'clock. I gave her money and told her to buy whatever she liked to cook and have something ready for us to eat when we returned.

"But I don't really like to cook anything," she said, amazed that I would ask. I pointed to the recipe books and happily stated, "Well, you'll have all day to come up with something."

I wondered all day what she would come up with and when we got back she had produced packaged macaroni and cheese and had Ken standing by the barbecue ready to throw on some burgers. It was an adequate meal and we all praised her efforts and mourned over the broken nail caused by "real work."

The next day Fred pulled Ken aside and explained that "Scripture says a man should support his wife; however, I'm supporting two and you're supporting none. There's something not quite right here."

Within a week Ken got a job that was beneath his education but that paid money. When they left quietly one morning, they said good-bye but added no words of thanks for the months of hospitality or the customized cooking. One day months later I was surprised to receive a letter from Barbie saying that the Lord had put it upon her heart to let me know she had forgiven me. She didn't indicate for what and I will go to my grave not knowing. We've heard nothing from them since that day and I don't know whether Barbie learned to cook or if Ken learned to work.

In the years since then we've had many other young people live with us, but we made the terms clear from the beginning. Then we had some standards to hold them to. Many of our friends have had funny experiences with sweet little saints of the faith. One young man had stayed at Elaine's for a week, and a year later he returned late one evening and asked to spend the night. Elaine was surprised that he hadn't called, but she agreed to let him in. He then called toward the car and said, "You can all come in now." Out rolled a little family; as Elaine stood aghast, a wife and three children filed in.

It was apparent in the morning that they were not leaving for a few days, and Elaine didn't know what to do about it. On the third day Elaine came home from marketing and met them walking out the front door carrying a chocolate cake Elaine had made that morning. When she asked where they were going with the cake, the man replied, "My sister invited us for dinner and it wouldn't be polite to go empty-handed."

The next morning Elaine and her husband suggested that the whole family go spend a few days with the sister who at least had some chocolate cake to feed them.

Many of us feel as good Christians we must take in every person who comes along or we're not going to be blessed by the Lord. I have taken in far more than my share, but I've learned that along with pilgrims knocking at our doors God gave us brains so we can make sensible choices about the best interests of our families. We can be hospitable without being stupid. We can't let people take advantage of our good nature in hopes that someday we'll entertain those angels unaware.

Is Your Doctor Taking Advantage of Your Ignorance?

I grew up in a time when women never questioned authority figures. A man of the cloth was considered only one step away from God incarnate. If he uttered a platitude it was as though the burning bush itself had spoken. If a lawyer placed a document before you, you signed. (I sometimes wonder if any of those past ponderous parchments I've autographed without reading will come back to haunt me.) If the doctor told you to take one pill each morning, you took two in hopes you would get better twice as fast. In each situation we were taught to respect the opinion of the professionals and do what we were told. After all, what do we know? We're only women.

When I was a child our family physician was Dr. Sweetsir, and he was spoken of with hushed reverence. I can remember my little grandmother standing in a pious position looking up toward the heavenlies and opening an important sentence with "Doctor says . . ." He was never "the doctor" or "Dr. Sweetsir"; he was DOCTOR. There was an aura of spirituality about the tone of that word, DOCTOR, and not one of us would have disputed the wisdom that followed. DOCTOR came when a baby was born or an elder was dying, and whatever he said was what we did.

Doesn't that sound like another world? Today with our healthcare in such a confused state, we can hardly find any doctor, let alone one we can trust and respect. When we do, we are impressed with how much more he or she knows than Dr. Sweetsir did, but all that knowledge is confined to one part of us. We have to go to someone else for the rest. Sometimes

modern-day physicians are so busy they make us feel we should have somehow healed ourselves and not bothered them with such a prosaic problem.
Even though we had another appointment just last week, they often look
at us as through a glass darkly, peering quizzically at us, groping for some
faint flicker of recognition, which rushes in the minute the nurse hands
them our folder full of secrets we aren't allowed to learn. We make foolish statements in a squeaky voice (caused by the fact that we're freezing
because our bare rear is being quick-frozen by the cold steel table). We're
embarrassed the gown won't go around us and they're seeing us like this
when we wore a perfect little form-fitting ensemble that is now in a
wrinkled heap on the chair. Oh, where is Dr. Sweetsir?

Books could be (and have been) written on the medical mistakes
perpetrated on women. We could start with the five weeks I spent in one
of the country's top hospitals dying of heart attacks, my arm strapped to
a board so I could receive blood thinner intravenously, only to find out
I needed my gallbladder out and my blood was too thin to coagulate. Or
when I was locked into a huge radioisotope machine and forgotten for
four hours until a night watchman came in and asked, "What are you
doing here?" As if I'd had a choice!

My purpose here is not to malign doctors—as the saying goes, some
of my best friends are doctors—but to ask you women to think.

Get a Second Opinion

Don't just assume the first doctor you go to is right. If you don't feel
right about the diagnosis, get another opinion. Meg got the results of her
PAP test and was frightened when they indicated she needed surgery; as
a twenty-five-year-old woman she didn't want a hysterectomy. At a
friend's suggestion she came to our nutritionist. Over the years we have
seen this talented healthcare professional be the instrument for healing
in many people who had not received help from regular methods. She
set up a program for Meg to follow that she knew from experience would
make a difference. The next day Meg called to say that her husband, "a
real doctor," wouldn't allow her to continue to see the nutritionist, and
because she was under his "headship" she had to do his will. The nutritionist told Meg if she could at least follow the program without coming in to see her she'd counsel her on the phone.

The husband allowed her to do that much, and when Meg went for
her one-month checkup, the problem had disappeared. Here was a
woman who wanted to do the right thing but because of her husband's
belief in headship almost had unnecessary surgery.

Some of us don't dare question professional opinions; we've bought the lie that we women don't understand our own bodies. *We must study up on our type of ailment.* We should learn the latest information for ourselves; we can't just assume the physician has had time to read *Prevention* magazine.

We must think preventively and take care of ourselves. Much information is available these days on the dangers of smoking, the need for exercise, and the dangers of food additives and poisons. (Given all the warnings, don't you sometimes wonder if there's anything left you can eat?) We don't need to take nutrition courses to be knowledgeable about our bodies, but none of this information makes any difference if we don't read it and act upon it.

We should listen to our friends. Often our best friends can see negative changes in us that we don't notice ourselves. Glenda had friends who said, "You're killing yourself working like this!" But Glenda didn't listen. She had a driving need to achieve more than anyone else and to perform it all to perfection. She didn't think about her childhood experiences and dysfunctional family; because of her compulsive behavior, she was able to keep herself so busy she didn't have to look at the past. She grew up the eldest of seven in an alcoholic home where she was forced to be the parent of her siblings. Glenda learned to be supermom and supersister combined.

When Glenda married Dan she continued her frenetic pace. She had two babies eleven months apart and worked two full-time jobs—one caring for the babies and one as a nurse. As a submissive wife she didn't ask Dan to help. Wasn't she superwoman?

Glenda worked six nights a week on two hours of sleep a day and became progressively thinner and weaker. She earned enough money to buy a house but achieving her goal didn't slow her down. In her words,

> I continued the frantic pace even when my friends warned me of the dangers. I needed to prove myself to me and I became the best in my professional field while adding two more children to our family.
>
> The wake-up call came in 1978 when I became ill with a rare blood disorder for which there was no cure. Wonder Woman had been struck down. My life had to be prioritized. A dead nurse wasn't going to be much help to four teenagers. My pace slowed somewhat temporarily but the work frenzy flared when I began to feel better, even though I wasn't cured . . . there was no cure.
>
> Six years later, I was diagnosed with chronic lymphocytic leukemia. Again I prioritized my life and made some changes

in work schedules, but as soon as I began to feel better the pace resumed.

Now, two rounds of chemotherapy later and after some serious introspection, God, yes God, has convicted me that I must do the emotional work that has been so pitifully neglected and begin to deal with the cause of my compulsive behavior. Last August, when I was unable to speak after having a stroke in a grocery-store parking lot, I knew I must address my self-destructive behaviors and stop asking my physical body to bear the brunt of unresolved emotional pain. Through counseling I have begun to face, experience, and resolve my very deep, emotional wounds by taking God back into those places and discovering His incredible loving hand. Unexpectedly and very gratefully, my cancer is in remission and I am healthier than I have been in ten years. My oncologist is amazed and believes me when I say I am better . . . spiritually, emotionally, and physically, as my blood count confirms.

How I wish I had listened to my very wise friends years ago. Maybe I wouldn't have cancer and wonder at my future.

Wake up, women! If the people who care the most for you are warning that your behaviors are destructive, have the courage to investigate your motives and begin the healing process before it costs you your health.

Have Basic Checkups

Some of us are so preoccupied with our jobs and caring for our families that we neglect ourselves, as Glenda did. Some feel it's better not to know. "What you don't know won't hurt you." But in fact, what you don't know can kill you.

According to the National Breast Cancer Coalition there are 2.6 million women in this country with breast cancer, but one million of them don't know it yet and may not until it's too late.[4]

Mammograms and self-examinations are considered essential along with regular medical checkups. When it's time for your mammogram it is wise to go to a clinic accredited by the American College of Radiology. To check this, call the National Cancer Institute's information line, 800-4-CANCER, for the name of a certified lab near you.

Please take care of your health, both physical and emotional. We need to wake up and think. No one else is going to do it for us!

10

Dealing with Divorce and Widowhood

For every day I stand outside your door,
And bid you wake, and rise to fight and win.
from Walter Malone's "Opportunity"

Widowhood might be an expected topic in a book of this sort. But many readers will think it is daring for a Christian author to discuss divorce in a book dealing with Christian principles. I'm including it because, despite how we feel about it, divorce is an issue we must face. I am in no way teaching that if we're not happy with our husbands or wish to go "find ourselves" we should get a divorce. No. Those divorces are plentiful, but they are not the situations I am addressing here.

Surviving an Unwanted Divorce

The majority of Christian women I see each day who are going through divorces didn't want them. The majority never even thought it was a possibility and were totally unprepared to deal with the stark reality when it hit them. In many cases the traditional advice they received from their church leaders was to be submissive, hang in there, and pray more. Because they were ashamed to tell anyone and often did not have the money to get legal counsel, many have ended up broke, on welfare,

living in substandard housing, and leaving children uncared for while
they try to earn a living.

We would all like to look the other way and utter platitudes about trusting the Lord, but we can't play ostrich anymore. We must wake up to the
fact that good, dedicated, Christian women are in financial and emotional
trouble because of divorce. We can no longer treat them as fallen
women—as so many report they are made to feel—but to help them face
the harsh reality of life as a single woman. Of the divorced women I talk
with, none are out nights carousing in singles bars. Instead they are home
helping with homework and doing housework after a long day with low pay
while trying to convince their children that the Christian life is exciting.

It is for these women, who find themselves in circumstances they
never expected, that I have written on divorce. This is not to suggest
divorce as a simple alternative to marriage problems or to condemn those
going through it, but to touch base with reality and help the church, the
Bible study teachers, the counselors, and the victims themselves to be
aware of the pitfalls and show them how to get proper advice. As people
untutored in divorce law we cannot possibly make judgments on the
proceedings, but we must know someone who can.

The Faults of No-Fault Divorce

When no-fault divorce was initiated it was supposed to ease the agony
of court hearings and dignify the process of dissolving a marriage. But it
hasn't worked that way. A 1986 *Woman's Day* article on no-fault divorce
said:

> Instead of becoming simpler, divorce legislation has multiplied
> into a tangle of laws and regulations that even divorce lawyers
> cannot always find their way through. No two states have the
> same laws, and so many statutes are under scrutiny in the courts
> that interpretations change from one month to the next.
>
> Most disappointing of all, the changes in divorce laws have
> let down women in their expectation of better financial treat-
> ment. Perhaps such a hope never was realistic—when an or-
> dinary family's financial pie is cut in two, neither half is very
> large. Often there is just not enough money to go around. But
> today, as in the past, most women still come out poorly, even
> when the laws dictate what looks like a reasonable split.[1]

Almost all of us suffer some emotional damage from our childhoods
and we enter into marriage full of holes we hope our mates will fill. Since

their emotional holes are in different places than ours they don't notice ours, and because we don't articulate what our needs are, they don't often find them. Dr. Harville Hendrix, a practicing psychologist and author of *Getting the Love You Want*, counsels his patients to look at marriage as a reparenting, with partners helping each other heal the wounds of childhood. "I'm trying," he adds hopefully, "to help people understand they have to cooperate with the unconscious and meet each other's childhood needs. If they do, they can have the marriage of their dreams; if they don't they will have the marriage of their nightmares."[2]

Let's pretend that you have been served divorce papers and are in a state of shock. You are trying to wake up and you need some help. If you have worked through chapter 5, "Managing the Money," and followed the suggestions there you are probably somewhat protected. You have copies of expenses and records of all financial dealings. You'll be glad you did if, in a few days, you discover your departing husband has taken all the papers and put them in his lawyer's hand before he sues you for divorce. Unfortunately this is an increasingly common practice. If you have copies of records of real estate deeds, properties, insurance, etc., you will be better prepared to fight for what you deserve. It costs money to have a lawyer search out hidden or misplaced documents. Don't automatically take your suing husband's word that you don't need a lawyer because his lawyer, a fine and fair man, will take care of you both. There may be exceptions, but in general his lawyer is interested only in him. You need someone on your side.

Is "Equitable Distribution" Really Equitable?

In the past spouses seeking divorce had to prove adultery or extreme mental cruelty. People worked overtime to find evidence to be used against each other, even staging what appeared to be adultery—with photographers handy. On January 1, 1970, California was the first state to institute no-fault divorce, meaning spouses no longer had to find something scandalous about their mates to get divorced. Irreconcilable differences became the new measure of divorce, and those differences could be stretched to fit around almost anything. By mutual consent a couple could get divorced and, with any luck, receive what is called "equitable distribution" of their properties and assets. *Equitable*, of course, depended on the judge or mediator making the decisions. If this person was a man who had just been taken to the cleaners by his wife, he probably wouldn't be inclined to favor you! This is where your records of all major purchases become valuable.

Another term that has developed is "spousal contribution." If you put your husband through medical school or worked to build his business, you could be entitled to some recompense in the settlement. However, you will need documentation of what you have done. A wife named Josie learned that the hard way. She helped in her husband's car business, working for no salary for ten years. When he divorced her and she tried to get "spousal contribution" she could show no records of the hours she had worked and it wasn't allowed.

With these new divorce laws, which were intended to give women equal distribution of property, came some losses. In the past most divorced women got alimony and child support to some degree, but in today's system only 15 percent of the women going through divorces get any alimony. There are four kinds of alimony: *permanent, lump sum, remunerative* (for the wife who put money into the marriage or put the husband through school), and *rehabilitative* (designed to help you learn a skill so you can support yourself). If you look too intelligent and competent you may not win rehabilitative alimony. In fact, if you look strong enough to bus tables at McDonald's you may be perceived as skilled enough to support yourself and the little ones without further training.

Women, in general, earn 71 percent of what men earn for comparable work and on the executive level only 42 percent of what men receive. So the financial outlook for a divorced woman rearing children is not optimistic. Most women settle for too little too quickly in order to stop the pain of the divorce proceedings; many women get small awards because they have no records. A lawyer will help you, but he can't produce your records.

Don't Let Yourself Be a Victim

In looking for an example of a woman who handled the divorce procedure as positively as possible, I called my friend Sheila, a Christian writer. I had known her before, during, and after her divorce, and I felt she would have some encouraging words for those women facing these difficult times. When she wrote me, I felt what she said was so well crafted that I'm quoting her directly:

> One of my first concerns was credit because Les, my ex-husband, had canceled my name on all our credit cards without warning. Fortunately, I did have a MasterCard in my own name that had been offered to me at some time prior to the separation. I had forgotten I even had it and am not sure why

I did, but it turned out to be my salvation. Also, of all the other cards, J. C. Penney contacted me and offered me a card in my name based on a good past credit history. If a woman contacts the companies where she and her husband have had joint credit, she can explain the situation and at least some of them will issue her credit in her own name. As it turned out, because I had the one major credit card in my name I had no problem establishing my own credit. I used it to set up several credit accounts and used them a little so I could begin to establish my own credit history. As a result I was able to buy a home in my name (two years later) based on that credit history.

Shortly after we separated, my husband's accountant invited me to lunch to offer me what amounted to a divorce settlement. He tried to convince me that Les's business was in serious trouble (so it was not worth very much), but Les was willing to take the business and give me the house (valued then at $250,000). He tried to assure me that this was a good deal for me. Les was hoping I would agree to this settlement and he wouldn't have to get a lawyer. I turned it down because I didn't want to keep the house (I had already moved out), I wasn't sure if it would sell or for how much, and I didn't have the resources to maintain it in the meantime. I also was not ready to file for divorce and didn't want to be pushed into something before I was ready. As it turned out, that was a wise decision.

Next, I found a book on legal issues for women. It explained that if I settled for alimony, I would have to pay taxes on the monthly payments, but if I took a property settlement, I did not have to pay taxes on the principle (just the interest). As it turned out, I did get a property settlement that amounted to monthly payments for several years. When the house sold I was to get a lump-sum payment of half of whatever he got as a cash down payment up to a maximum of thirty thousand dollars, which would offset part of what he was to pay me in the property settlement. He tried to sell the house and each time he got a potential buyer, he tried to get me to carry the loan so he could get out from under it, but I refused each time. Even though I would have made more money on the interest, etc., and he tried to assure me I could resell the house and make even more if the buyers defaulted, my main concern was the expense of maintaining the house and grounds if there had been a problem. As it turned out, he decided to keep the house and is still living there, so I continue to get monthly payments on the property settlement. Fortunately, he has always kept up-to-date on the payments, so collecting payments for what will be a total of eleven years hasn't been a problem. However, if a woman has serious concerns about her husband skipping out or not making the monthly payments, this might not be the wisest option. The other advantage of having the property settlement is that it is counted as a tangible asset by banks, etc.

At one point I had to meet with Les and the lawyers so they could take a deposition on our assets (to make sure neither of us was hiding any assets the other didn't know about). Prior to that meeting, I did my homework and went into the meeting knowing everything I needed to know to answer their questions. I had moved out of the big house into an apartment so I made up a list of what furnishings I had taken with me, which ones Les had, what I'd given to the children, etc., along with the estimated value of each piece. Since I was not getting any support from him at that time and was asking for it, I had a detailed copy of my budget and projected income. Les came to the meeting with no notes and could only guess when asked a question. I was so well prepared that even though his lawyer did his best to rattle me he wasn't able to ask a single question I wasn't prepared to answer. As a result I got the financial support I asked for, and his lawyer found out I couldn't be intimidated into doing what they wanted.

I let my lawyer know up front that I only wanted my fair share and I wasn't interested in taking Les for everything I could get, and he honored that; but he always let me know how to best handle the requests or what was fair. For example, Les had taken my car away several months before we separated because he wanted me to be forced to ask to borrow his car so he'd always know where I was. I contended that I should have my own car as I had for years, so eventually I got back the car without paying for it.

My advice to other women is to not let yourself become a victim or to play the role of a victim. I realize that in some cases they don't have a choice, but I know there are also a lot of women who become victims simply because they don't find out their rights and stand up for them. There is no excuse for a woman not knowing about the family assets, etc., and knowing how to handle the family finances. In my case, being well prepared and informed at each juncture is what helped me come out as well as I did. I would not let them intimidate me into doing what they wanted if it was not advantageous to me as well. I found it best never to give an answer on the spot, but to wait until I could think it through logically and unemotionally.

I went for counseling and felt it was important to get myself to a place where I felt well and whole again before I got into the really emotional garbage of actually getting the divorce. It was about eighteen months after the separation that the divorce went through. I am grateful I was able to take it slowly. Don't ever rush into a divorce.

How fortunate that Sheila had done her homework and had the stamina to hang in there until a fair settlement was reached. She is a role model for other women going through this ordeal.

Avoid Ungodly Counsel

Sheila mentioned going for counseling for her own well-being. It is always helpful to receive another person's opinion on what we are going through and to have someone to talk with who really seems to care. However, as women we must be very cautious about the kind of counseling we accept when we are lonely and vulnerable, as Theodora's story illustrates.

Theodora grew up in an alcoholic home with a family that attended church regularly and pretended they had no problems. The pastor was the authority figure for the family, and the church was the one place where Theodora felt safe. As an adult Theodora continued to hide the victimization she suffered as a child because she was afraid the truth would cause people to turn away from her. In her thirties, after an unwanted divorce, she became increasingly depressed and feelings of loneliness crept up on her.

She was cautiously excited when her church announced the formation of a support group for those who had come from dysfunctional homes. She didn't want to accept the idea that her childhood had any bearing on her adult problems, but as she heard the tales of others she had to recognize she fit the pattern of the victim. For the first time in her life she was in a group of people who were all genuine, *real*. No one was trying to impress anyone else. Bit by bit she began to open up and trust the others in the group.

She made friends and felt as though she were no longer alone in the world. Theodora felt particularly safe because the meetings were held in a church and the leader was a church member who had completed his psychology courses and was volunteering his time to meet his internship requirements. It was like receiving free counseling.

Theodora was at work one day when a panic attack swept over her. She didn't know what had happened, and in desperation she called her support-group leader. He listened to her and then recommended that those feelings would be eliminated if she would masturbate whenever she began to be anxious and panicky. She was surprised at his suggestion and at his instructions. She didn't feel right about it, but she'd been told to trust, open up, share, and change her old ways of dealing with life.

After all, wasn't this man knowledgeable, trained in such things? Wasn't he a member of the church? Hadn't he been compassionate, kind, and so willing to listen to her? After all he'd done for Theodora, wasn't she obliged to be obedient and follow his advice? Theodora thought so, but after a couple of months of this type of behavior, she stopped going to her support group. She was so embarrassed at her actions and her inability to stop this newly established habit she couldn't look the man in the face. Thus, she quit attending the group without an explanation and without calling this "compassionate" counselor on the carpet!

Theodora needed the support of a caring group she could trust. She thought looking for it in a church would be safe. I wish that could always be the case. However, just as in anything else, we must look more deeply and carefully than strictly on the surface. There have always been wolves in sheep's clothing, even in our churches, unfortunately. Paul understood this when he said, "Therefore take heed to yourselves and to all the flock, among which the Holy Spirit has made you overseers. . . . For I know this, that after my departure savage wolves will come in among you, not sparing the flock. Also from among yourselves men will rise up, speaking perverse things, to draw away the disciples after themselves" (Acts 20:28–31 NKJV).

We must *wake up* to the fact that we must seek out help and support that is godly and sound. Even if we can't tell at first, we must realize that any time a person gives us counsel that is sexual in nature and suggests we do anything we question in our spirit, we must watch out! Unfortunately, victimizers can recognize a vulnerable person, especially one who is newly divorced or widowed, and they move in with perverted advice.

This often satisfies their own sick need and binds the victim to them as authority figures. Many individuals who were victimized themselves go into counseling in hopes of finding solutions for their own problems. Before entering into any suggested activities we don't feel entirely comfortable about, we should seek out a second opinion from another trusted, objective source. Get confirmation that this is the way to go and pray about it. Do you lack wisdom? God says we need to ask Him (James 1:5) and He will give generously! (For further information on choosing a counselor, read chapter 16 in *Get a Life Without the Strife*.)

Remember to test the advice you receive; if in doubt, don't!

Surviving Widowhood

Kathryn had it all. She was married to a doctor, had a big house and fancy cars, plenty of money, and no need to work. Her husband loved her and the children and wanted them to have what he'd been deprived of as a child. Let's read Kathryn's words about what happened to her fairy-tale marriage:

> I was married to a general surgeon whose temperament was super Choleric. He wanted to control and take care of his family in the way he had dreamed of as a child but never had a chance to live. His desire was to let me just have fun and take care of the four kids as they grew up—and *eventually*, he said, he would teach me about money. I was Sanguine enough to say, "Great! That's easy enough!" So I let it happen.
>
> But one day my bubble burst. He died suddenly of a massive coronary. I had to grow up fast and close his office, refer patients, take care of all the business and funeral arrangements, *before* I could even *grieve*. My husband never wanted to admit he was mortal, so he never wrote a will or taught me the ropes. I had to become Choleric (which I was underneath, but didn't realize). Now I really like my personality, but it was hell getting there.

Shelley's story was different than Kathryn's. She had worked side by side with her counselor husband for many years, handling all the bookkeeping for his practice. Eventually their son joined the firm as a counselor also and her husband taught him all he knew.

When Shelley's husband died suddenly, she didn't know who owned what. They'd never discussed this possibility. The will stated that the proceeds of the practice were to be divided equally between Shelley and her son James. James asked if he could make monthly payments to her out of the profits of the practice as he did not have enough money to give her a cash settlement. Since she was doing the books and could keep tabs on the financial condition of the business, Shelley felt comfortable with this agreement.

But soon after her husband's death, James hired a part-time bookkeeper under the guise of "giving Mom some free time." Shelley didn't really feel she needed any free time, but the leadership of her church told her she should comply with her son's requests and let him be her leader. She was under his umbrella, they said. After a few months James had cut Shelley's hours completely, and the part-time bookkeeper had become full-time. One day when Shelley stopped by the office, she noticed there was new furniture and each room had been completely redecorated. Then she found out James had borrowed money against the business, which he claimed was to pay for the redecorating.

Eventually the monthly payments to Shelley stopped. When she inquired, he told her that business was slow, he had a lot of debts, and she would have to wait for her money. That's when Shelley came to me. When I suggested she contact a lawyer immediately, she asked, "As a Christian, is that all right for me to do?" Shelley's husband thought he had provided for her, but he didn't take into account that his son might become greedy. Shelley needed someone to give her permission to stand up for her legal portion of her husband's business. Of course, the problem was compounded because the person who was cheating her was her son.

Widows have to make many decisions very quickly and, as we have cited here, often times they are completely unprepared to become the sole decision-maker in their family.

The American Association of Retired Persons (AARP) recognizes how common this situation is and has published a book entitled *Survival Handbook for Widows*. It provides this helpful list of ways to protect yourself against those who would like to help you spend your deceased husband's money.

1. Learn to say no.

2. Deal with responsible, reliable local dealers or services.

3. Never buy on a door-to-door salesperson's first trip to your home.

4. Don't be afraid to ask what you may think the other person will think are dumb questions. They are cheaper than dumb mistakes.

5. Never buy sight unseen.

6. Read and understand contracts before signing.

7. Check with someone who knows the product before you buy, not after.

8. Stay within your income. Do not be oversold.

Suspect a phony if any of the following apply:

1. You are asked to sign your name—*now*.

2. The prices are too good to be true.

3. The salesperson discredits others who sell similar products.

4. A cash payment is necessary.

5. The contract has vague or tricky wording.[3]

Actually these suggestions from the AARP apply equally to those of us who are divorced, single, or just plain naive. We tend to expect the best of others and can easily be taken in by a smooth salesman preying on vulnerable women.

Remember, if it seems too good to be true, it probably is!

Dating Again

As women, we can be led by our emotions and thus make wrong choices and decisions if we are not awake and alert to life.

Lyndsay was married with three children when her twenty-four-year-old husband was diagnosed with cancer; he died a short time later. Convinced that her children needed a dad and she needed a husband to take care of her financially, she began dating and frantically searching. She let all her relatives and friends play matchmaker and she wasn't discriminating or particular on the qualifications. Eight months to the day after her husband's death, Lyndsay married a man she hardly knew, but he looked good, said the right words, and went to church each Sunday.

Lyndsay's emotional needs and the fear for her children's future led her to make a tragic choice. Her new husband later developed incestuous relationships with both her daughters, and her son now tells her about dreams he had after she remarried about a man tying him up, beating him, and arousing him sexually. Her son thinks he's becoming a homosexual.

Lyndsay has had to pay a great price for what she hoped would be financial and emotional security, and so have her children.

When I asked Lyndsay what her advice would be for other widows or divorcées facing a newly single life, she gave me this list:

1. Grieving takes time; don't panic!

2. Know who *you* are so you can discern who *he* is.

3. Don't allow others to be matchmakers—*you* have to live with the person you marry!

4. God can meet all your needs in *His* time—financial, emotional, and security—and He can even fill your heart where it is empty.

5. Don't rush in—take your time! Know all you can about him first.

6. Wake up, women!

Look at His Financial Report

Soon after I talked with Lyndsay, I met with a group of women who had been divorced and remarried. As we relaxed together after a seminar I asked them what advice they would give someone heading into a second marriage. They all said in unison: "Do a credit check on him." "Do a Dun and Bradstreet. " "Look at his TRW report." They all laughed at the similarity of their answers and then told me their stories.

Each of them had met a man who was attractive, well-dressed, successful, and sensitive. Ironically, all of them had met these men at Christian singles groups and they had eventually prayed together about getting married. The other similarity was that the men had all been deceptive about money. Even though they weren't exactly Christian con men, they had not told the truth.

One man had lied to his wife-to-be that he had a job when he didn't. In fact, he still hadn't gone to work yet even though they had been married quite awhile; she had ended up supporting him. One woman found out after the marriage that her new husband owed sixty thousand dollars in back taxes and was in trouble with the IRS. One man had a very close relationship with his secretary, who paid the couple's bills and refused to give the new wife any money without a written request. Each of these women felt betrayed and knew they could never totally trust the person they had pledged to live with forever. When we got beyond their case histories and back to their advice, they all had plenty to say based on their experiences. Here's a summary of their suggestions:

• **Check his finances.** Even though it sounds unromantic, the time to discuss finances is *before* the wedding, not after. If you are considering marriage, you should each get your own TRW (or similar) report, then sit down without stress and share them with each other. Sometimes you will be surprised at what information TRW has on you. Fred and I recently found we had a negative rating on something our son had not handled correctly and it had mistakenly been put on Fred's account. When you both expose your ratings before marriage, there are no ugly surprises later on.

- **Discuss how you will handle your monthly expenses.** You need to agree ahead of time who will pay for what. Are there child-support obligations from a first marriage? Who will handle taxes, rent, car payments? Don't be afraid to ask questions. If he turns you down because you want to discuss finances, you know he has something to hide or he is a very insecure man and you don't need him.

In the book *Love and the Law* author Gail Koff considers it mandatory for those going into second or third marriages to have a prenuptial agreement. These are relatively simple legal preparations that spell out finances, ownership, and responsibilities and, according to Koff's experience, are more than worth their weight in gold. Prenuptial agreements serve two major purposes: They get emotional issues over money settled when you're both positive, and they set at ease the concerns of both families. Prenups, as they are called, supersede state laws and will save future grief. Don't fall for the line, "If you really loved me you wouldn't ask these things. Just trust me."

- **Check pensions, wills, and insurance policies.** Don't wait until you are married to find out that all his insurance goes to his first wife, that his pension fund is in her name, and that the sole beneficiaries of his will are his children. He has a right to do with these policies as he will, but you should understand ahead of time. I frequently hear women say, "If I'd only known, I wouldn't have married him." Once you have discussed these issues you can record the details of the agreement in your prenups.

- **Meet with his first wife.** If you're considering marriage to a man who has been married before, see if his first wife will talk with you, or meet with one of her good friends. (Of course if you were "the other woman" in the divorce, this would not be advisable.) Although the perspective you get may be weighted against your prospective husband, the information may save you from a costly mistake. Ask why the marriage failed and what he should have done differently. One woman found out from the first wife that her fiancé was homosexual and was marrying her as a cover. Another learned her intended husband was so attached to his mother that she controlled his every move. Still another found out the man was a compulsive liar and had abused his daughter. It is not rude of you to learn all you can about a man who is going to live with you and your own children. Save yourself surprises. In 1989 in Massachusetts a survey done by the legal professions showed that only 35 percent of the financial statements submitted by men were accurate. Are you going to be fortunate enough to find an honest man out of that 35 percent?

Fear Will Always Destroy You

After her husband left her for her best friend, Suzanne met Hank at a Sunday school class in his church where he and his parents and other family members had been very active since its inception and were considered pillars of the church. She eventually met them all and felt warmly accepted and loved by this well-known, Christian family.

Soon after they met, they began to make wedding plans. When I talked with her recently she reminded me that their fifth anniversary was to be the following Sunday. We giggled over how I had teased her on her wedding day when we were getting dressed just before the ceremony. I'd said to her, "Well, I guess you have a choice. You can go with him on your honeymoon or you can go with us and have a hot-fudge sundae. It's not too late to change your mind."

Suzanne had called me when she returned from their honeymoon and said, "I should have gone with you girls for a hot-fudge sundae."

In the intervening years I had watched Suzanne lose herself, desperately trying to adapt and have the perfect Christian marriage. I had watched her "do the dance" so she wouldn't have to endure his cruel tongue. I knew it wasn't good, but I didn't know how bad it really was until the day she began to share with me about the mental and emotional abuse she had suffered from this very angry man who had never resolved issues from his past. She became his victim as he showered his lifetime collection of venom on her.

She confessed that what changed her life was when a friend confronted her about the cauldron of anger that she sensed was boiling up inside Suzanne. Her friend expressed concern for her health and even went so far as to say she feared an early death for her unless Suzanne faced and dealt with what was making her so angry. Suzanne then chose to get help, rationalizing that she must do whatever it took to stay in this Christian marriage. She couldn't endure a second failed marriage. She felt trapped and believed there were no options except to continue to control herself. She reasoned that she would have to suppress her disappointment and pain so as not to bring shame to Hank's saintly family.

After ending up in the hospital for three weeks for treatment of depression, she went back home to try again. This time the difference was that she had learned to stand up for herself and stay true to herself. The only problem was that Hank was not willing to live with the new Suzanne or get help for himself. He refused to meet her ultimatum: "Either deal with your issues of anger or I am no longer willing to invest in this relationship." He just didn't get it.

As we talked, Suzanne and I both agreed that hindsight is always twenty-twenty, but I asked her, "What advice would you give women who are faced with the possibility of remarriage?"

Suzanne answered quickly, "Don't give yourself away and don't be afraid to be yourself. Fear will always destroy you. It will transform you into a nonperson, and he won't like you any better."

She continued, saying, "Don't rush into it just to be married. Be willing to pay the price to get the knowledge you need to make a wise decision."

When I asked, "How would you do that?" Suzanne listed five steps she would take to gather information about the man she was considering as a marriage partner:

"First, I would meet his ex-wife and get her perspective on why their marriage didn't work. I wouldn't just take his side of the story," she said.

"Second, I would take an objective third party with me, someone capable of emotional detachment, to help me sort out any sour grapes. Third, I would date someone at the very least a full year before jumping into a new marriage. By dating a full year we would experience holidays, birthdays, Mother's Day, and any anniversaries together, giving me the opportunity to observe him and his reactions to different situations. I would also see how his family related on holidays, what expectations they had, and where his children from the first marriage fit into the picture," she said.

Suzanne's fourth suggestion was "listen to my close and trusted friends," she said. "I would be more open to their opinions, concerns, and advice. I would need their blessing before I would feel comfortable about moving ahead. So often the adage 'Love is blind' is so true. Knowing that should make us even more cautious.

"If I had it to do over again I would stay true to my own Sanguine personality. I would look inside myself to find my own emotional needs. I would get to know and understand myself instead of getting caught up in the excitement of being in love and living the happily-ever-after syndrome."

Suzanne summed up her experience this way: "I realize I wore a Phlegmatic mask, pretending to be sweetly submissive in both marriages, and it just about killed me, physically and emotionally."

She should have gone out for that hot-fudge sundae!

Don't Be Blinded by Your Neediness

"Sometimes I think this Sunday school class is a Christian singles bar." These were the words of the singles pastor of a large church where I was about to speak. "They come in here with one thought on their minds, and I'm helpless to do anything about it."

This pastor was doing his best to teach God's principles to adult singles, but he shrugged his shoulders in a gesture of hopelessness. "At least the ones they pick up are Christians, so I guess that's better than going to the bars." By the time he'd shared his frustrations with me, we'd arrived on the platform and I was facing a bright, attractive group of singles who were all singing their hearts out.

After the service the pastor turned me over to Lucy, who was assigned to take me out to lunch. "She's the most faithful of all and will do anything to help," he said as he introduced her. Off we went to lunch, where Lucy told me her story. I asked if I could take notes as her experiences were right for this book. "If you can save one woman from going through what I've experienced, feel free!" she said.

Lucy had met Jeff at this church. Both had been divorced three years and had children the same ages. Tall, dark, and good-looking, Jeff was deeply involved with the ministry . . . making pancakes on Sundays, inviting single parents over for potlucks at his house, leading singles events. He was the obvious catch of the group.

As Lucy gravitated into a leadership position, their contact was more frequent and a friendship began to bloom. After a few months the singles director of their division asked them to teach a class together on "How to Have a Healthy Relationship." Since neither one had ever had one of those, both were intrigued. They met and began working on approaches to take. By the end of their second meeting, it was obvious that they were attracted to each other. He was perfect. A strong Christian, a devoted single dad. She, too, loved the Lord and was dedicated to His service and to her children. Both loved to hike, body surf, cook, and travel. It was truly a match made in heaven.

After the third date, Lucy sensed he was about to kiss her. She said, "I hadn't been touched in a loving way for so long . . . I was ready. But the kiss was rough. He shoved me into the kitchen counter and began tearing at my clothes, going for it. I said, 'No.' He didn't stop, but he did become more gentle. The next day he called me, full of remorse, and bemoaned the way his 'flesh' had gotten the better of him.

"Red flag!" Lucy said, waving her arm. "I saw it in my peripheral vision, but I'd been alone for what felt like forever. So I ignored it. Mistake."

They were practically inseparable after that. Their children bonded. Jeff's daughter called Lucy Mommy. They became, in the singles director's words, the shining stars of her ministry, planning and running events ranging from a single-parents camping trip to Mother's Day and Father's Day parties.

A few months later Jeff's daughter had a birthday. Who showed up uninvited to the party? Jeff's former girlfriend, Danielle. Everywhere they went for the next week or so, Danielle managed to be there. Jeff assured Lucy that they were merely talking through some old issues, that it was no big deal. She did her best to be pleasant, but underneath felt a perplexing, overwhelming sense of impending doom.

"I'd wake up in the middle of the night in a panic . . . wondering, wondering, wondering. Then Danielle called me one morning and informed me that she'd had sex with Jeff four times since that birthday party. I hung up on her. She called again and threatened to go to the church with her story and destroy him. I hung up and called Jeff."

Lucy continued, getting more angry as she relived these moments. "He began to cry and beg for forgiveness, saying that Danielle had manipulated him into bed and that he loved me, only me. He kept calling her the 'ex-girlfriend from hell.'"

Lucy forgave him. They went to the singles director and shared their story with her, and Jeff asked for forgiveness there too. Danielle also repented. Restoration was achieved in the Christian way. Lucy even hugged Danielle one Sunday after church and offered her forgiveness.

All seemed to be back to normal until three weeks later, when Jeff confessed that he'd spent the evening with Danielle.

Wake up, Lucy!

She told him, "I'm not into triangles. I didn't sign up for this ride! Either you quit seeing her or you have to stop seeing me!"

Jeff flipped. His whole personality changed when he felt threatened. He called Lucy a "controlling bitch" who wanted to put him in a little box, make him her prisoner. Suddenly, Lucy was the evil one, Danielle the angel.

In her pain, Lucy asked the singles director to excuse her from being in leadership at the next few events. She attended, however, and to her chagrin, Danielle and Jeff were up front, being publicly commended for their hard work. She had taken Lucy's man and her place in the ministry. What was going on here?

Lucy recounted, "Every time I went to the church after that, at least one of my children would leave in tears. Hysterical, awful tears. Not only was I out, but my kids were being rejected and humiliated too. I went to the singles director, but my pleas for intervention fell on deaf ears.

"When should I have awakened?" Lucy asked me. "After he practically raped me on the kitchen counter? If not at that point, then how about after Danielle's phone calls? I could have saved myself and my kids immeasurable heartache.

"But no, I was so desperate to be loved that I ignored the warning signals, and there certainly were enough of them! I fell for a self-sacrificing, religious man who appeared to be the perfect daddy. I believed his words of love, family, and forever. I gave myself to him sexually even after I knew he'd cheated on me." Lucy burst into tears.

What can we learn from Lucy's unfortunate experience?

There are two issues to ponder here. The first is that we can't be blinded by a man's apparent piety. All of us must walk our talk.

Single women . . . you may be lonely and longing for love, but do not let your judgment be blinded by neediness! By succumbing to Jeff's sexual advances and believing his promises, Lucy became intimately involved with him before she had a clear idea of his character. And his goodness was counterfeit.

God instructs us to refrain from sexual activity until marriage. His reasons for this are to protect us from wounding ourselves and each other and to prevent us from contracting serious disease. And in the case of single parents, God wants to protect the children from being wounded as well.

Single women . . . so many of you came of age in the sixties and seventies. You left the churches of your youth and became part of the sexual revolution. Although you probably remained faithful in your marriages, if you once again face single life, your sexual behavior may revert back to that of the seventies. Even though you're a Christian now, you're still looking for love in physical relationships. In your yearning for connection and affection, you may bypass the vital steps of verifying the other's integrity.

Not all pious men are true! It is possible to be deceived and used as Lucy was. If this story sounds familiar . . . if you're involved with or are contemplating involvement with someone in your church . . . slow down! He may be using religion as a facade, a tool for seduction.

There is a hopeful ending to Lucy's story. Her church did not abandon her. She wrote a letter to her pastor, the one I had met, and he responded in love and wisdom. Jeff and Danielle were exposed and removed from the singles ministry. The singles director was replaced by a healthy married couple . . . a couple who had been through divorce, been down in the trenches, who had suffered and made mistakes comparable to those of the people they were ministering to. Their compassion and true Christian maturity have been a gift to the singles ministry of their church.

Cohabitation

As many of us grew up we had no concept of some of the things that are now everyday topics of conversation. My mother lived and died without ever knowing what the word *homosexual* meant. I went through college without a thought of date rape. Decent people didn't spend so much as a group weekend at the beach together without a chaperone watching over them, and living together outside of marriage was out of the question. We knew people who smoked and we had an alcoholic barber who lived in our attic, but none of these problems were ours. Drugs were no more drastic than aspirin, and aids were young women who assisted nurses in hospitals.

How times have changed!

Is it possible that some of us have managed to look the other way and avoid the reality of the world about us? We have to wake up. That doesn't mean we have to condone them or live them, but we must be aware and forewarned of some things that now are accepted as the norm.

Even though I feel I've been told about every sordid fact of life imaginable, I still blanch when some men and women who come to CLASS to learn to be Christian speakers openly mention how they live together. Somehow the two ideas don't add up to me. Perhaps the funniest was the woman who called our office to ask if she and the man she lived with could get the couple's discount for CLASS even though they weren't married. When we said no, she brought him anyway and he sat in the hall outside, listening through the crack in the door and coming in for each of the coffee breaks and lunches at no charge. Financially we would have been better off to let him come at a discount than lose money on his peripheral attendance, but somehow it didn't seem quite right.

Probably you are not in one of these arrangements today, but you may have a friend who is. Don't we all have that friend? Or you may have a son who's moved in with a woman with two children. *How could he do this to me?* you think. Or you might even have a mother who's moved in with old Joe; they're both still single because if they get married she'll lose your father's pension and who knows what else. Do you have any idea of the legal and financial problems this arrangement could bring upon this pair or possibly on you?

Whose House Is This Anyway?

Even though states have different laws about cohabitation, there are certain questions that need to be asked. When a couple decides that two can live cheaper, better, sexier than one, they don't often say "Let's discuss the rent first," but when it comes due, someone's got to pay it. Should it be the one who already lived there, giving the guest a free room? Should they alternate months? Should they get a new lease with both names? Problems like these may take the romance out of this whole idea in a hurry.

What if both pay on the mortgage and they split up? Does the one who leaves get his or her investment back? Do they have to sell the house and divide up what each put in? Or do they call on Solomon to come and cut the house down the middle?

What if this is *your* family home and old Joe moves in with Mother? Might he con her into signing it over to him—and ultimately his children? What if it's his house and Mother sells her house to move in with him? What if he decides later to cohabitate with someone else? Can he evict Mother? Might she end up homeless on your doorstep? Or what if he dies and his children get the house? Will they be generous of spirit and let her continue to live there?

When couples live together outside of marriage even the furniture can become a problem. Who paid for the couch? Do you still have proof? Such seemingly trivial matters can become major issues. That's what happened when Kevin became infatuated with the secretary at work. They were each newly divorced and didn't want marital entanglements, so Sue moved in with him. Her ex had custody of her children and the arrangement seemed ideal. She had no furniture but Kevin had an apartmentfull. They would each pay part of the rent and live happily ever after.

Then came the day when the ex-husband decided to marry a sweet young thing who wanted no part of his children. Suddenly Kevin's life changed. Instead of carefree love with play-now-pay-later expectations, Kevin had an apartment bursting with angry children. By the time he realized this was far more than he bargained for, Sue and the children were firmly planted in *his* place. They were enrolled in the local school and Sue was doing all she could to win back their affection after having abandoned them for her new life of free love. Her attention, which had been 100 percent focused on Kevin, now was scattered, and her guilt made her depressed and close to dysfunctional. Suddenly Kevin wasn't sure what he'd seen in Sue in the first place.

But how could he get out of this? And how would Sue feel when she perceived Kevin was rejecting her and her misplaced flock?

The magnetic attraction Kevin and Sue had felt for each other diminished as reality dropped heavily upon them: The grim facts jumped out before them. Sue had nowhere to go, no money for a rental deposit, continual baby-sitting bills so she could work, and minimal child support from an ex-husband who was off enjoying his freedom as she had done. Sue was angry at her ex for ruining her free-love fest, at her children for being born, and at Kevin for rejecting her. Kevin found Sue to be high strung and irrational; he knew he couldn't live like this any longer. He also had his own underlying guilt for having left his wife and one little girl whom he never saw. "Why am I raising her kids," he asked himself, "and abandoning my own daughter?"

One evening he came home to a mess of candy and chips on *his* white couch and he blew up. The kids all began to cry. Sue walked in on this scene and screamed, "That's it. You're out!" "You bet I am!" Kevin yelled. He grabbed a suitcase, threw in some shirts and shorts, pulled two suits off their hangers, and walked out.

He found himself sitting in *his* car in front of *his* apartment full of *his* furniture. *How did I get in this mess?* he wondered. He drove over to his mother's house, knowing he'd get a lecture but seeing no alternative. Sure enough, her first words were, "I told you so! You let that cheap woman move in with you and now she's stolen your furniture." Then a flash came to her. "And remember that white couch is mine!"

Neither mother nor Kevin ever saw that white couch again.

What if Kevin were your son or Sue were your daughter? What if they wouldn't respond to the Scripture verses you recited or your pleas for a celibate life? What if it were one of your parents? My friend Pat called me in a state of nervous breakdown. Her mother had died a few months before and her father had already moved a local waitress into her mother's bed! Worse than this shocking news was the fact that he saw nothing wrong with it and had just come over to show her the new sexy silk briefs he had purchased with little red hearts all over them. "Wouldn't your mother die if she saw me in these!" he had told her, laughing at the thought and sending Pat into orbit.

"She's already dead, you fool," Pat cried. "Grow up! What's the matter with you?"

When Pat called me, she was hysterical. Once she calmed down we decided she should go over to her father's house and remove the jewelry and special objects her mother had left for her. She had refrained from doing this so as not to look greedy, but the time had come. She went in while they were out and retrieved what was rightfully hers. It was several weeks before her father noticed anything missing and by that time the waitress was missing also.

We are living today with circumstances many of us never expected to face, and we have to accept lifestyles that we can no longer control. If possible, when we see arrangements we cannot change, we can suggest what is called a "cohabitation agreement," a relatively simple legal document stating the financial independence of each partner, what possessions of value each entered the relationship with, future financial obligations, property ownership, the debt obligation of each party, shared expenses, will, and estate plans. In effect, it spells out who owns the white couch.

Gail Koff, author of *Love and the Law*, writing about cohabitation agreements says, "All too often people neglect to face questions like these, questions that may conjure up unpleasant situations and eventualities. Some people are superstitious, thinking that to discuss potential problems will only make them real. And yet, as a rule, it's always better to be prepared for the worst, even while expecting and hoping for the best."

Wake up, women, wake up!

11

I Can Always
Get an Abortion

In the fall of 1993 a Texas high school made national news when it barred pregnant teenagers from being cheerleaders. The mothers of these girls were on TV crying that the school-board decision was prejudiced against girls who just happened to be a little different—as if being pregnant were hereditary. To further complicate the matter, one of the girls had gotten an abortion. Since she was then no longer pregnant, the new rule didn't apply and she was reinstated. This infuriated the other already-emotional mothers who saw this as promoting abortion.

Obviously, there is no easy solution to unwanted pregnancy. Abortion leaves guilt and pain in the heart of the could-have-been mother. Becoming a teenage single parent can ruin the entire future of a girl and make her bitter as she sees the young man continue on with his life unscathed. Giving up the baby for adoption seems to remove the problem, but often the young woman continues to be haunted by the fact that there is a child somewhere that should be hers and isn't. This causes her to feel cheated. Some women continually search crowds for a young face that looks like theirs.

The Post-Abortion Syndrome

As abortion has become legal, we have been told that the process is simple and it is a finite answer to a minor inconvenience. But is that

true? I think the answer will be obvious as you read the stories in this
chapter from women who have had abortions.

"But This Is Different"

Valerie grew up in a fine Christian home, went to college, and got
pregnant in her senior year. She went home and told her parents and
they all agreed that the only thing to do was have an abortion. If not, it
would hurt the family reputation, it would set a bad example for the teens
in the church, and it would keep Valerie from graduating and getting on
with life. They also told her that having a child outside of marriage would
hurt the cause of Christ. Even though the family was against abortion in
general, this was different. They all rationalized around the issue and
concluded "too many people would be hurt" if Valerie's pregnancy continued. Besides, abortion is legal; therefore there can't really be anything
wrong with it, right?

Valerie's mother comforted her by saying, "It won't be any worse than
having a tooth pulled, and once it's over we can put this whole thing
behind us and no one will ever know." The decision was made quickly
and the father, wise church elder that he was, concluded, "There really
is no other option."

Valerie accepted the family decision and went, as they suggested, to
another city to have this done. "We'll all feel better knowing that it
won't get out around town."

Valerie had learned to repress negative truth from early childhood
when her mother had taught her, "God only wants us to look on the good
things." When Valerie had stolen a doll from a friend, her mother explained, "You didn't steal it; you just borrowed it. When you're through
with it, just take it back." When she lied and was caught, her mother said
she had a creative imagination. Valerie had lived a charmed life, and this
momentary problem would soon be over, never to be mentioned again.
We can soon go back to our loving family life, she thought.

Valerie tried not to think of what she was going through as the abortion was performed; she quickly recovered, missing only two days of
classes. "See, dear, how strong you are?" her mother said with pride. The
abortion doctor had a charming personality, and Mother was thrilled
when he personally called to see how Valerie was recovering. "I don't
usually do this," he explained to Mother, "but Valerie seems like a very
special young lady."

"Oh, she is. You're right."

Dr. Somers called again right after Valerie graduated from college and asked her out for dinner. She was so flattered, and her mother was ecstatic. "I always thought you would marry a doctor."

The good doctor, however, wasn't interested in marriage. He was in the process of a costly divorce and was not about to try marriage again. But he was lonely, and Valerie's new job was near where he lived and his home was lovely and lavish.

Mother and Valerie discussed Dr. Somers's proposal that Valerie move in with him. She could have her own room, and surely Valerie was smart enough by now, having learned her lesson the hard way, to stay out of trouble. Mother had been quite critical of Valerie's friend Susie when she had moved in with Joe. But that was different. Joe lived in a cheap apartment, hadn't gone to college, and obviously had no future. Surely, sharing an elegant home with a doctor was different.

So with Mother's blessing, Valerie got free room and board from Dr. Somers. Of course there were some services that went along with the bargain, but as we all know, there's no such thing as a free lunch. Despite this convenient arrangement, Valerie didn't seem as happy about life as Mother thought she should be, so Mother frequently sent her cheerful little verses like "a merry heart doeth good."

Within two years it was obvious even to Mother that Valerie was depressed. Mother called a Christian counseling group and made an appointment. "My daughter has a problem," she said.

When they arrived, the counselor gave them a symptoms chart to fill out. Mother helped refresh Valerie's memory on her early-childhood diseases and worked through the list with her. At the end it had a place to add any situations that might possibly contribute to depression and Valerie whispered, "Do you think I should write in 'abortion'?"

"I don't know why you should," Mother said firmly. But remembering how agreeable she always was with Valerie, she added, "unless you want to."

When the counselor read over the list, she concluded that Valerie was a classic case of depression. "We'll be able to have you all well and happy within a month," the counselor chirped almost as cheerfully as Mother. This month of well-and-happy live-in therapy was to cost twenty-four thousand dollars.

As they were evaluating this commitment Valerie asked, "Does my abortion have anything to do with my depression?"

"It used to be a problem with some people," the counselor explained, "but now that it's so common, we don't deal with it." Mother was relieved.

Saving the Family's Reputation

Let's leave Valerie in Mother's capable hands for the moment and move on to Donna, who attends the same church. Donna's whole family had always been stalwart saints in this church; there had been no black sheep in their pasture. Donna had suffered with childhood arthritis but by her late-teenage years the symptoms had eased enough that she could live a near-normal life. She got engaged in her senior year in college; her mother was thrilled with Luke, who even had a biblical name. They planned to be married in the fall. Donna had always been the typical good girl but Luke told her it was all right to have sex if you were planning to get married. For all his worldly ways he wasn't all that smart, and Donna got pregnant. She couldn't believe this had happened to her.

She and Luke discussed what they should do about this unfortunate situation. The wedding was five months away and Donna knew the bridal gown her mother had already made wouldn't fit by then. Donna also knew her mother had grandiose plans for her only daughter's wedding in the fall and she didn't want to ruin it. Her whole life Donna had wanted to please her parents, and now she was in this terrible predicament.

Donna asked a close family friend for advice. "This would just kill your parents if they knew," the friend said. "They'd never recover if they thought their perfect daughter had to get married. It would be a blot on the whole family." The friend didn't think Donna had any option but to get an abortion.

The year was 1975, two years after Roe vs. Wade caused abortions to be legalized. No one knew anyone who had had one, but living in a big city made finding a doctor who would perform an abortion fairly easy. In fact, everything happened so smoothly the abortion and pregnancy really didn't seem like such a big deal after all.

She and Luke got married in the fall as Mother had planned, and they began their happily-ever-after life together. Right from the beginning, though, Luke told Donna she was not as exciting a love partner as some of the other women he'd had sex with in the past. While she knew she was no sex kitten, she was shocked that he'd had so many others and that he'd compare her with them. This put her in a frightening position, and instead of making her a better love partner, it made her worse.

Luke didn't want any children, but Donna did. She had to make up for the lost one. When she got pregnant Luke seemed supportive, but after the baby was born he didn't care much about the child. He often made Donna feel guilty by saying she was no longer his lover now that she was a mother. Luke never did bond with the child; he had affairs and ultimately walked out on Donna, bringing shame to her family.

As Donna grappled with the failure of her marriage, she began to examine herself in a realistic way. She had denied her situation for so long and tried to make everything look good for her family and church that getting honest with herself was like learning a new language. When people would ask, "How are you doing with the divorce?" her habit pattern caused her to say, "Oh, fine, no problem." To recover, she now had to stop herself, rewind her tape, and say, "This is very painful and I appreciate your concern."

It was at this point that Donna came to CLASS and heard about the personalities. This gave her a new tool to use; she realized that she was born to be a Choleric and had an innate desire to be in charge. But because she had two strong parents and a code of performance that fit their plan for her life, she had never had a chance to be in control of her own life. She had married a man who made her feel worthless and her situation was way out of control at this point. Donna realized she had been wearing a Phlegmatic mask all her life: agree with everyone, offer no opinions, take the easy way, and deny problems. Realizing the self-deceit she had lived with was the first step in her healing process.

The second step was to go back over her life bit by bit, writing her feelings from her heart to the Lord Jesus and asking Him to show her what to do next. When she got to the abortion, she began to sob. She thought it hadn't bothered her, but she suddenly saw clearly that she had chosen to kill her child in order to keep up her family's reputation. "How could I have done it," she cried out to the Lord, "and for such a phony reason?"

As Donna continued to seek the Lord daily, looking for truth she'd never known, she saw clearly for the first time why she had suffered with arthritis at such a young age. She had worked so hard at suppressing reality that her pain had come out in her body. She thought of the times she was nearly in a wheelchair and the years of taking strong drugs to alleviate her pain. She'd been treating the symptoms and not even looking for the cause.

In Donna's search for answers she found verses in Scripture that showed her she had violated God's principles and that she had to make it right. Not so that He would forgive her—He already had—but so that she could receive His peace. Donna came up with the following outline to use in sharing with others. She based it on the idea that God has given us His *principles* for our *protection* and His *provision* for our *purity* that we might know His *peace*.

Principles. There are certain basic fundamentals that God teaches us in His Word. When we violate one that we know better than to disobey, we suffer the consequences that range from guilt and shame to repeated violations to emotional and even physical pain. To begin healing we need to confess that we have disobeyed God's Word. In Donna's case she had sex outside of marriage and chose to have an abortion. Even though the world and the law allow both of these as a woman's right to control her own body, the consequences of guilt and pain still occur.

Protection. God gives us a conscience and a brain for our protection so that we will know instinctively what we should and should not do. Once we willfully do what we shouldn't, no matter how we rationalize around it, no matter how few people know, we step out from under God's protection. Donna realizes now that if she had refused to have sex with Luke he would have dropped her. That seemed like a negative at the time, but in God's protection of Donna, He wanted to save her, as a virgin, for some man who had not already had sex with many of her friends.

Provision. God does provide our needs when we are faithful to His principles. This does not mean that He will send each one of us a dashing prince in a white Corvette, but He will provide what is best for us. Donna realizes she gave up God's best by entering a sexual relationship when she knew better.

Purity. God didn't instruct us to avoid fornication and adultery as an arbitrary rule but for our own protection. (A visible example of disobedience is the AIDS epidemic spread by wanton disregard of God's laws.) Donna has suffered emotionally and physically for years because of the guilt she bears. Once she admitted her abortion as a sin, God washed her white as snow—pure once again. (See Psalm 51:7.) Now she says, "I reclaimed the ground I had given up to Satan and my Lord gave me back the territory."

Peace. We all want peace of mind, but not all of us realize that it is only the peace of the Lord that passes all understanding. (See Philippians 4:7.) God is not a big bad bully enjoying our pain and wanting to make us worse. He is a benefactor who wants the best for His children. He is the only one who can give us peace even in adverse circumstances, but we have to do our part. We need to reprogram and renew our minds. We need to get rid of the lies we've believed and get honest with ourselves and our Lord. We may also need to go to others and confess what we've done if it relates to them. By discussing the situation honestly we may be used to bring peace to others who were involved in or related to the problem. Donna went to her mother and father and told them what had happened. At this point they reflected, "Why didn't you tell us then?" Donna asked, "How would you have felt about it?" They admitted it would have been difficult. And it is still difficult; it is often unpleasant to face the truth.

By sharing with her parents, Donna was freed to talk about her abortion openly. Not to air her dirty laundry in public but to let others who are still suffering know that there is hope. Donna gave this testimony in her church, and it has been replayed on radio programs in this country and in New Zealand. Now we rejoin Valerie's story. It was when Donna shared her experiences in church that Valerie's mother heard her and came to talk with her later.

By that time Valerie was deeply depressed and without hope because she could not afford the month of therapy that had been prescribed and she did not understand why she was depressed. She had her degree, a promising career, and Dr. Somers's great house to live in. Valerie also had a lifelong ability to rationalize around unpleasant circumstances and deny negative reality.

When Valerie met Donna it was like meeting her emotional twin. Valerie couldn't believe someone could understand her pain and yet not condemn her. Sitting with Valerie, Donna went through the steps of her outline, "God has given us His *principles* for our *protection* and His *provision* for our *purity* that we might know His *peace*." When she asked what Valerie had done to violate God's principles and have Him remove His protection, Valerie cried, "It's the abortion." Even though the counselor had told her the abortion was "no big deal," Valerie knew in her heart it was wrong.

When they got to the part about purity, Valerie asked, "Do you think that my living with a man I'm not married to could be part of my problem?" Donna hid her smile at the obvious answer and replied gently, "That could have something to do with it."

Both Donna and Valerie started out as Christian teenagers who didn't ever expect to get in trouble. When they got pregnant, they each had an abortion to save their families' reputation. Each one thought this simple, legal procedure would free them from embarrassing consequences but instead it caused them to have long-range depression along with unexplainable burdens of guilt and shame.

Symptoms of Post-Abortion Syndrome

As Donna has worked through her own recovery and become a friend and counselor to other girls in need, she has studied the clinical subject now called post-abortion syndrome. She speaks to women's groups, letting them know that abortion may be legal but it can cause a lifetime of emotional pain.

Is there any reason for us fine Christian women to wake up to this problem? Or do we think it always happens to someone else? Do we teach our daughters that the choice should be made *before* getting pregnant, not after?

Would we be like Valerie's mother and rush our daughter off to an abortion clinic? Do we believe it's a simple procedure with no lasting effects? Would we be against abortion until it hits home?

The rapid increase in abortions over the last twenty years has more to do with the elimination of moral restraints than any other reason. With freedom of choice to do what we will with our bodies, we have created a whole generation of post-abortion women who are suffering emotionally and don't know why.

At the time, many women feel guilt, remorse, and anguish over their decision to have an abortion, but many don't get hit with symptoms until ten years later. Even though having an abortion today is as common as catching a quick burger while driving to your desired destination, the feelings of suppressed guilt often fester inside, waiting for an excuse to come forth, producing disappointment, depression, or divorce and triggering self-condemnation. The abortion may have bothered them a little at first, but with time they became desensitized to what really happened; they tried to forget the pregnancy ever existed.

This is called "psychological numbing," and it often occurs in reaction to a highly stressful event. In order to protect their mental stability, many women must rationalize the need for an abortion and therefore repress any initial feelings of guilt. As a result, emotional reactions to abortion are delayed, sometimes for as long as five to ten years.[1]

Statistics show that 1.6 million abortions are performed in the United States each year and fewer than 1 percent are due to rape or incest. One-third of all abortions are performed on teenagers, usually without parental knowledge or consent.[2] It is estimated that more than 46 percent of American women will have had at least one abortion by the time they are forty-five. These women are faced with a tremendous amount of fear, embarrassment, and anxiety about their unwanted pregnancy, and they seek fast solutions to their dilemma. Women are afraid of what their families will think of them when the pregnancy is revealed. Will they be exiled from their church? What will their friends say? Will everyone desert them in their time of need? Will they lose their job and control of their lives?

Since abortion is legally and socially sanctioned, it is the choice one in every four women make,[3] even if it means violating her morals to do so. Immediately after the procedure the women will usually feel relief that the crisis is over. But eventually any struggle they felt prior to the abortion will resurface, at which point most women will question or regret their decision. In many cases, this may be prompted by their learning more about fetal development or by their change in moral perspective. Some women may develop destructive ways to protect themselves from these uncomfortable and haunting feelings that derive from their abortion. A Focus on the Family booklet shows there is an alarming and dramatic increase in the number of women with post-abortion syndrome. Their defense mechanisms include rationalization, repression, and compensation.[4]

Rationalization. This is a convenient ability of the mind to let us think what's wrong really isn't. In post-abortion syndrome, women spend time discovering well-founded reasons or logical explanations or justifications for having had the abortion.

Repression. This is a way of blocking out or stuffing any memories of the painful emotions surrounding the abortion. When symptoms arise years later, very few women connect them with the past abortion.

Compensation. Women make up for the loss caused by abortion by overachieving or working extremely hard in the hopes that keeping busy will keep them from facing the truth. Many go into Christian or social services, hoping to relieve their guilt by helping others.

Like survivors of rape or incest most women who have had abortions experience certain symptoms at one time or another. These symptoms, described below, may not necessarily appear at the same time, and the woman may not experience all of them. The reason for reviewing these symptoms here is to help you, your daughter, or your friend find the source of the pain instead of being treated for the wrong problem as Valerie was. If three or more of the following symptoms describe what you are feeling, you may be experiencing post-abortion syndrome.

1. Self-condemnation. Even if you have repressed the memory, you still have an underlying feeling of low worth and a nagging question of *What's wrong with me?* If the memory is clear this question often moves to *How could I have done it? I must be a terrible person. Will God ever forgive me?* When bad things happen to you, you feel you deserve them. You pick up the typical victim-style thinking: *Everything that goes wrong is my fault.*

2. Depression. A little black cloud travels with you and you see no silver lining. The depression increases in intensity, and sometimes you are shocked to hear yourself say, "I guess I'll kill myself." *Where did that come from?* you wonder. You have occasional periods of relief when you proclaim yourself happy. Then the sight of a baby-food jar in the supermarket brings the cloud back. You may have sought help for depression and been given drugs to lift your spirits.

3. Anger. The woman who has had an abortion has an abundance of anger, much of it misplaced. If this is your situation, you may be mad at yourself for allowing this to have happened in the first place. You're mad at him ("He told me he loved me, but where was he when I needed him?") You're mad at your parents, even though they had nothing to do with it; you're doubly angry if one parent made you get the abortion. You may be mad at whoever counseled you to do this and even the doctor who performed the abortion. This anger, often unexplainable, eats away at you and may cause people to pull away from you, increasing your depression.

4. Rejection. Because you rejected your unborn child by having an abortion, you may have deep feelings of rejection that suddenly well up in you. If a parent ever did anything to make you feel rejected, these acts, possibly insignificant in the grand scheme of life, may come surging up and you may find yourself needing affirmations from your mother that you are acceptable. If your anger pushes your mother away to another sibling, you may sink into hopelessness, believing, *Mother has never really loved me.* The resulting sibling rivalry may cause further family rifts that no one understands.

5. Fear. "What if someone finds out?" "My mother would die." "The church would reject me." The fear that your dark secret will be discovered creates duplicity in your hurting life, causing you to cover up things that don't need to be hidden. Unintentionally, you develop a look of fear.

6. Sleeplessness. This problem may not manifest itself for years until triggered by such flashes as, *he'd be starting first grade* or *she'd be graduating.* This late grieving may cause added guilt and sleeplessness.

7. Fear of losing control. Although abortion proponents preach of free choice and control of your own body, the opposite is apt to happen if you have an abortion. Somehow you begin to feel that the abortion caused you to be out of control and you fear ever letting anything get out of control again. If you are a Choleric personality to start with, this thought will amplify your need for control. You will have a close-to-compulsive need to keep everything tightly in line and you may be apt to snap at people who offer their own opinions.

8. Physical problems. When you suppress your emotions and refuse to look at your problems, the pain ultimately comes out somewhere else. It's as if you filled a wooden barrel with liquid and put pressure on it. When enough force comes to bear on it the barrel either bursts or the fluid starts seeping through the cracks. It's the same with humans. Given enough pressure we either blow up or the pain comes out in a different form such as physical problems.

9. Suppressed feelings. When you work hard to shut down your guilty feelings, over the years you become quite good at it. At first it seems like a positive thing not to react to daily traumas, but after a while you become numb, believing, "I never want to feel pain again." This coldness can affect your marriage and keep others from becoming close to you. They sense a wall around you. No one enjoys trying to relate to a cold, unfeeling statue.

10. Dislike of babies. If you have terminated a pregnancy you may feel ill at ease around pregnant women. Perhaps you tend to make derogatory remarks about impending motherhood and avoid holding babies or attending baby showers. You may cry easily at TV stories involving children. You may make excuses for why you don't want to have a baby yourself. If you do have children you may alternate between overattention to one and cold indifference to another, setting them up for sibling rivalry. However, be aware that some women swing totally in the other direction and reach out for every baby they see, hoping to fill the maternal void inside.

It is always important to review all the symptoms for any problem, physical or emotional, and not build a case on only one or two signs. But if, when you read this list, you see yourself or your daughter clearly and the Lord puts a spotlight on an abortion one of you had in the past, it may be time for you to face the issue head-on.

What Can You Do about It Now?

As you begin your recovery from post-abortion syndrome, you may need to spend some time in prayerful self-examination. The following suggestions may be helpful as you move through the recovery process:

Write down every symptom you have from the previous list. Add any others such as eating disorders or habits you are ashamed of. Ask the Lord to show you the source of your troubles. Be aware that all of the symptoms described here can manifest themselves as adult symptoms of childhood abuse. Read *Freeing Your Mind from Memories That Bind* for more understanding. If as you have read this chapter you see your own life spread before you, it is time to begin your healing process. If it describes someone else, perhaps you can be her instrument for healing.

Reread the steps that Donna went through (page 167) and apply them to your life.

Start a prayer journal in which you write to the Lord daily and express your true feelings of guilt and blame. Keep your prayer book hidden so you can be honest with God and not fear the judgment of others.

Begin a study of the book of Psalms. Commiserate with David as he cries out to the Lord for forgiveness and healing. You may have a whole new appreciation for David when you realize your similarities.

Accept the memory of your abortion, even if you've suppressed it. The Lord will bring it back clearly when you are ready and willing to ask. Walk yourself through it again, feeling the pain. This will release your pent-up emotions.

Cry if you feel like it. God tells us He keeps our tears in a bottle because they are so precious to Him.

Grieve in whatever way is comfortable for you. Sanguines may need some friends to cry with them. Melancholies will probably want to be alone. Whatever it takes, grieve over the death of what might have been.

Name the baby if you would feel better about it. Donna spent time with her son explaining to him that he would have had a sister but that she had had an abortion. They discussed the age the sister would have been and together they named her.

Have a funeral to bring this guilt to a close if you would be comfortable doing so. This does not need to be a public affair. It could be you alone, reading Scripture and praising the Lord for His forgiveness.

Pray through your list of symptoms and confess them one by one. Perhaps in this prayer you would say, "Lord Jesus, I see now why I have been so angry. Take this anger from me. Forgive me. Heal me. I love You, Lord, and thank You that You give grace to those of us who have sinned against Your laws."

Forgive those you've been angry at. This act alone will open you up to being able to restore relationships.

Join or start a support group for others in similar circumstances. Many times knowing you aren't alone is a great step toward healing.

Help others. As you begin to heal and can see that your symptoms are lessening, be open to sharing with others. You don't have to be a platform speaker or hunt around for sad cases. When you are ready, the Lord will drop people on your doorstep. Donna says she can hardly believe the number of women in her church who have come forward, seeking her help.

Remember God is in the restoration business. He forgives, loves, protects, and renews the mind. "Be ye transformed by the renewing of your mind" (Rom. 12:2). (Also see Ephesians 4:22 and 23.)

Recapture your youth. Many women who have had abortions feel as if they lost their youth when suddenly they went from being a child to having the burdens and blame of an adult. The fun and joy of youth were wiped out; yet there is the hope of loving life again. Psalm 103 tells us God forgives us, heals us, redeems us from destruction, crowns us with lovingkindness and mercy, and satisfies us with good things, "so that thy youth is renewed like the eagle's" (v. 5).

Receiving God's Grace in a Personal Way

Stephanie, a tanned California blonde, walked up to our book table. When I complimented her on her beauty and confidence she looked back at me in quick amazement as tears came to her eyes. She said with a real lift in her voice, "You have made my day." I sensed there was a whole volume of meaning behind her words. Later, when we had a chance to visit, she asked me to tell her about the new book I was working on. When I said the title was *Wake Up, Women!*, she said, "I have something I'd like to share, especially with girls my age. It might help them wake up before they make the same mistake I did."

Stephanie was a very mature twenty-five-year-old and held a position of importance on the staff of a very large, well-known church. She began by telling me some of her background, including her parents' divorce when she was two. Her mother had remarried when Stephanie was six, at which time her real dad's sparse visits completely stopped. Her stepdad was not affectionate; nor was he available to her. In essence she had been both physically and emotionally abandoned by any father figure in her life. So when Stephanie got into high school and college, if a young man had any physical contact with her, she thought that meant he must love her. This led to sex and vows of "I love you." When she became pregnant at age eighteen all she could think of was how to fix it. She opted for an abortion and decided not to marry the young man. In fact, he made a fast exit from her life.

For four years she totally numbed out her feelings and thought she was doing just fine. Then she fell into a severe depression; she stopped functioning altogether and was sleeping all the time. She said, "I knew I couldn't retrieve my child, but neither could I retrieve my innocence."

She was diagnosed with post traumatic stress disorder and got into some intensive counseling that helped her confront her past trauma. She was led through some steps similar to those we just listed (see pages 173–175) and as she dealt honestly with her past, her depression lifted. She told me, "I received and experienced God's grace in a very real and personal way."

Stephanie had grown up in a Christian home. Jesus was no stranger to her, but she now had to ask Him to forgive her and help her learn to live with a choice she had made and go on with her life. I asked her how she was doing that. Stephanie was honest with me as she admitted, "At times I still have feelings of sadness and shame. Then I pray." Sometimes because she has not yet found a husband, she feels like God is punishing her. But she has chosen to surround herself with friends who have been very nurturing and have helped her feel safe and express her feelings.

I asked her what she had learned from this that she would like to share. She answered with two important lessons:

"First, my security doesn't lie in other people. It's within me. Someone else can't tell me I'm OK until I believe it myself," she said. "And second, God's 'don'ts' are because He loves me—not to punish me."

Stephanie truly believes that if God denies us in one area He has planned something better for us in another area. She went on, "Now I know God has very real and practical reasons to deny singles sex outside of marriage. It's for our own protection."

I said to Stephanie, "I feel that you know God's forgiveness now."

She said, "Yes, I feel He has healed me and allowed me to start over again."

Then she added, "I have a message for the women who read your book: Think, think, think. Look at the consequences. Count the cost! There are consequences to every choice we make. Wake up, women, wake up!"

Before we close this chapter about the long-range effects of abortion, one postscript is necessary: It is essential that we support the girl who chooses not to have an abortion and goes through the unplanned pregnancy. Amazingly, some of us Christians would find it easier if these girls would quietly have abortions and not let us know about it. Don't we sometimes feel a little awkward when that single girl in our Sunday school class shows up obviously pregnant? Yet she has chosen the better way. We should affirm her in that decision.

One such girl told me that the response of the people in her church was so judgmental that she wished she had gone for an abortion. "I was looked upon as the fallen woman while my sister who had an abortion that no one knew about was being praised."

Doing the right thing can be difficult, especially when those you turn to for support let you down. When Nora found out she was pregnant she told the future father, and he was angry at her for letting this happen. Within the week his mother appeared to talk with Nora, graciously offering to help pay for the abortion. When Nora said that as a Christian she wouldn't have one, the woman got angry and told her if she wouldn't have an abortion she could expect no help from them. She finally gave up pleading with Nora, washed her hands of the whole unfortunate situation, and left, never to be heard from again. Neither the young man nor his mother have even checked to see if the baby was born or what happened to it.

Fred and I spent the afternoon of Christmas Eve with Nora. She was considering putting the baby up for adoption, but she wanted our advice. We wouldn't tell her what to do, but we assured her if she kept the baby we would serve as grandparents and help her financially. When Elizabeth was born, we all fell in love with her, and Nora is so proud of her adorable little girl.

The pregnancy and humiliation weren't easy for Nora, and she knows it was not God's will for her to have sex outside of marriage. She also knows that God redeems the fallen and makes beauty out of ashes.

Elizabeth is beautiful.

12

I'll Pray about It

All good Christian women believe in prayer. How frightening it would be to think there was no one up there to call on in time of need! Yet some of us have a cloudy view of a God afar off and a Jesus who is somehow untouchable. When we hear of someone who has a "prayer life," we feel guilty over our "prayer minute." When there's a prayer meeting at church with no refreshments, we rush to the mall instead for some urgent item. When we tell a friend, "I'll pray about it," do we?

Oswald Chambers wrote: "Never say you will pray about a thing; *pray about it.* Our Lord's teaching about prayer is so amazingly simple but at the same time so amazingly profound that we are apt to miss His meaning. The danger is to water down what Jesus says about prayer and make it mean something more like common sense; if it were only common sense, it was not worth His while to say it."[1]

Does Prayer Really Work?

Let's wake up and be honest. We don't really pray that much. We believe in it, but does it really work? Is it worth the time and effort when we've seldom seen actual results? Does it make sense?

In the last few years Fred and I have included some lessons on written prayer in our CLASS and Promise of Healing seminars. We teach people to write a letter to Jesus each day and get acquainted with Him.

From this simple segment in our seminars we have received many testimonies of changed lives when people start to pray sincerely. Writing forces us to concentrate on what we're doing instead of allowing our minds to wander to our grocery lists or the TV schedule. Writing to Jesus makes us think about Him as a real person who cares about us. Writing keeps us accountable each day. Either we wrote in our notebook or we didn't. We can't just sort of pray as we weave through traffic.

We also teach "listening prayer" by encouraging the participants to write out a question to the Lord and then record everything that comes to their minds. As we ask them to share, we are amazed at what God has said to individuals, giving custom-tailored answers that affirm the power of God.

Achieving Two-Way Communication with God

Marilyn Heavilin teaches the following five steps to help CLASS participants begin to develop a pattern of two-way communication with God.[2] Consider adapting these steps for use during your prayer time:

Affection. Many times because of damage in our childhood, the hardest words for us to receive from the Lord are "I love you." Listen quietly. If the first words you hear are words of condemnation, write them down in your notebook, and then write across those words, "These words are a lie! Romans 8:1 states, 'There is therefore now no condemnation to them which are in Christ Jesus, who walk not after the flesh, but after the Spirit.'"

Keep listening until you hear that still, small voice whisper, "I love you!" Then write it down and thank Jesus for His everlasting love.

Reflection. Often we get in the middle of a mess and we think, *How in the world will I ever get out of this?* In Deuteronomy 5:6 the Lord states, in essence, "Remember that you were slaves in Egypt and that the Lord your God brought you out of there with a mighty hand and an outstretched arm."

Take time to reflect on the Egypts God has brought you out of and write them down. Thank God for rescuing you then, and thank Him for how He is going to rescue you this time. Write down the thoughts He gives you.

Correction. First we need to examine ourselves to see if there is something we need to confess, someone we need to forgive, or someone we need to ask to forgive us. Also, this is a time when we can ask God if He wants to change our perspective on something. This could be a current situation or something that happened to us in our childhood. As God brings a memory to our minds, we can invite Him into the scene and ask Him to give us His perspective. In your prayer time, write down what the Lord shows you. "Behold, thou desirest truth in the inward parts: and in the hidden part thou shalt make me to know wisdom" (Ps. 51:6).

Direction. "I will instruct thee and teach thee in the way which thou shalt go; I will guide thee with mine eye" (Ps. 32:8). As we learn to ask the Lord specific questions, He will give us specific answers. "Your teachers will be hidden no more; with your own eyes you will see them. Whether you turn to the right or to the left, your ears will hear a voice behind you, saying, 'This is the way; walk in it'" (Isa. 30:20–21 NIV).

Inspection. We must always compare what we hear with Scripture. Scripture is the final and true authority for the Christian, so if what we hear contradicts Scripture, we should ignore what we hear and hang on to Scripture. Job 12:11 states, "Does not the ear test words as the tongue tastes food?" (NIV). It is also wise to consult with other Christians if there is any question about the validity of what we have heard. "Where no counsel is, the people fall; but in the multitude of counsellors there is safety" (Prov. 11:14).

Vera, the woman described in chapter 7 who lost her son when she fled without him from an abusive husband, attended one of the CLASS sessions when Marilyn presented this prayer message. Afterward Vera wrote,

> I've realized over the years that I have a lot to share but have never been able to get it out. I've felt blocked . . . nothing seemed to flow. I chalked it up to "God's timing." During the guided prayer time led by Marilyn Heavilin last Wednesday afternoon, during the time of "correction" when Marilyn asked us to ask the Lord to show us His view of us and give us a correct view of ourselves, I remembered the time twenty-five years ago when my ex-husband tried to strangle me. He stopped just short of killing me. In the prayer time, the Lord was with me and in my mind I could see Him take my ex-husband's fingers from around my neck! It wasn't until this morning that I realized why, at long last, I've finally been able to sit down, pull together thoughts on what to speak about, and begin writing brief summaries and an information sheet. I attribute this directly to the healing of that memory during the CLASS prayer time.
>
> Please ask the staff to pray for me that the Lord will use all that's now released after being "strangled off" for so long and

that God's creativity will flow through me to be a source of healing in the lives of others. Praise to His name! Now I can dare to dream of being a speaker for Him.

Vera now has a deep, two-way prayer life. As God gave her a quick answer to her concerns, He also healed her memory and set her free.

Seeing the World through God's Eyes

Becky also found great meaning in a CLASS prayer message. She was having trouble relating to her teenage son and during the section on correction she asked the Lord to let her see her son as He sees him, not from her own point of view. Immediately she saw her son as a lonely boy without real friends. "He was standing on a beach, looking out to sea, and I began to cry for him. I'd never seen him that way before and I began to pray in earnest that I could reach out to him, that I could have a new understanding instead of a critical spirit, and that he would get a real friend. I can hardly believe how quickly the Lord answered me when I asked to be able to relate to my son. I have a much better relationship with him now that I am in tune to his needs, and as a bonus God gave my son a special friend. I no longer talk about prayer, I pray."

Tapping into the Power of Prayer

One evening after a CLASS seminar Monica shared with our staff how much she had enjoyed CLASS and how restful it had been for her. Since CLASS is very intense training, conferees seldom use the word *restful* in describing the seminar. So we all laughed, and I commented, "Your life must really be hectic for CLASS to seem restful."

Monica smiled and said, "hectic is an understatement. My husband has just sued me for divorce and he is doing everything he can to make my life a hell on earth."

Monica's husband of more than twenty years had apparently been planning the divorce for quite some time. He had managed to shift all their finances to his control, and he had even turned in a change of address for Monica at the post office so he would receive all of her mail, apparently to make sure she had no financial holdings he hadn't claimed yet.

Monica told how he was spreading lies about her to ruin her reputation and make things look better for him in court. She noted that everything about him seemed very dark and secretive. Marilyn suggested that Monica rid her house of anything that belonged to this man and walk through her house praying, "In the name of Jesus, I demand that everything evil leave this house. I commit this house and everything in it to holiness."

Marilyn then also suggested that as Monica prepared for court she should pray that only the truth would be spoken. If her husband began to speak anything but the truth, she should pray that God would confuse his words so they would be completely ineffective.

Later Monica wrote me and said that's exactly what happened. Her husband had chosen to represent himself in court, and twice as he began to make accusations against her, his words became confused and finally, in utter frustration, he stopped talking.

God gave the power of prayer equally to men and to women, and in this situation Monica learned that when you have God and prayer on your side, there's no such thing as helplessness.

Praying with Fervor and Faith

In a head-on collision with a van Linda was thrown out the door of her car; she remembers the feeling of flying through the air and landing in a ditch. Her husband, Ron, who was asleep on the passenger side, was hurled through the windshield and landed face-down in a deep mud puddle. Their car was so totally destroyed that the police didn't think anyone could have escaped alive. They found Ron first and pulled his face out of the mud so he could breathe. Then the police searched around, eventually finding Linda, who was praying silently in the ditch, unable to make a sound. As she told me about her plight she said, "The first thing I had to do was accept the reality that I was in a ditch and that I was alive. I couldn't see and I couldn't move, but I knew I was alive."

By the time Linda arrived at the hospital her eyes were swollen shut. One eye was pushed back into her head behind shattered facial bones. Upon examining Linda, the doctors found several breaks in her back and one leg so smashed that the bones were in splinters. Linda was put in a body cast and leg casts and is still awaiting eye surgery. Her pain is beyond anything she could have imagined, and she can barely see through a slit in her good eye.

Through this experience Linda has learned to pray with fervor and faith believing that the Lord is going to restore her health in His time. "He must have something great in mind for me or He wouldn't have kept me alive," she told me by phone. "It's a miracle that both Ron and I lived through what should have killed us."

When I asked Linda how she was getting through each day she explained that when she wakes each morning, she reestablishes the reality of her situation. She doesn't deny her pain or cry over it; she accepts where she is and then prays to move on.

"What has helped me the most is setting a realistic goal for each day," Linda said. "One day it's to move my right big toe, the next day to flex my wrist. I write the goal in big print on a piece of paper and when my mind wanders because of the medication, I pick up the paper and reread my goal."

Each day Linda forces herself to get in the wheelchair and move to a new spot so she doesn't get overwhelmed with the bleakness of one hospital room. "It's a lot easier to just lie there, but I would get depressed if I couldn't see some people. Some days I sit near the front door and watch the people—people wearing real clothes."

Linda started writing her prayers and keeping a journal of her feelings as soon as she could use her wrist. She can't read what she's writing, but she knows in the future, after the two scheduled eye surgeries, she will be glad she forced herself to record these difficult days and write to the Lord.

What can those of us who are not in a body cast, who are not in physical pain, who are not facing surgery, learn from Linda?

1. Assess the situation realistically. We should not deny we have problems or weep and wail as if we were chosen by God to suffer like Job. We must put our pain in perspective and look at our situation as God sees it.

Earlier I described Becky, who was having trouble relating to her teenage son. Just as Becky prayed, "Show me my son from Your point of view, Lord" we must all seek God's perspective of our circumstances.

2. Set a reachable goal each day. When we are discouraged or depressed, things tend to seem impossible. We look at the whole world and know we are unable to right the wrongs or fight the foes. It's all too much for us to face. But could we determine to achieve one small feat a day, wiggle a toe, flex a wrist, get dressed, clean a closet? Could we write it down on a piece of paper and look at it now and then? Can we keep a positive focus on at least one potential? If Linda can scrawl out a goal and peer at it through a slit couldn't we make some strides ourselves?

3. Pray when it's not an emergency. Linda prayed in the ditch when she thought life was over, but she also prays each day in a heartfelt cry to the Lord who saved her. An emergency prayer now and then is acceptable to the Lord as long as He knows who we are. It's a little late to get acquainted. Linda is writing her prayers each day even though the process is painful. She knows she needs to stay in close touch with her Lord.

4. Get a new look on life. When we get depressed, sometimes over trivial problems, we find it easier to stay in bed and not get dressed, but this lack of drive makes us feel worse about ourselves. If Linda can sit alone in a wheelchair and move herself from one spot to another, can't we "lift up our eyes to the hills from whence cometh our help"? Can't we move on and encourage someone else, as Linda does?

5. Ask a question of the Lord and listen. Linda wonders what God has in mind for her since He spared her life. She's waiting patiently for His answer. When Vera asked the Lord why she wasn't making progress, He showed her the scene of her ex-husband choking her. She had to release both him and the memory so she could be free in turn to help others. As we'll see in the next story, Katie's life has also been changed by prayer.

Experiencing Personal Healing

When I first met Katie she had come to CLASS to improve her writing and speaking skills. She already was a leader among the women in her denomination, but she knew there was something missing in her ministry. Katie was sincere in her search and open to my suggestions. First, we looked at her personality strengths and weaknesses and saw that her Choleric need to be in control and make decisions was too strong for those she was hoping to inspire. Katie agreed to pray that the Lord would soften her nature and make her less adamant in her statements. She also asked that He would show her any other areas in her life where adjustments were needed.

It is amazing that when we genuinely want to know, pray believing God can speak to us, and then listen for His answer, He will respond. Katie heard from the Lord that she needed to examine her childhood hurts and pray through them. She was to cease denying the presence of her pain and get real.

If the Lord said that to you, would you act upon it? Katie did. Over several years I've observed the changes in her. I've seen her personality soften, her determination mellow, her marriage improve, her search reach conclusions, and her training succeed. Because she was willing to ask the Lord about His will for her life and then listen to His answers, Katie is a new person today, and she enjoys a deeper relationship with her Lord.

Katie wrote me on New Year's Day 1992, saying:

> This year holds within its days many goals—personal and professional. However, I have only one New Year's Resolution: completion of the cycle of training as a Christian leader and speaker, using the lessons you have taught me.

Because you taught me to use words more effectively, my writing has improved and my outlines for public presentations come quickly (and have a better chance of being remembered by my audiences). You have given me healing information to foster hope, and I have experienced much personal healing because I've been willing to see my past pain and drop the present pretense.

When I first met you, Florence, I had pain in my eyes and in my life. Now, due to much prayer, trust in the One who lets no memory emerge before its time, and my willingness to let the river of life flow at its own pace—without my trying to cross its current, swim upstream, or move too fast ahead of the flow—I can rest in the Lord. While I have no complete picture of what this training at CLASS means for the future, it is enough to have completed it. Thanks!

Prayers of Intercession

Tricia has two daughters who have been on drugs, and she has had to learn unconditional love in each situation. She has been involved in their lives through arrests, court cases, forced counseling, and twelve-step programs.

After one of her daughters was placed on house arrest for two weeks, God showed Tricia she needed to take a new approach in her own personal devotional time and in her prayers for her daughter. Although she had been a Christian for many years, she had never read all of the Bible, so Tricia decided to read through the Scriptures using a one-year Bible. Each day after she read the Scripture passages, she wrote in her journal, noting the truths from Scripture that pertained to her daughter; then she spent as much time as she could in prayer. She also began using the book *Praying God's Will for My Daughter* by Lee Roberts in which he provides hundreds of Scriptures that parents can pray over their family members.[3] Often Tricia would spend hours simply praying Scripture, inserting her daughter's name where appropriate.

We had Tricia speak at a Promise of Healing Workshop and tell about her daily prayer time. She explained how prayer helped her change her attitude from blame and anger to power and joy, even in less-than-ideal circumstances. Her situation is different from the physical trauma Linda suffered in the car crash, but her process is the same. Each day she faces the reality of her family problems. She doesn't lie about them or deny them. She is honest with God and others. She has set a daily goal of spending time with God in prayer whether or not there is a current emergency. Tricia is not wallowing in self-pity; instead she is teaching workshops to other mothers who are in similar circumstances.

Within four months of her daughter's house arrest, Tricia's daughter had renounced her lifestyle of drug use and made her peace with God. At the time of this writing the daughter has been completely drug free for five months, is attending church regularly, and has a good relationship with her family. As Tricia spent time in prayer she learned how to model Christ to her daughter, and she now understands that God's Word is truly the sword of the Spirit. In Tricia's words, "I have learned to glance at my circumstances and gaze at God."

We won't know until we get to heaven why we can do our best and still have our children go astray, but we can't waste our time on self-pity. We must come to our Lord and Savior daily and wake up to the power available to us when we take the time to ask.

Our Goal: To Become Like Christ

In Philippians 3:10 Paul sums up the aim of the Christian life: "All I want is to know Christ and to experience the power of his resurrection, to share in his sufferings and become like him" (TEV).

For those of us who are functioning as believing Christians and yet not experiencing the excitement of a daily walk with the Lord, perhaps it's time to wake up and get serious about our commitment. Like Paul, we need to get to know Christ. Paul had a passion to spend time with Jesus each day. He didn't wait until he was drowning in a shipwreck or hanging by a thread in a basket to call out to the Lord. Paul faced reality every day and yet was able to focus on the Lord and get to know Him intimately. How do we get to know someone? We have to spend time with him or her.

If we look out one morning and see a moving van unloading next door, we instantly get curious. We peer through the curtains and make judgments on our new neighbors based on their furniture, their looks, their children, and even their dog. We have assessed their status before we've even met them, but we don't really know them. How can we get to know them? We have to go next door and introduce ourselves. We have to spend time with them and get acquainted. How do we get to know Jesus? We must spend time with Him in daily prayer and Bible study. How many of us come to Him when it's not an emergency? Are there some of us who just peek at Jesus through the curtain now and then to make sure He's still there? Do we have no more than a windowsill relationship with our Lord?

Paul not only spent time with Him, but he felt His power. You can't feel the power of someone you don't spend time with or you are estranged from. Yet all of us know someone who makes us feel good, who lifts us up when we're together. That's what Jesus wants to do with those of us who care to get acquainted. Are some of us hoping to pick up the power while sitting next door?

Paul was willing to share in the sufferings of others because he knew his Jesus in a personal way, and his single aim was to become like Him. Even though human nature sends so many of us scurrying in the opposite direction to look out a different window with a better view we need to discipline ourselves to look straight up to Jesus.

In this chapter we've seen several women who learned to do that by developing two-way communication with the Lord. The results have brought new strength, new courage, and new joy to their lives:

• Vera is free to get to know Jesus in a closer way and free of the anger and fear that filled her marriage to an abusive husband. She's no longer looking at the Lord through the curtain but face-to-face.

• Becky knows the power of the Lord to reveal her teenage son's needs in a clear scene with no curtains to confuse her.

• Monica has learned that God can confound the words of the wicked, as He did when she prayed for truth in the courtroom.

• Linda says she'll never complain about minor problems ever again. As she's been lying in constant pain recovering from the devastating car crash, she has spent time with Jesus and experienced His power. Now she's anxious to get well so she can share her experience to ease the sufferings of others. Only those of us who have come through traumatic situations seem to have a heart for those in pain.

• Katie has heeded the Lord's answers to her questions and by doing so has become a new person, an instrument of His love as she continues her work in His ministry.

• Tricia still prays in intercession for her daughter, asking God to give the girl the strength to keep away from her former drug-dominated life. As Tricia spends time with Jesus each day she feels His power to lift her up, and she is willing to share what she's learned to help in the suffering of others.

Scripture tells us that when we desire to know Jesus, get so close that we feel His power, and are willing to share in sufferings instead of turning the other way, we will ultimately become like Him.

We women need to stop playing church and wake up to the power available to us when we genuinely care to know Jesus. Let's not say, "I'll pray about it." Let's pray!

APPENDIX A

A Comparison of
Three Views

	WORLD VIEW	BALANCED CHRISTIAN VIEW	LEGALISTIC VIEW
WOMEN'S PLACE	All women should be out in the workplace fulfilling their potential. They should dress for success and keep up with the latest trends.	Intelligent women need to evaluate their situation. Family comes first but single mothers or those in debt may need to work at least part-time. They should dress suitably for the occasion	All women should be at home with their children. They should dress modestly, wear high-necked blouses, avoid make-up, and eliminate jewelry.
MEN	Men are inferior and often abusive. Don't let them get the best of you. Fight your way to the top and show them who's boss.	Even well-meaning men don't get it at times. We need to make ourselves clear and help them understand us.	Men are superior and God speaks through men to their wives, who must be quiet and obedient.
EMOTIONAL NEEDS	Think of yourself first. It's a dog-eat-dog world. If you don't watch out for yourself, who will?	We all have emotional needs and we should prayerfully find the source of our pain so we can bring it to the Lord for healing.	If you were really a Christian, you wouldn't have any emotional needs. God would have filled them all.
DYSFUNCTION	Wallow in your miseries. Repeat your problems to all. There can't be a God or this wouldn't have happened to you.	Not all families are perfect but we need to look at the situation honestly, take human steps to improve our situation, and know that God won't allow us to suffer more than we can bear (1 Cor. 10:13).	Deny any problems. Pretend you are happy. Don't let any-one know if you are hurt. God is testing your patience and building your character.

	WORLD VIEW	BALANCED CHRISTIAN VIEW	LEGALISTIC VIEW
MONEY MATTERS	Don't let him get his hands on your money. You earned it and you deserve to spend it whatever way you want. Take charge of the money as quickly as possible.	Decide together who has the time and ability to handle the family finances. Keep in touch and make major decisions and purchases in unity. Know where all the important papers are.	Only men should handle money. They should make all the decisions because God has appointed them to be ruler of the family. Trust your husband to do the right thing.
HUSBAND'S ACCOUNTABILITY	Men can't be trusted. Watch him like a hawk. Check up on his every move. If you suspect he's unfaithful, hire a detective. If you mutually agree to date others and stay married, this will broaden your relationship.	Believe your husband is an honest, faithful man, but don't be so naive that you can't recognize obvious signs of infidelity. Face the problem immediately and don't just look the other way and hope things will be better tomorrow.	Marriage is built on trust. You should never check up on your husband. If you are the wife you ought to believe he will not stray. If you're suspicious confess it quickly to the Lord as a sin. If he has an affair accept it as God's discipline for you and forgive him.
SUBMISSION	Women are now liberated and must make up for the years they have been demeaned by men. We've come a long way, baby, but not far enough. Don't let any man tell you what to do.	Scripture tells us to be submissive one to another and to put the other person's needs before our own. It does not teach that we women are to be doormats and refuse to use our minds. Submission doesn't mean stupidity.	The wife's role is to be the helpmate no matter what. Submission is God's plan for the woman and she must display a subservient attitude at all times. The man is the Lord of the house and the woman is to do his will.

	WORLD VIEW	BALANCED CHRISTIAN VIEW	LEGALISTIC VIEW
PHYSICAL ABUSE	If he lays a hand on you, call the cops. Report him to the authorities. If he does it again, throw him out and consider divorce. Tell all your friends what a rat he is. Find a feminist counselor who will defend you.	If you are being hit, pushed, slapped, or beaten, you are being abused. Report the abuse to your pastor or counselor and don't make excuses for your husband's behavior. If abuse continues there needs to be a separation until appropriate help can bring about change.	If you had been more submissive and done what he wanted, he wouldn't have hit you. Realize this is your cross to bear and you will get your rewards in heaven. Don't let anyone know what he's done because you probably provoked it.
VERBAL ABUSE	If your husband yells at you, yell back! Always be thinking of what ammunition you can use against him. Learn some strong words that will stop him in his tracks. Tell your girlfriends; they don't like him anyway.	If your husband insults you, points out your faults in public, demeans you in front of your children, this is verbal abuse. This shows his insecurities and probably reflects what he received as a child. Refuse to accept this harsh treatment, pray for wisdom, and seek counsel.	If your husband insults you, realize you have not been submissive enough. It is our place to accept whatever our husbands say because God speaks through them and is trying to teach us something. We should not think too highly of ourselves. Learn to grin and bear it and God will bless you.
DIVORCE	Divorce is a legal option for troubled marriages. You can always get a divorce if you're not happy. It's better for the children if you separate than stay and fight.	Divorce is a last resort and should not be jumped into quickly. Seek legal counsel before it's too late. Have copies of all deeds, wills, and trusts, and know where they are. Be sure you have a credit card in your own name.	Christians never get divorced under any conditions. There is no divorce in the eyes of God. Watch out for divorced women. They're after your husband. It's better to take abuse than to separate.

	WORLD VIEW	BALANCED CHRISTIAN VIEW	LEGALISTIC VIEW
TAKING ADVANTAGE	Don't put yourself out for others; they don't appreciate it anyway. Why should you let these people into your house when they've never had you to theirs? Don't give a nickel to your adult children; you supported them long enough. It's time they grow up.	Be hospitable, but not foolish. Be in control of the situation and don't become the maid to your guests. Make basic rules for dinner hour, chores, and baby-sitting. Don't let visiting children trash your home. Set departure dates for guests, especially your own adult children. Help them financially in emergencies.	You are called to selfless service and must have the attitude of a servant. You must open your home to strangers, the lame, and blind. You must be sacrificial and put other people's needs ahead of your own. You must always keep the door open for your adult children, no matter how old they are, and continue to bail them out when they need money.
DATING AGAIN AFTER DIVORCE OR WIDOWHOOD	The sooner you get out into the social scene the faster you will recover. Realize in today's world sex outside marriage is acceptable. If you live together you will save money and test your compatibility.	Don't rush into dating again. Realize not every man in the church singles group is a balanced Christian. Don't date—or marry—someone because the pastor says it's God's will. God can find you and tell you personally. Don't get quickly involved with a man and his children. Don't leave a new boyfriend alone with your children.	Trust all men you meet in church. Consider them as Christian brothers. Assume the pastor has divine wisdom in choices for your happiness.

	WORLD VIEW	BALANCED CHRISTIAN VIEW	LEGALISTIC VIEW
ABORTION	Abortion is legal and acceptable. It's no more trouble than going to the dentist. We need abortion clinics to keep girls from having illegal procedures. They are going to have sex anyway so give out condoms and provide free abortions.	Realize that while abortion is legal, there will be an emotional price to pay somewhere down the line. Don't sneak off to have an abortion and not expect guilt to go with you. Realize abstinence is the only safe sex, and teach this to your children.	Abortion is murder. Extreme measures are needed to eliminate this crime. Burning down clinics or threatening physicians is acceptable behavior if the motive is pure. If an abortion takes place, hide it so you won't hurt the cause of Christ.
PRAYER	It doesn't hurt to pray, but be sure you take control of the situation. Don't just trust luck or expect God to change your circumstances.	Approach solutions with both prayer and action. *"Faith without works is dead."* Believe God hears and answers prayer. The *"fervent effectual prayer . . . availeth much."* Write your prayers as David did the Psalms. *"Pray without ceasing."*	When you pray about it, you don't need to do anything about it. Leave the praying to the clergy who know how to do it right. Prayer is more effective in church or at healing meetings.
CHURCH	Women should be ordained in all denominations and be allowed to be pastors and priests. Women have their rights and should fight to achieve leadership positions. They have been second-class citizens too long, and they should put aside the old-fashioned idea of submission.	Women should be gracious, not belligerent, and they should not try to usurp authority. Women should be accepted as equal in the sight of the Lord, and church women with a gift for leadership should be allowed to share their wisdom with men, women, and children. Women should be allowed to serve on boards where their natural discernment should be taken into consideration.	Women's place is in the home and not in church leadership. Women can only serve in roles that don't need divine wisdom. Women should keep quiet in church and not offer opinions. Women should *never* be allowed to preach, exigete the Scriptures, or pray out loud in church. Women must remember their place and know God speaks to them through their husbands. Single women should take direction from their pastors as from the Lord.

APPENDIX B

Survey of
Emotions and
Experiences

Check each item that applies or *ever has applied* to you. Note that the blank for each statement falls under one of the four column headings, which will be explained in the "Scoring Your Survey" section. Leave blank any items that do not apply or you are not sure of. For the men's version of this survey, see *Wake Up, Men!* by Fred Littauer (Word Publishing, 1994).

	Clear	Strong	Possible	Group
1. Abusive spouse			_____	
2. Afraid of big or black dogs				_____
3. Alcoholic parent		_____		
4. Anorexia/bulimia or other eating disorders		_____		
5. Being chased in dreams	_____			
6. Brother or sister molested as a child	_____			
7. Candles in dreams				_____
8. Childhood "bad houses" or "bad rooms"	_____			
9. Childhood depression			_____	
10. Date rape	_____			
11. Dislike roses or their smell				_____
12. Don't like full moon				_____
13. Downcast looks as a child		_____		
14. Dreams of snakes	_____			
15. Early-childhood anger		_____		
16. Early-childhood masturbation (before age ten)		_____		
17. Emotionally abused as child			_____	
18. Emotions suppressed in childhood			_____	
19. Fear of being alone		_____		
20. Fear of knives				_____

	Clear	Strong	Possible	Group
21. Fear of losing weight		____		
22. Fear of rape	____			
23. Feel unworthy of God's love	____			
24. Feeling dirty	____			
25. Fits of rage	____			
26. Guilt feelings			____	
27. Hate Halloween				____
28. Hate men	____			
29. Hear chanting or laughing in dreams				____
30. Hide real feelings			____	
31. Lack of trust		____		
32. Low self-worth		____		
33. Marital sexual disinterest			____	
34. Memory gaps in childhood	____			
35. Migraine headaches		____		
36. Panic attacks	____			
37. People wearing hoods or robes in dreams				____
38. PMS (called PMT in some countries)		____		
39. Poor teenage relationships with boys			____	
40. Recurring bad dreams		____		
41. Rejection feelings			____	
42. Same-sex attraction	____			
43. Scared by bells, chimes, or gongs				____
44. Self-hatred	____			

	Clear	Strong	Possible	Group
45. Sexually abused or molested as child	_____			
46. Sexual compulsions	_____			
47. Sometimes hear voices				_____
48. Spiders in dreams	_____			
49. Strange feelings about "the cross"				_____
50. Suicidal feelings			_____	
51. Teenage promiscuity			_____	
52. TMJ (a jaw problem)		_____		
53. Temptation to touch children sexually	_____			
54. Uncomfortable with nudity in marriage	_____			
55. Uncontrollable anger		_____		
56. Uncontrollable crying		_____		
57. Undiagnosed pains and aches		_____		
58. Unexplained fear of darkness				_____
Your totals:	_____	_____	_____	_____
Possible:	21	14	11	12

Grand total (add all four column totals): _____

Note: This Survey of Emotions and Experiences for Women and the following scoring analysis are adapted from *Get a Life Without the Strife* by Fred and Florence Littauer (Thomas Nelson, 1993). All rights reserved. Used by permission. This form may be reproduced.

Scoring Your Survey

Add up your responses in each of the four columns and enter your score on the Totals lines (the number under each Totals line indicates the possible number for that column). Then add up your four column totals to get your Grand Total of responses.

The first thing to realize in looking at your scores is that every statement on the list is a possible symptom of childhood sexual victimization or interference, with one exception: "Sexually abused or molested as a child" (No. 45). It is not a symptom. It is a fact. The survey, therefore, is simply a list of these symptoms, which lead us to the source.

The first of the four columns, labeled "Clear," is of special significance. This means in our judgment every statement answered in the first column is a clear symptom of childhood sexual violation.

Responses in the second column, labeled "Strong," mean these responses are frequently seen in people who have suffered childhood trauma, but these symptoms could also come from other sources. They are important, but of lesser significance in getting to the bottom line quickly.

The third column, identified as "Possible," shows that these symptoms are of still lesser importance. Their roots are even more apt to have come from nonsexual abuse and usually indicate rejection. However, these symptoms do give an enhanced picture of the overall issues that you may be facing.

The fourth column is used to indicate "Group Symptoms." Your marks in this column may be an indication that when violation occurred, it could have been by a number of perpetrators, or a group, rather than a single violator. If you checked several of the fourth-column symptoms, you have most likely checked many in the first three columns as well. Generally, people who have checked five or six in the fourth column will have checked ten or more in the first column. They are also apt to have a grand total of about thirty-five or more responses. The symptoms in the fourth column indicate an even more traumatic form of victimization.

For a more complete analysis of your survey responses, see "How Can I Know If I Was Sexually Violated as a Child?" in *Get a Life Without the Strife* (Thomas Nelson, 1993).

NOTES

Chapter 1 Back When Father Knew Best and We Left It to Beaver

1. "The Birth and—Maybe—Death of Yuppiedom," Walter Shapiro, *Time*, 8 April 1993, 65.

2. Ibid.

Chapter 4 Who Are All Those Dysfunctional People?

1. Mary Kay Blakely, "Psyched Out," *Los Angeles Times Magazine*, 3 October 1993, 28.

2. Dr. Harriet Lerner, *Dance of Deception* (New York: Harper Collins, 1993).

3. Sir Walter Scott, "The Lay of the Last Minstrel," stanza 17.

4. *New York Times* Service reported in the *Los Angeles Times*, 3 October 1993.

Chapter 5 Managing the Money

1. Shelby White, *What Every Woman Should Know about Her Husband's Money* (New York: Turtle Boy/Random House, 1992).

2. Ibid., 14.

Chapter 7 When Submission Allows Abuse

1. *Time*, 29 June 1992.

2. Gail J. Koff, *Love and the Law* (New York: Simon and Schuster, 1989).

Chapter 8 Sticks and Stones Can Break My Bones, and Words Can Also Hurt Me

1. Isaac Black, *Assault on God's Image* (Winnipeg: Windflower Communications, n.d.).

Chapter 9 Is Someone Taking Advantage of You?

1. *USA Today*, 26 August 1993.

2. "Women's Feminine Skills Are a Plus in Today's Corporate America, *Newsweek*, 17 March 1986.

3. Margaret Carlson, "Even Feminists Get the Blues," *Time*, 20 January 1992, 57.

4. *Mirabella*, October 1993, 183.

Chapter 10   Dealing with Divorce and Widowhood

1. *Woman's Day*, 27 May 1986, 36.

2. Harville Hendrix, *Getting the Love You Want* (New York: Harper and Row, 1990), quoted in *ITA* (an Australian magazine), August 1990.

3. Ruth Jean Loewinsohn, American Association of Retired Persons, *Survival Handbook for Widows (and for relatives and friends who want to understand)* (Glenview, Ill.: Scott, Foresman and Company, Lifelong Learning Division, 1984), 33.

Chapter 11   I Can Always Get an Abortion

1. Terri K. Reisser, M.S., and Paul C. Reisser, M.D., "Identifying and Overcoming Post-Abortion Syndrome" (Colorado Springs, Colo.: Focus on the Family Publishing, 1992).

2. Wirthlin Group Polls, Allen Gottmacher Institute.

3. Statistics courtesy of the Center for Family Life, San Diego, California, June 1992.

4. Reisser and Reisser, "Identifying and Overcoming Post-Abortion Syndrome," 8.

Chapter 12   I'll Pray about It

1. Oswald Chambers, *Our Brilliant Heritage*, quoted in *The Best from All His Books, Vol. 1, Harry Verploegh, ed. (Nashville: Oliver Nelson, 1987)*, 253.

2. Marilyn Willett Heavilin, *I'm Listening, Lord* (Nashville: Thomas Nelson, 1993). Used by permission.

3. Lee Roberts, *Praying God's Will for My Daughter* (Nashville: Thomas Nelson, 1993). Versions of this book are also available for praying for wives, husbands, sons, and for yourself.

Bibliography

De Angelis, Sidney M. *You're Entitled! A Divorce Lawyer Talks to Women*. Chicago and New York: Contemporary Books, 1989.

Barnes, Bob, and Emilie Barnes. *The 15-Minute Money Manager*. Eugene, Ore.: Harvest House Publishers, 1993.

Barnes, Emilie. *The Spirit of Loveliness*. Eugene, Ore.: Harvest House, 1992.

Enroth, Ronald M. *Churches That Abuse*. Grand Rapids, Mich.: Zondervan, 1992.

Ketterman, Grace. *Verbal Abuse—Healing the Wound*. Ann Arbor, Mich.: Servant Books, 1992.

Koff, Gail J. *Love and the Law*. New York: Simon and Schuster, 1989.

LaSourd, Sandra Simpson. *The Not-So-Compulsive Woman*. Tarrytown, N.Y.: Chosen Books/Fleming Revell, 1992.

Lerner, Harriet Goldhor, Ph.D. *The Dance of Deception—Pretending and Truth-Telling in Women's Lives*. New York: Harper Collins, 1993.

Miller, Holly G., and Dennis E. Hensley. *How to Stop Living for the Applause* (help for women who need to be perfect). Ann Arbor, Mich.: Servant Books, 1990.

O'Connor, Karen. *When Spending Takes the Place of Feeling*. Nashville: Thomas Nelson, 1992.

Patterson, Rosemarie. *Money Makeover*. Nashville: Thomas Nelson, 1991.

Pryor, Austin. *Sound Mind Investing*. Chicago: Moody, 1993.

White, Shelby. *What Every Woman Should Know About Her Husband's Money*. New York: Turtle Boy/Random House, 1991.

Wright, Linda Raney. *A Cord of Three Strands*. Old Tappan, N.J.: Revell, 1987.

Recommended Resource Order Form

Number Ordered   **Total**

____ 1. *Wake Up, Women!* Florence Littauer $11.00   ____

____ 2. *Wake Up, Men!* Fred Littauer $11.00   ____

____ 3. *Get a Life Without the Strife,* Fred
         and Florence Littauer $11.00   ____

____ 4. *Personality Plus,* Florence Littauer $9.00   ____

____ 5. *Your Personality Tree,* Florence Littauer $9.00   ____

____ 6. *Personalities in Power,* Florence Littauer $9.00   ____

____ 7. *Personality Puzzle,* Florence Littauer and
         Marita Littauer $10.00   ____

____ 8. *Freeing Your Mind from Memories That Bind,*
         Fred and Florence Littauer $10.00   ____

____ 9. *The Promise of Healing,* Fred Littauer $10.00   ____

____10. *Raising Christians Not Just Children,*
         Florence Littauer $10.00   ____

____11. *Hope for Hurting Women,* Florence Littauer $9.00   ____

____12. *How to Get Along with Difficult People,*
         Florence Littauer $8.00   ____

____13. *Silver Boxes,* Florence Littauer   (Hardback) $13.00   ____

____14. *The Best of Florence Littauer,* compiled by
         M. Heavilin   (Hardback) $10.00   ____

____15. *Dare to Dream,* Florence Littauer $10.00   ____

____16. *Make the Tough Times Count,* Florence Littauer $10.00   ____

____17. *Your Personality Tree* Video Album, 8 half-hour
         lessons with book and study guide $80.00   ____

____18. *Personality Profile Tests,* Fred Littauer
         (6 for $5.00) $1.00   ____

                                                          SUBTOTAL   ____

Shipping and Handling (please add $1.50 per book, $5.00 for the video album)   ____

                        California residents please add 7.75% sales tax   ____

                  TOTAL AMOUNT ENCLOSED (check or money order)   ____

CHARGE: MasterCard/Visa # _____

Name on card _____   Expiration Date _____

Make checks payable and mail to: CLASS Book Service
                                    1645 S. Rancho Santa Fe Road #102
                                    San Marcos, CA 92069

Payment plan may be made by sending three checks, each for one-third of total amount,
one payable currently and the other two dated a month and two months later. International
Orders: Please send checks in U.S. funds only and add $5.00 per book for shipping by air.